# READING IN DETAIL

Figure 1.   Ilya Schor.   Bracelet.

# READING IN DETAIL

*Aesthetics and the Feminine*

Naomi Schor

METHUEN:  New York and London

First published in 1987 by
  Methuen, Inc.
29 West 35th Street, N.Y. N.Y. 10001

Published in Great Britain by
  Methuen & Co., Ltd.
11 New Fetter Lane, London EC4P 4EE

Copyright © 1987 by Methuen, Inc.

Printed in the U.S.A.

Library of Congress Cataloguing in Publication Data

Schor, Naomi.
  Reading in detail.

  Bibliography: p.
  Includes index.
  1. Aesthetics.   2. Femininity (Philosophy)
I. Title.
BH39.S355  1987        111'.85        86-28641
ISBN 0-416-01511-5
ISBN 0-416-01521-2 (pbk.)


British Library Cataloguing in Publication Data

Schor, Naomi
  Reading in detail : aesthetics and the
  feminine.
  1. Aesthetics   2. Feminist aesthetics
  I. Title
  111'.85        BH39


  ISBN 0-416-01511-5
  ISBN 0-416-01521-2 Pbk

*Pour mes morts*

# NOTE ON PERMISSIONS

The author wishes to acknowledge the cooperation of the following in granting permissions to reprint articles or to reproduce works of art: *New York Literary Forum* for "Duane Hanson: Truth in Sculpture" in the issue "Fragments: Incompletion & Discontinuity," vols. 8–9, edited by Lawrence D. Kritzman; *Poetics Today* for "Details and Realism: *Le Curé de Tours*" in vol. 5, no. 4, 1984; Princeton University Press for "Fiction as Interpretation/Interpretation as Fiction" from *The Reader in the Text: Essays on Audience and Interpretation*, edited by Susan Suleiman and Inge Crosman, 1980; Union Générale d'Editions for "Le délire d'interprétation: Naturalisme et paranoïa" from *Le naturalisme: Colloque de Cerisy*, 1978; *Dada/Surrealism*, vol. 6, for "Dali's Freud," 1976; the Metropolitan Museum of Art for Schor, Bracelet, and for Brouwer, *The Smokers*; The Brera di Milano for Rubens, *Last Supper*; the Louvre for Veronese, *Marriage at Cana*, and for Millet, *L'Angélus*; the Alte Pinakothek, Munich for Murillo, *The Melon Eaters*; and O. K. Harris Works of Art for the Duane Hanson figures.

# CONTENTS

# ACKNOWLEDGMENTS

This book has been long in the making and many are those who have contributed to its coming into being. A generous grant from the National Endowment for the Humanities permitted me to spend 1981 in France and to do the reading that became Part I. As a result the final product bears little resemblance to the original project funded, for which I trust I am forgiven. A semester of released time as the Spring 1984 Faculty Fellow of Brown University's Pembroke Center for Research on Women provided both the time to polish the manuscript and a wonderful forum in which to present work in progress. Similarly my presentation of portions of the manuscript to the Williams College Faculty Seminar in Critical Theory produced many useful comments and leads. All along I have been fortunate in my readers—though some of the anonymous ones would have been more helpful had they been less curmudgeonly. I wish to acknowledge with particular gratitude the meticulous annotations of Neil Hertz, Sandy Petrey, and Arden Reed. My thanks also to Mira Schor, my sister, who read the manuscript with an artist's eye. To Nancy K. Miller, who kept after me to include the chapters on the detail that form Part II, I owe in a certain sense my title. I received invaluable expert help in obtaining some of the illustrations from Norine Cashman, Margaret Weinstein, Mary Ann Doane, and Alex Arvo, all of Brown University, as well as from my indefatigable French connection, Philippe Hamon. Holly Dawkins was a most gentle and accurate typist. It was a joy as always to work with my editor, William P. Germano. My husband Paol Keineg's contribution is, of course, immense: he not only read the manuscript with a keen, critical eye, he lived with the author and that baggy monster, her "detail book," for more years than either of us cares to remember.

# LIST OF FIGURES

To see a world in a Grain of Sand
And Heaven in a wild flower
Hold infinity in the palm of your hand
And eternity in an hour.

William Blake


I do not doubt but the majesty & beauty of the world are latent in any iota of the world . . . I do not doubt there is far more in trivialities, insects, vulgar persons, dwarfs, weeds, rejected refuse, than I have supposed . . .

Walt Whitman


Let us not take it for granted that life exists more fully in what is commonly thought big than in what is commonly thought small.

Virginia Woolf

# INTRODUCTION

We live in an age when the detail enjoys a rare prominence. Responding to a questionnaire on "The Adventures of Reason in Contemporary Thought and Science," Jürgen Habermas sketches some of the recent trends and tendencies that have contributed to the widespread legitimation of the detail: "Contextualism is heretofore spelled with a capital C; the living world appears only in the plural; ethics has taken the place of morality, the everyday that of theory, the particular that of the general."[1] Nowhere have these tendencies been more spectacularly in evidence than in the writings of some of the major figures of post-structuralist France. Himself a historian of the detail, Michel Foucault, writing in *Discipline and Punish*, called for the writing of a "History of the Detail," which would chart its passage from a theological category in the Age of Classicism to its present role as an instrument of both knowledge and power. Reflecting on his own painting technique, Roland Barthes confessed: "I have the (initial) taste for the detail . . . " And, last but not least, Jacques Derrida has elaborated a textual approach characterized by a strategic revaluation of neglected textual details: notes, epigraphs, post-scriptums and all manner of *parerga*. This pervasive valorization of the minute, the partial, and the marginal runs the risk of inducing a form of amnesia that in turn threatens to diminish the import of the current privileging of detail. For, as any historian of ideas knows, the detail has until very recently been viewed in the West with suspicion if not downright hostility. The censure of the particular is one of the enabling gestures of neo-classicism, which recycled into the modern age the classical equation of the Ideal with the absence of all particularity. The normative aesthetics of neo-classicism did not, however, simply fade away upon the advent of Romanticism; constantly reinscribed throughout the nineteenth century they continue to resurface well into the twentieth, constituting the indelible marker of nostalgics of the Ideal (e.g. Lukács and Baudrillard). Viewed in a historical perspective, the ongoing valorization of the detail appears to be an essential

3

aspect of that dismantling of Idealist metaphysics which looms so large on the agenda of modernity.

The story of the rise of the detail is, of course, inseparable from the all too familiar story of the demise of classicism and the birth of realism, but it should not, indeed cannot be reduced to that story, for to retell the story from the perspective of the detail is inevitably to tell *another* story. To focus on the detail and more particularly on the *detail as negativity* is to become aware, as I discovered, of its participation in a larger semantic network, bounded on the one side by the *ornamental*, with its traditional connotations of effeminacy and decadence, and on the other, by the *everyday*, whose "prosiness" is rooted in the domestic sphere of social life presided over by women. In other words, to focus on the place and function of the detail since the mid-eighteenth century is to become aware that the normative aesthetics elaborated and disseminated by the Academy and its members is not sexually neutral; it is an axiology carrying into the field of representation the sexual hierarchies of the phallocentric cultural order. The detail does not occupy a conceptual space beyond the laws of sexual difference: the detail is gendered and doubly gendered as feminine.

Many of the phenomena which contributed to and accompanied the rise of the detail are well-known and amply documented. They include secularization, the disciplining of society, consumerism, the invention of the quotidian, the development of means of mechanical reproduction, and democratization.[2] But so long as the history of the detail was viewed as a footnote to the history of realism and, furthermore, as sexually unmarked, a crucial factor in its current hegemony was overlooked: the breakdown of sexual difference. If today the detail and the wider semantic field it commands enjoys an undisputed legitimacy it is because the dominant paradigms of patriarchy have been largely eroded. Eroded, but not eradicated. By reversing the terms of the oppositions and the values of the hierarchies, we remain, of course, prisoners of the paradigms, only just barely able to dream a universe where the categories of *general* and *particular*, *mass* and *detail*, and *masculine* and *feminine* would no longer order our thinking and our seeing.

I did not start out to write on the detail as aesthetic category. A literary critic by training, I began by studying the function of the detail in nineteenth-century fiction, following in the formalist wake of Jakobson, Barthes, and other poeticians. My goal was to elaborate a taxonomy of the literary detail. Traces of my initial classificatory project subsist in *Reading in Detail*, notably in part II, but also in the chapter on Barthes. Gradually, however, I became aware that the detail had not always revelled in its current status, indeed that it had gained legitimacy only after a prolonged and hard-fought struggle that had broad sociopolitical ramifications. The question then became: how did the detail shake off its century-old censure to assume its commanding position in the field of representation? The feminist archaeology I have reconstructed in part I is by definition fragmentary—those seeking a totalizing, exhaustive *history* of the detail more congenial to male epistemological models will be disappointed—but not, I would like to think, arbitrary. The pivotal texts I have chosen to examine, notably the *Discourses on Art* of Sir Joshua Reynolds, Hegel's *Aesthetik*, the writings of Freud and Barthes, imposèd themselves on me with something like the force of necessity. This is not to say that other paths might not have been taken—one might, for example, have focused on such movements as the baroque and on such major detailists as Morelli or Walter Benjamin—but the shape of the emergent narrative would, I suspect, remain very much the same, a story of sublimation and desublimation.

Each of the five chapters in Part I is designed to function as a free-standing essay, while at the same time constituting an integral part of the whole. This organic or synecdochic structure presents certain obvious inconveniences: on the one hand, a minimal degree of repetition, on the other, a certain intermittence in the argumentation. Having established in the initial chapter the modalities of gendering that underpin neo-classical aesthetics, the alleged femininity of the detail and its collateral fields is assumed throughout the following pages. Though, for example, explicit references to sexual difference are largely absent from the chapter devoted to Hegel—as they are, significantly, from the *Aesthetik* itself—Hegel's idealism must, in the light of Chapter 1, be read as a rejection of the "nether world" of the Family and the particular in which women (as Hegel argues in the *Phenomenology*) are at home. Indeed, *Reading in Detail* assumes a persistent association of idealist aesthetics with the discourse of misogyny. Finally, while chronology informs the ordering of the chapters, the linearity of the overarching narrative line is occasionally disturbed by local incidences of achronicity and discontinuity.

In Chapter 1, I take Reynold's *Discourses on Art*, generally acknowledged to be the supreme formulation of neo-classical aesthetics, as the point of departure for a wide-ranging—some might say eclectic—inquiry into the over-determinations of the woman-detail association in idealist aesthetics. In the latter half of the eighteenth century this association culminates in the promotion of the sublime, an anti-particularist aesthetic whose fortunes parallel in modern times a rise of the feminine, when not (as today) the rise of feminism. The complex mechanisms by which the encroaching "world of prose" is sublimated into art forms acceptable to the norms of idealist aesthetics is the subject of the second chapter, closely focused on Hegel's *Aesthetik*. In Chapter 3, the method if not the focus changes. My concern here is the persistence of the principles of neo-classical aesthetics well into the twentieth century. And in order to make my point, this most archaeological of chapters brings together three very strange bedfellows: Francis Wey, a little-known nineteenth-century French novelist and rhetorician, but less obscure early writer on photography; Adolf Loos, architect and cultural critic of Vienna 1900; and Georg Lukács, the preeminent Marxist literary critic of the twentieth century.

A few words about the central yet eccentric position Freud occupies in my scheme of things: in light of the narrative I have constructed, my neglect in Chapter 4 of Freud's theory of sublimation, indeed of his writings on art altogether, may appear somewhat odd. And yet, I believe it is justified, for the leap from Hegel to Barthes would be unimaginable were it not for Freud's radical intervening formulation of the principle by which libidinal energy can be transferred from the significant to the insignificant (that is, displacement). It is the theory of displacement rather than that of sublimation that makes intelligible and, more important, legitimate the multiple modes of investment in the trivial everywhere at work in modern society.

The modern fascination with the trivial, the playground of fetishism, is exhibited throughout the variegated oeuvre of Roland Barthes which constitutes the text of Chapter 5. Though Barthes's deliberate undoing of the romantic sublimation of the detail appears here as a sort of happy end, spelling the demise or temporary retreat of idealist aesthetics, from a feminist perspective a new and nagging question emerges: does the triumph of the detail signify a triumph of the feminine with which it has so long been linked? Or has the detail achieved its new prestige by being taken over by the masculine, triumphing at the very moment when it ceases to be associated with the feminine, or ceasing to be connoted as feminine at the very moment when it is taken up by the male-dominated cultural establishment?

In a short story entitled "Funes, The Memorious," Borges describes the "dizzying world" of Ireneo Funes who, rendered hypersensitive to details by an accident that has left him blind, is "incapable of general, platonic ideas," hence of thought, for "to think is . . . to generalize, to abstract": "In the overly replete world of Funes, there was nothing but details, almost contiguous details."[3] This fiction of details run riot might serve as a cautionary tale for the devotee of the detail, because there is always the danger that to write *on* the detail is to become lost *in* it, unable to see the proverbial forest for the trees, or, as in the extreme case of Funes, the tree for the leaves: "In effect, Funes not only remembered every leaf on every tree of every wood, but even every one of the times he had perceived or imagined it."[4] Though it does hazard generalizations, *Reading in Detail* cheerfully runs the risk of the detail, for, as Borges's tale implies, there is a special beauty, a heroic dimension to his idiot savant's universe that the convinced Platonist cannot perceive. Each chapter in the first half is primarily a close reading of details of texts on the detail. Perhaps, too, the archaeology of the detail I have attempted is self-serving: an effort to legitimate my own instinctive critical practice, the readings in detail worked out in Part 2.

A sweeping generalization: all literary methodologies, all critical theories and histories of critical theory serve to validate idiosyncratic relationships to the text. Unless the poetician or hermeneut be mad, however, the laws she abstracts from her personal storehouse of myths and the interpretations she translates

from the hieroglyphs of her unconscious will encounter in other readers recognition and response. My own love of the detail—and like all loves this love
is shot through with ambivalence—is inextricably bound up with my Oedipus:
my father, a goldsmith, was a master of the ornamental detail, a Renaissance
artist in the age of high modernism and minimalism. Now, as Nietzsche writes
in a fragment of *The Gay Science* entitled "On the origin of scholars": "Once one
has trained one's eyes to recognize in a scholarly treatise the scholar's intellectual
*idiosyncrasy*—every scholar has one—and to catch it in the act, one will almost
always behold behind this the scholar's 'pre-history,' his family, and especially
their occupations and crafts."[5] In asserting the detail's claim to aesthetic dignity
and epistemological prestige, my motivation is then double: to endow with legitimacy my own brand of feminist hermeneutics, while giving value to my
father's craft.

 *Reading in Detail* and my earlier *Breaking the Chain: Women, Theory, and French
Realist Fiction* are imbricated texts, elaborations of the same feminist project. In
*Breaking the Chain* I describe my reading practice as a form of *female paranoia*, that
is the privileging of odd, eccentric textual details referring to parts of the female
body: eroticized wounds, bound limbs, the clitoris.[6] The essays that make up
Part 2 can be said to represent the more familiar masculine manifestations of
the pathology, for with the possible exception of "Duane Hanson: Truth in
Sculpture," which is primarily concerned with the uncanny, all are informed by
*male paranoia*: in the essay that is in fact the matrix of the entire book, "Dali's
Freud" (more accurately Dali *between* Freud and Lacan, since Lacan makes a
cameo appearance), I consider the implications for hermeneutics, especially the
psychoanalytic, of Dali's "paranoia-criticism." "Fiction as Interpretation/Inter-
pretation as Fiction" considers paranoid interpretation as it is thematized in the
fiction of James, Proust, and Kafka through the adventures of the interpreting
character, or "interpretant." Finally, in both "The Delusion of Interpretation"
and "Details and Realism," the persecution of the male protagonist is shown
to be a recurrent scenario in the realist and naturalist texts produced by the
disciplining of nineteenth-century French society. Though not written under the
sign of paranoia, male or female, "Duane Hanson: Truth in Sculpture" shares
with the other essays the concern inherent to paranoia and to any hermeneutics
patterned more or less consciously on that pathology: the relationship between
the detail and the truth. To read in detail is, however tacitly, to invest the detail
with a truth-bearing function, and yet as *Reading in Detail* repeatedly shows, the
truth value of the detail is anything but assured. As the guarantor of meaning,
the detail is for that very reason constantly threatened by falsification and misprision. *Reading in Detail* is thus both a defense of the detail and an illustration
of its lures.

# Part 1
*Archaeology*

# 1.

## GENDER:
## In the Academy

and the whole of beauty consists, in my opinion, in being able to get above singular forms, local customs, particularities, and details of every kind.
Sir Joshua Reynolds, *Discourses on Art*

A Folly! Singular & Particular Detail is the Foundation of the Sublime.
William Blake, *Annotations to Reynolds's Discourses*

In the room the women come and go
Talking of Michelangelo.
T. S. Eliot, "The Love Song of J. Alfred Prufrock"

Is the detail feminine? This question assumes a certain urgency when one recalls that one of the major debates in neo-classical aesthetics—whose legacy is still very much with us today—concerns precisely the status of the detail in representation, the practice of what I will call, after G. H. Lewes, "detailism."[1] According to Ernst Cassirer, "the problem of the relationship between the general and the particular" is "the basic and central question of classical aesthetics."[2] Nowhere is the problem more insistently foregrounded than in a work generally recognized as one of the most considerable and representative bodies of Academic aesthetics produced in Europe in the latter half of the eighteenth century, the *Discourses on Art* which Sir Joshua Reynolds delivered to the "Gentlemen"—Reynolds's addressees are definitely, exclusively male—of the Royal Academy between 1769 and 1790.[3]

Before turning to Reynolds's *Discourses*, I would like to make a brief reference to a lesser-known text of Reynolds's, indeed his only sustained work of practical art criticism: *A Journey to France and Holland*. In 1781, Reynolds travelled through the Low Lands, recording his impressions of the numerous paintings he saw in the churches and private collections he visited. Commenting on a Last Supper by Rubens, then hanging in the Cathedral at Mechlin, Reynolds notes:

Under the table is a dog gnawing a bone; a circumstance mean in itself, and certainly unworthy of such a subject, however properly it might fill a corner of such a picture as the marriage of Cana, by Paul Veronese.[4]

11

I take this passing note as exemplifying Reynolds's general aesthetic stance. The painter's practiced gaze is immediately drawn to a corner of the painting before him, to a trivial detail which is distinctly out of place in the lofty scene represented. Thus in one glance are conjoined the most traditional separation of high and low subjects and a thoroughly modern, not to say postmodern, fascination with the eccentric detail, referring to the refuse, so to speak, of everyday life.

As we turn now to Reynolds's *Discourses*, we shall do well to bear this vignette in mind, for it bodies forth the dual attitude toward the circumstantial which pervades the *Discourses*; as M. H. Abrams notes, Reynolds's aesthetics are bipolar,[5] oscillating between a strict anti-detailism consonant with classical Academic discourse, and a lucid recognition of the uses of particularity in keeping with the contemporary rise of realism. Nevertheless, as Abrams is quick to recognize, the general pole of Reynolds's aesthetics predominates over the other, the particular. My concern in what follows is with the logic of the discourse marshalled *against* the detail.

Summarizing Sir Joshua's general system "in two words" William Hazlitt writes: *"That the great style in painting consists in avoiding the details, and peculiarities of particular objects."*[6] Reynolds's censure of the detail is not quite as absolute as Hazlitt's summary suggests, but it persists throughout the discourses. It dominates in particular the Eleventh Discourse, which Reynolds himself outlined as follows in the Table of Contents: "Genius—Consists principally in the comprehension of A WHOLE; in taking general idea only."[7] Indeed the entire discourse on Genius takes the form of a protracted and sinuous argument against confusing detailism and Genius: "a nice discrimination of minute circumstances, and a punctilious delineation of them, whatever excellence it may have, (and I do not mean to detract from it,) never did confer on the Artist the character of Genius" (XI, 192). Whereas the second-rate artist loses himself in the servile copying of nature in its infinite particularity, the Genius extends his "attention at once to the whole."

The opposition of Genius and second-rate artist corresponds to a distinction Reynolds draws elsewhere between two forms of mimesis. There are, he writes in his annotations to a translation of Du Fresnoy's poem, *The Art of Painting*, "two modes of imitating nature; one of which refers for its truth to the sensations of the mind, and the other to the eye."[8] Not only is the purely visual form of mimesis inferior, worse it is regressive, for it produces a trompe l'oeil effect which harks back to the infancy of painting: "Deception, which is so often recommended by writers on the theory of painting, instead of advancing art, is in reality carrying it back to its infant state."[9] For whereas poetry in its primitive state eschewed the representation of the common life in favor of the supernatural and the extraordinary ("heroes, wars, ghosts, enchantment and transformation"), painting began by showing off its capacity to transform indifferent objects into seemingly three-dimensional figures capable of fooling even the canniest observers. This archaic stage of painting might be described as the birds and

Figure 2.   Rubens, *Last Supper*

grapes stage, in reference to Pliny's oft-cited anecdote about art and illusion in classical antiquity.

The story runs that Parrhasios and Zeuxis entered into competition, Zeuxis exhibiting a picture of some grapes, so true to nature that the birds flew up to the wall of the stage. Parrhasios then displayed a picture of a linen curtain, realistic to such a degree that Zeuxis, elated by the verdict of the birds, cried out that now at last his rival must draw the curtain and show his picture.

Figure 3.   Veronese, *Marriage at Cana*

On discovering his mistake he surrendered his prize to Parrhasios, admitting candidly that he had deceived the birds, while Parrhasios had deluded himself, a painter.[10]

Reynolds's strictures against detailism fall into two distinct groups which must be clearly distinguished if the subsequent destiny of the detail as aesthetic category is to become intelligible: on the one hand there are the qualitative arguments (those according to the Ideal), on the other the quantitative (those according to the Sublime). In the first instance, Reynolds argues that because of their material contingency details are incompatible with the Ideal; in the second he argues that because of their tendency to proliferation, details subvert the Sublime. But while the rise of realism will entail the legitimation of the contingent detail, it will remain to modernity to embrace the dispersed detail.

Let us pay close attention to his use of language. For though Reynolds himself was an outspoken believer in the instrumental nature of language—"Words should be employed as the means, not as the end: language is the instrument, conviction is the work" (IV, 64)—his writing is laced with figures, notably extended metaphors. The following passage from the Third Discourse provides us not only with one of Reynolds's most fully articulated statements on the difference between the particular and the general, but also with one of the most elaborate deployments of his metaphorics of the detail:

All the objects which are exhibited to our view by nature, upon close examination will be found to have their *blemishes* and *defects*. The most beautiful forms have something about them like *weakness, minuteness,* or *imperfection*. But it is not every eye that perceives these *blemishes*. It must be an eye long used to the contemplation and comparison of these forms; and which, by a long habit of observing what any set of objects of the same kind have in common, has acquired the power of discerning what each wants in particular. This long laborious comparison should be the first study of the painter, who aims at the greatest style. By this means, he acquires a just idea of beautiful forms; he corrects nature by herself, her imperfect state by her more perfect. His eye being able to distinguish the *accidental deficiencies, excrescences,* and *deformities* of things, from their general figures, he makes out an abstract idea of their forms more perfect than any one original; and what may seem a paradox, he learns to design naturally by drawing his figures unlike any one object. This idea of the perfect state of nature, which the Artist calls the Ideal Beauty, is the great leading principle, by which works of genius are conducted. (III, 44–45; emphasis added)

The "selection" procedure Reynolds recommends the painter follow in abstracting the Ideal from brute Nature is not unlike the technique devised by structuralist analysts of myth and folktales to extract the invariant structure of the narrative from its variable concrete manifestations. The Ideal, like the Structure, is a construct arrived at by conceptual rather than perceptual means. But what differentiates the contemporary structuralist from the eighteenth-century idealist is their use of language: whereas the language of the structuralist strives toward objectivity in the manner of a pseudoscientific discourse, in this characteristic treatise of Augustan aesthetics the metaphorics of the detail is heavily freighted with the vocabulary of teratology, the science of monsters. In its unreconstructed state, nature is a living museum of horrors, a repository of genetic aberrations, which can take the form either of lack (*deficiencies*) or excess (*excrescences*)—the logic of the particular is the logic of the supplement. The particular becomes a vehicle for pollution; to practice naive mimeticism is to risk introducing the Impure into the space of representation, for as Reynolds writes in his Third Paper for *The Idler:* "if it has been proved that the Painter, by attending to the invariable and general ideas of Nature, produce beauty, he must, by regarding minute particularities, and accidental discrimination, deviate from the universal rule, and *pollute his canvass with deformity*."[11]

Deformity is the key word in Reynolds's qualitative argument against the particular. It is through his insistent use of the word that we begin to grasp the link between particularity and the feminine. For though Reynolds never explicitly links details and femininity, by taking over a metaphorics grounded in metaphysics—and Reynolds's debt to both Plato and Aristotle is well-documented—he implicitly reinscribes the sexual stereotypes of Western philosophy which has, since its origins, mapped gender onto the form-matter paradigm, forging a durable link between maleness and form (*eidos*), femaleness and formless matter. This equation pervades Greek theories of reproduction, notably Aristotle's. According to his founding myth of sexual difference, woman's sexual desire only serves to confirm her *lack:* "matter longs for form as its fulfillment, as the female longs for the male."[12] As this passage illustrates, the always imperfect nature which awaits the (male) artist's trained eye to attain the beauty of the Ideal is in the idealist tradition in which Reynolds participates, feminine. "*He* corrects nature by *herself*," writes Reynolds, revealing the pedagogical role of the male artist who cunningly instructs female Nature by homeopathic means.

The alignment of woman and (devalorized) nature is, of course, not limited to classical metaphysics or neo-classical aesthetics; it is, according to anthropologist Sherry Ortner, a universal phenomenon. The relationship of woman and nature is, Ortner emphasizes, one of proximity rather than identity. Women are viewed cross-culturally as closer to nature than men, who are associated with the more prestigious term, culture, that is anti-*physis*. Ortner lists three reasons for linking woman and nature: woman's physiology (childbearing); woman's social role (childrearing), and woman's psyche. Both as a social being and an individual, woman is seen as more embedded in the concrete and the particular than man:

the family (and hence woman) represent lower-level, socially fragmenting, particularistic sort of concerns, as opposed to interfamilial relations representing higher-level, integrative, universalistic sort of concern.

One relevant dimension that does seem pan-culturally applicable is that of relative concreteness vs. relative abstractness: the feminine personality tends to be involved with concrete feelings, things, and people, rather than with abstract entities; it tends toward personalism and particularism.[13]

The unchallenged association of woman and the particular spans not only cultures, but centuries, extending from antiquity to the present day; along the way, however, it has acquired the trappings of scientific fact, and it is on this semimythical, semiscientific association that modern-day critics have based their assessments of men's and women's respective contributions to the arts. Thus Jean Larnac, the author of the classical *Histoire de la littérature féminine en France* (1929), grounds his unshakeable belief in the absolute difference between men's and women's writing on what must have passed in his time for the latest in scientific evidence. According to one Iastrow, writes Larnac, it has been shown that: "while female students are attentive to their immediate surroundings, the finished product, the decorative, the concrete, the individual, men prefer what is most distant, the constructive, the general and the abstract."[14] Viewed as congenitally (rather than culturally) particularistic, the woman artist is doubly condemned to produce inferior works of art: because of her close association with nature, she cannot but replicate it. The law of the genre is that women are by nature mimetic, incapable of creating significant works of art in nonrepresentational art forms—notably music. This law is clearly enunciated by the father of modern French poetics, Paul Valéry:

> Women have been absent neither from the field of painting nor of letters; but, in the order of the more abstract arts they have not excelled.
>
> I say of an art that it is *more abstract* than another when it requires more imperatively than that other art the intervention of completely ideal forms, that is forms not borrowed from the world of sense . . . *the more abstract an art, the fewer women there are who have made a name for themselves in that art.*[15]

But the gendering of the detail in Reynolds—and Reynolds, it should be clearly understood, is the proper name for the idealist aesthetics he promotes—is a complex operation; the feminization of the detail is, in Freudian terms, overdetermined. It is produced not only by associating the particular with brute Matter and genetic malformation, but also by setting the detail against the Sublime. The Sublime in Reynolds is an anti-detailism because, like Jansenist grace, the Sublime produces its characteristic effect with the speed of lightning, while the attention required by details acts as a break on perception:

> . . . it is impossible for a picture composed of so many parts to have that effect so indispensably necessary to grandeur, that of one complete whole.

However contradictory it may be in geometry, it is true in taste, that many little things will not make a great one. The Sublime impresses the mind at once with one great idea; it is a single blow . . . (IV, 65)

The sublime object is not built on the organic model so essential to Romanticism which ensures the transmutation of quantity into quality; no patient piling on of details can produce a sublime object. On the contrary, which is why the rhetorical manuals of the period are full of descriptions of sublime objects displaying two complementary attributes: grandeur and uniformity. In his pioneering *Essay on the Sublime* (1747), John Baillie explains why uniformity is an essential attribute of the sublime object:

> Where an Object is *vast*, and at the same Time *uniform*, there is to the Imagination no Limits of its Vastness, and the Mind runs out into *Infinity*, continually *creating* as it were from the *Pattern*. Thus when the Eye loses the vast Ocean, the Imagination having nothing to arrest it, catches up the Scene and extends the Prospect to *Immensity*, which it can by no means do, were the uniform *Surface* broke up by innumerable little *Islands* scattered up and down, and the Mind thus led into the Consideration of the various Parts; for this adverting to dissimilar Parts ever destroys the creative Power of the Imagination. However beautiful the Hemisphere may be when curled over with Silver-tinged Clouds, and the blue Sky ever where breaking thro', yet the Prospect is not near so grand as when in a vast and uniform Heaven there is nothing to stop the Eye, or limit the *Imagination*.[16]

For Baillie it follows that the ideal natural sublime object is huge and without asperities, in short "an Alp." The singularized Alp represents the hyperbole of uniform grandeur: "A flowery *Vale*, or the Verdure of a *Hill*, may charm; but to fill the Soul, and raise it to the *Sublime* Sensations, the Earth must rise into an *Alp* . . . "[17] For Burke, on the other hand (and it is, of course, his theory of the sublime that has prevailed), smoothness is counterproductive of the sublime *frisson*: "the effects of a rugged and broken surface seem stronger than where it is smooth and polished."[18] Furthermore, grandeur is not for Burke the unique attribute of the sublime natural object; there is also in Burke, as in Pascal, a sublime of the infinitely small. As Burke goes on to say: "as the great extreme of dimension is sublime, so the last extreme of littleness is in some measure sublime likewise" (ibid.). Yet however much Burke may have diverged from his predecessor, he did take over Baillie's emphasis on uniformity, recasting it as "the artificial infinite," which rests on the double principle of succession and uniformity. The prime example of the "artificial infinite" is the "rotund":

> For in a rotund, whether it be a building or a plantation, you can no where fix a boundary; turn which way you will, the same object still seems to continue, and the imagination has no rest. But the parts must be uniform as well as circularly disposed, to give this figure its full force; because any difference,

whether it be in the disposition, or in the figure, or even in the colour of the parts, is highly prejudicial to the idea of infinity, which every change must check and interrupt . . .[19]

To value the sublimities of the rugged and/or the small is not to valorize the detail, whose distinctive feature from the perspective of the sublime is not its wondrous "minuteness," but rather its uncanny tendency to introduce eye-catching differences within the mind-expanding spectacle of perfect uniformity and proportion.

By dividing and dispersing the spectator's attention—and if the argument according to the Ideal is focused on the Artist, the argument according to the Sublime is a reception aesthetics, focused on the pole of the receiver, the de-coder—the detail blocks the dynamic rush of the Imagination, fatigues the eye, and in the end induces anxiety rather than the elevating pleasure of the Sublime. "In a composition, when the objects are scattered and divided into many equal parts, the eye is perplexed and fatigued, from not knowing where to rest, where to find the principal action, or which is the principle figure . . . The expression which is used very often on these occasions is, the piece wants *repose;* a word which perfectly expresses a relief of the mind from that state of hurry and anxiety which it suffers, when looking at a work of this character" (VIII, 147). The sit-uation of the spectator confronted with this restless, anxiety-producing work is similar to that of the critics of the ornament-laden decorative arts who, according to E. H. Gombrich, feel "overwhelmed by the assault on their senses made by the profusion of ornament."[20] That this should be so is not surprising, for at the same time as the detail militates against the production of the Sublime, it produces by its very anarchic proliferation another style, the Elegant or Orna-mental: "what may heighten the elegant may degrade the sublime" (IV, 63). For Reynolds, there are two main schools of Italian painting: the elegant school of Ornamental art centered in Venice (Titian, Veronese), and the grand and noble school of Sublime art, centered in Rome (Raphael, Michelangelo). The *relative* inferiority of the Venetian school—for, typically, Reynolds is lavish in his praise of its qualities—is due to the privilege it accords sensuality over reason, dazzle over affect, color over line, ornament over severity. Now as Gombrich reminds us, the "identification of crowded ornament with feminine taste"—an identi-fication which is always devalorizing—goes back to the rhetorical manuals of classical antiquity and extends well into modern treatises on taste.[21] Thus, in his chapter on "Gardening and Architecture," Lord Kames dramatizes the taste-lessness of excessive ornamentation in houses and gardens by comparing it to a peculiarly feminine form of personal over-ornamentation:

> In gardening as well as architecture, simplicity ought to be the governing taste. Profuse ornament hath no better effect than to confound the eye, and to prevent the object from making an impression as one entire whole. An artist destitute of genius for capital beauties, is naturally prompted to supply

the defect [ornament is supplementary and enlisted to compensate for a lack] by crowding his plan with slight embellishments. Hence in gardens, triumphal arches, Chinese houses, temples, obelisks, cascades, fountains, without end [cf. Bouvard and Pécuchet's garden]; and hence in buildings, pillars, vases, statues, and a profusion of carved work. Thus a woman who has not taste, is apt to overcharge every part of her dress with ornament.[22]

The matching up of sexual and aesthetic hierarchies is apparent in Reynolds's association of the sublime style with virility, it is for him "the more manly, noble, dignified manner . . . " (VIII, 153). But the polarization of art history along the lines of sexual difference does not end there, for the detail features prominently not only in the sensual Ornamental style, but also in the vulgar style of the Dutch school. Indeed the split between the Roman and Venetian schools is but an internal manifestation of the difference which opposes two national artistic traditions, the universalist tradition of Italy and the particularist tradition of Holland: "the Venetian school . . . may be said to be the *Dutch part* of the Italian genius."[23] Svetlana Alpers has shown that the persistent privileging of Southern art over Northern art, the exclusion of Dutch Art from the great tradition of art history is accountable to a covert association of Dutch art with the feminine. This association goes back to the Renaissance, indeed to a remark attributed to Michelangelo—whose very name is for Reynolds productive of a sublime-effect—where he dismisses Dutch art as appealing to a particularly benighted class of viewers:

> Flemish painting . . . will . . . please the devout better than any painting of Italy. It will appeal to women, especially to the very old and the very young, also to monks and nuns and to certain noblemen who have no sense of true harmony.[24]

Alpers goes on to comment: "To say an art is for women is to reiterate that it displays not measure or order but rather, to Italian eyes at least, a flood of observed, unmediated details drawn from nature."[25]

The irreconcilability of details and the sublime and the concomitant affinity of details for the effete and effeminate ornamental style point to what is perhaps most threatening about the detail: its tendency to subvert an internal hierarchic ordering of the work of art which clearly subordinates the periphery to the center, the accessory to the principal, the foreground to the background. Given the persistent association of all manner of devalorized or threatening details with the feminine, it is scarcely surprising to find the insubordinate detail singled out as distinctively feminine in one of the very first works of criticism devoted to female specificity in writing. In his turn-of-the-century book on *The Feminine Note in Fiction*, William L. Courtney boldly asserts that: "a passion for detail is the distinguishing mark of nearly every female novelist"; "The feminine intellect has a passion for detail; that is a quality which belongs to all the best work done by female writers.''[26] Unfortunately, not all woman writers are blessed with the delicate sense of proportion of Jane Austen, that master miniaturist. In most instances the feminine privileging of the detail entails a dangerous blurring of the line between the principal and the incidental event, the main protagonist and the secondary characters:

> The passion for detail conflicts in many ways with the general scope of a novel. The subordinate personages are apt to be too highly coloured, the inferior incidents are put, as it were, into the front place, and therefore interfere with the proper perspective of the whole.[27]

The complaint that a profusion of details leads to a loss of perspective was in 1904 hardly novel: Courtney is merely adapting to his own ends a veritable leitmotif in contemporary critical responses to realist fiction (see Chapter 3). Baudelaire's catas-troping of the detail in his section on ''Mnemonic Art'' in *Le peintre de la vie moderne* may stand as the most revelatory statement of the threat posed by the proliferation of details inherent in copying from nature. Baudelaire is arguing here the superiority of what we might call *deferred mimeticism*, of drawing from memory rather than from the model. Recollection, as it is practiced by Constantin Guys, screens out parasitical details. Thus when a mnemonic artist like Guys is confronted with the model, he is overwhelmed by the multiplicity of details the model presents:

> In this way a struggle is launched between the will to see all and forget nothing and the faculty of memory, which has formed the habit of a lively absorption of general colour and of silhouette, the arabesque of contour. An artist with a perfect sense of form but one accustomed to relying above all on his memory and his imagination will find himself at the mercy of a *riot of details* all clamouring for justice with *the fury of a mob* in love with absolute equality. All justice is trampled under foot; all harmony sacrificed and destroyed; many a trifle assumes vast proportions; many a triviality usurps the attention. The more our artist turns an impartial eye on detail, the greater is the state of *anarchy*. Whether he be long-sighted or short-sighted, *all hierarchy and all subordination vanishes*.[28]

Baudelaire's troping of the detail as revolutionary mob overtly politicizes the aesthetic; the peril posed by succumbing to the invasion of the barbaric or feminine upstart detail—the crowd and the female are on the same continuum in the nineteenth-century male imaginary—is nothing less than the end of civilization itself.

However much Reynolds may have called for sacrificing of the detail to the higher ends of the Ideal and the Sublime, his strictures were far from absolute. For him the complete absence of detail or ornament is no more desirable than

their excessive presence. Just as the so-called Scottish rhetoricians of the sublime—Lord Kames and Blair among them—exempt the rhetorical figure hy-
potyposis from their critique of circumstantiality in recognition of its mimetic
power, Reynolds repeatedly asserts that details do produce a truth effect, and
ornaments provide needed contrast with *repose:*

> I am very ready to allow that some circumstances of minuteness and par-
> ticularity frequently tend to give an air of truth to a piece, and to interest the
> spectator in an extraordinary manner. Such circumstances therefore cannot
> wholly be rejected. (IV, 58)

> . . . absolute unity, that is, a large work, consisting of one group or mass of
> light only, would be as defective as an heroick poem without episode, or any
> collateral incidents to recreate the mind with that variety which it always
> requires. (VIII, 147)

What Reynolds's *Discourses* reveal is that by the latter half of the eighteenth
century the detail had already invaded the precincts of the academy; the problem
for him is not so much to exclude the detail altogether as to moderate the effects
produced by its indiscriminate profusion. "Rules," he remarks knowingly, "are
to be considered fences placed only where trespass is expected."[29] The Sublime
can in this perspective be seen as a masculinist aesthetic designed to check the
rise of a detailism which threatens to hasten the slide of art into femininity,
because unquestionably for Reynolds, the decadence of art since the Renaissance
is bound up with its loss of virility: "Parmigiano has dignified *the genteelness of
modern effeminacy* by uniting it with the simplicity of the ancients and the grandeur and severity of Michel Angelo" (IV, 72; emphasis added). Indeed, as we
shall have ample opportunity to observe, the association of details, femininity,
and decadence is perhaps the most persistent legacy left to us by Classicism.
That Reynolds's strategy for containment was not successful is a matter of historical record, not because the detail overwhelmed the sublime, rather because
the detail was to become, as Blake had predicted it would, the very "Foundation
of the Sublime."

# 2.
# SUBLIMATION:
## Hegel's *Aesthetics*

Hegel still, always . . .
Jacques Derrida, *Writing and Difference*

Hegel's *Lectures on Aesthetics* is a notoriously underread text, but it is also one of the most influential treatises on aesthetics in our Western heritage. The paradoxical status of Hegel's *Aesthetics* is wittily summed up by Paul de Man: "Few thinkers have so many disciples who have never read a word of their master's writings."[1] The neglect of Hegel's monumental work surely is due in part to its unwieldy form. Like Saussure's *Cours de linguistique générale*, the *Aesthetics* is a posthumous composite of manuscripts and student lecture notes which, while heavily edited by Hegel's pupil Heinrich Gustav Hotho, appears both repetitive and digressive, awash in a hodgepodge of empirical details drawn from an encyclopedic range of sources. The following attempts to tease out of this mass of details what is in fact a remarkably consistent and coherent discourse *on* the detail, for the detail as aesthetic category undergirds the entire edifice of the *Aesthetics*, serving as a means of distinguishing both between periods of art (Symbolism, Classicism, Romanticism) and between major artistic modes of representation (e.g. sculpture, poetry, painting). The detail ordains both the diachronic and the synchronic axes of the *Aesthetics*, enabling generic distinctions as well as periodization.

Synchronically the detail serves to distinguish among the arts, for Hegel does not assign the same role to the detail in the different artistic media:

> It is true that there is an essential distinction between the different arts according to the medium in which they are expressed. The fullness and detailing of external fact [*Ausführlichkeit und Partikularität des Äusseren*] lies further away from sculpture because of the peace and universality of its figures . . . Epic, on the other hand, says *what* is there, *where* and *how* deeds have been done, and therefore, of all kinds of poetry needs the greatest breadth and definiteness of the external locality. So too painting by its nature enters especially in this respect upon detail [*Partikuläre*] more than any other art does.[2]

Diachronically the detail operates as an essential discriminant between the successive artistic epochs. It is the passage from a quasi-total absence of details to an excess thereof that allows Hegel to distinguish earlier from later epochs of art, as well as early from later moments of a single epoch. For, as Steven Bungay writes: "Hegel accepted a model of stylistic development which goes back to Vasari, was adopted by Winckelmann, and had become a commonplace in the early nineteenth century, the model of growth, flowering, and withering. Arts, epochs, and styles have a period of groping imperfection, reach a peak, and decline into decadence, and Hegel uses the terms 'streng,' 'ideal,' and 'angenehm' or 'gefällig' for these periods, which he introduces as a perfectly usual set of distinctions."[3] Thus whereas Symbolic art forms and/or classical Greek sculpture in its "streng" or "ideal" phases eschew "the fullness and detailing of external fact," Romantic art forms and/or classical sculpture of the decadent Hellenistic age embrace particularization.

Hegel is here reinscribing the traditional association between details and decadence constantly at work in Academic aesthetic discourse, but this does not in any way diminish the interest of his model of periodization. For, to quote de Man once again, "the name 'Hegel' stands here for an all-encompassing vessel in which [so] many currents have gathered and been preserved."[4] In other words, what makes Hegel's discourse so very precious to us is that the *Aesthetics* is, in René Wellek's congruent formulation, "the culmination of the whole astonishing development of German speculation on art."[5]

But Hegel's *Aesthetics* claims our attention for yet another reason. Not only does Hegel chart the passage of one aesthetic age to another, his own writings are themselves situated at a moment of aesthetic crisis, on the cusp between neo-classicism and romanticism, in its conventional, un-Hegelian meaning. (Hegel, it will be recalled, collects under the rubric "Romanticism" all art since the Middle Ages.) Fredric Jameson has eloquently described the extraordinary "transitional period" which both produced and was memorialized by Hegel (and Beethoven): "it is to such a moment of possibility, such a moment of suspension between two worlds, that the philosophy of Hegel is the most ambitious and profoundly characteristic monument."[6] The *Aesthetics* bears the stamp of what we might call Hegel's double aesthetic allegiance, for Hegel refuses to opt between the perfections of the Classical and the seductions of the Modern; and, further, between the assertion that art is dead and the rival claim that "the wide Pantheon of art is rising." This double split is what leads Sir T. M. Knox, the translator of the *Aesthetics* into English, to qualify them as a puzzle.[7] Hegel's fetishistic refusal to decide explains why the *Aesthetics* is not infrequently described as a split text, "a double and possibly duplicitous text" in de Man's words.[8] Wellek, for his part, concludes: "Hegel thus presents a curious double face, a Janus head, one side looking back into the past, yearning for the Greek ideal of serenity and ideal art . . . and the other side turned toward the future, looking with unconcern and even satisfaction at the death of art as a past stage of humanity."[9] If we consider the prominence of the detail in the writings of some of those who name pivotal moments in the history of modern aesthetics—Reynolds, Hegel, and Barthes—it would appear that at moments of aesthetic mutation the detail becomes a means not only of effecting change, but of understanding it.

As more than one of Hegel's critics has noted, his systematic aesthetics are flawed by the awkward mapping of his system onto history, of the triadic art forms (Symbolism, Classicism, Romanticism) onto the five particular arts: architecture, sculpture, painting, music, and literature, in that order. And yet, for all their misgivings, Hegel's critical commentators have respected his organization and espoused his chronologies. In what follows I do neither. Guided by the fate of particularization in the *Aesthetics*, a kind of Ariadne's thread, I have adopted a circular rather than a linear mode of exposition: my dis-ordered discussion of the arts is framed by Hegel's considerations on portraiture and those on Dutch genre painting, the central focus of this chapter.

Hegel's *Aesthetics* is based on and tends toward the Ideal, which is to say the Idea of Beauty. The total adequacy of form and content that is Beauty consigns to the realm of the un-beautiful any superfluous sensuous element not fully invested by the soul. Accordingly, the Ideal implies "the negation of everything particular" (1:157); for Hegel, as for Reynolds, the Ideal is that which escapes the contamination of "chance and externality" (1:155). The Ideal is always bound up with the divine, since only God avoids completely the impure universe of the contingent: "The ideal work of art confronts us like a blessed god" (1:157). By making the quasi-divine Ideal the telos of all artistic endeavor, Hegel forecloses any access by women to the higher spheres of art. Elaborating on his theory of sexual difference in *The Philosophy of Right*, Hegel writes: "Women are capable of education, but they are not made for activities which demand a universal faculty such as the more advanced sciences, philosophy and certain forms of artistic production. Women may have happy ideas, taste and elegance but they cannot attain to the ideal."[10]

It follows from this ideal of the Ideal that Hegel condemns any art—and especially any representation of the human figure—that remains mired in the material and the contingent. Thus, like Reynolds, he condemns particularly the portrait painters who are content merely to imitate their models without improving on them, without raising them up to the Ideal. But whereas Reynolds banishes particularities in the name of a general effect, Hegel displaces the question, shaking by the same gesture the foundations of the very neo-classical aesthetic he appears to be reinscribing. In Hegel the censure of the detail is motivated not by a concern with the *general*, but rather with the *spiritual*, which is not at all the same thing. That is what emerges from two similar but not identical passages which are spaced a few pages apart, demonstrating that Hegel's repetitions are not always on the order of repetitiousness, but on occasion of insistence:

> But even the portrait-painter, who has least of all to do with the Ideal of art, *must* flatter, in the sense that all the externals in shape and expression, in form, colour, features, the purely natural side of imperfect existence, *little hairs, pores, little scars, warts*, all these he must let go, and grasp and reproduce the subject in his universal character and enduring personality. It is one thing for the artist simply to imitate the face of the sitter, its surface and external form, confronting him in repose, and quite another to be able to portray the true features which express the inmost soul of the subject. For it is throughout necessary for the Ideal that the outer form should explicitly correspond with the soul. (1:155–56; emphasis added)

> In the case of the human form, for instance, the artist does not proceed, as may be supposed, like a restorer of old paintings who even in the newly painted places reproduces the cracks which, owing to the splitting of the varnish and the paint, have covered all the other older parts of the canvas with a sort of network. On the contrary, the portrait painter will omit *folds of skin* and, still more, *freckles, pimples, pock-marks, warts* etc., and the famous Denner, in his so-called "truth to nature," is not to be taken as an example. Similarly, muscles and veins are indicated indeed, but they should not appear in the distinctness and completeness which they have in reality. For in all this there is little or nothing of the spirit, and the expression of the spiritual is the essential thing in the human form. (1:164–65; emphasis added)

To single out Denner—known as *Poren-Denner* to critics scornful of the extreme of slavishly mimetic portraiture his work represents—is by Hegel's time a topos of German neo-classical aesthetics. What is nonetheless striking about these two passages is the extraordinary fascination exerted over Hegel by the very details that must be suppressed. In contrast to the very general and abstract terms in which Reynolds's condemnation of the particular is couched, Hegel's normative vocabulary exhibits a spectacular specificity. By means of a sort of preteritio—a rhetorical figure which is particularly apt to take over the oscillations of the fetishist Hegel is—Hegel succeeds in embodying the most natural, not to say naturalistic details, even as he consigns them to erasure. It is as though in Hegel's text details are, to borrow Derrida's expression, "under erasure": both absent and present at the same time.

But that is not all: equally striking in these passages in the choice of details Hegel makes. They are not just any details, but dermal details. Nor are these passages unique; in a passage on the human body, Hegel locates in the human skin's capacity to reveal at every point man's "ensouldness" man's superiority to animals. But, he adds:

> however far the human, in distinction from the animal, body makes its life

appear outwardly, still nevertheless the poverty of nature equally finds expression on this surface by the non-uniformity of the skin, in *indentations, wrinkles, pores, small hairs, little veins* etc. (1:146; emphasis added)

Hegel's obsession with human skin is in itself not remarkable, for ever since Ulysses's scar fleshly marks and mimesis have been closely linked. No, what arrests the attention of the reader is the manner both perfectly predictable and yet somehow unexpected—considering Hegel's strictures against particularity—in which the dermal details progress from the natural to the pathological. The notoriously unreliable French translation of the *Aesthetics* presents an interesting and so far as I can make out totally fanciful interpolation in the series of dermal blemishes, adding to the list "des cicatrices consécutives à la vaccination, taches produites par une maladie de foie."[11] Now, as we have seen, it is consonant with the metaphorics of neo-classicism to imagine that any natural detail is in constant danger of a morbid mutation, indeed, that the natural is finally indistinguishable from the pathological.

The question then becomes how can the spiritual be made manifest without the intervention of the mutant detail, for the work of art exists only from the moment the Idea is given sensuous form. Or, to phrase the question otherwise: *can there be representation without particularization?* In order to answer this question, let us consider the exemplary case of sculpture which in the Hegelian system—just as in Reynolds's, who writes: "sculpture is formal, regular, austere"[12]—functions as the degree zero of the detail.

Degree zero of the detail, certainly—but providing one distinguishes, as Hegel does not always do, detail and *detail*. For, as Hegel will repeat tirelessly, if sculpture—art of the classical ideal carried to perfection by the Greeks—is, by definition, "incompatible" with the figuration of natural details, it can in no way do without a certain degree of particularization; thus an art of "abstract generality," such as Egyptian sculpture, is an art of death. In fact, Hegel's sculptural ideal is informed by a pneumatic metaphysics, and individualization are the wages of vitality:

In looking at such works the eye cannot at first make out a mass of differences and they become evident only under a certain illumination where there is a stronger contrast of light and shade, or they may be recognizable only by touch. Nevertheless although these fine nuances are not noticed at a first glance, the general impression which they produce is not for this reason lost. They may appear when the spectator changes his position or we may essentially derive from them a sense of the organic fluidity of all the limbs and their forms. This breath of life, this soul of material forms, rests entirely on the fact that each part is completely there independently and in its own particular character, while, all the same, owing to the fullest richness of the transitions, it remains in firm connection not only with its immediate neighbour but with the whole. Consequently the shape is perfectly animated at every point; even the minutest detail [*das Einzelnste*] has its purpose; every-thing has its own particular character, its own difference, its own distin-guishing mark, and yet it remains in continual flux, counts and lives only in the whole. The result is that the whole can be recognized in fragments, and such a separated part affords the contemplation and enjoyment of an un-broken whole. (2:725–26/669)

The lifelike effect produced by the sculptors of the fifth century is due to the proliferation of minute details, "fine nuances" situated just beneath the range of immediate perception or outside the field of perception altogether, in the shadowy, corporeal realm of the tactile. And yet it is from their very subliminal situation that these details derive their illusionistic power. Hegel insists on the impossibility for the spectator of taking in in the same glance both the details and the lifelike impression they produce: just as in Gombrich, the spectator is condemned to an alternative mode of perception, seeing now the illusion, now its mainsprings. It is by arresting perception in its second stage, the stage of disillusionment, that Hegel gives us his ideal of the detail. Abandoning the neo-classical framework in favor of the aesthetic of the part object elaborated by German Romanticism,[13] Hegel links the fate of the detail to that of the frag-ment, lending to the humble detail some of the prestige of the noble fragment, all the while stressing their mutual dependence on each other.

In Hegel's modulation of organicist theory there exists a relationship of "dou-ble synecdoche"—to borrow a term from the μ Group's *Rhétorique générale*—between detail and fragment. In other words, to the extent that both are distinct parts referring to the same totality, they are equivalent. At the same time, how-ever, detail and fragment are in a hierarchical relationship, because it is the equal distribution and high density of purposeful details that insures the integrity of the fragment. If each fragment is a microcosm of and acceptable aesthetic sub-stitute for the whole, it is due to the animation of every inch of the sculpture in its entirety by the play of differential nuances. Put another way: it is in the virtuality of the fragment that the detail finds its finality, gains some measure of its legitimacy. In an aesthetic of an essentially archaeological order, where any totality is but a temporary assemblage of potential fragments, the detail is the guarantor of perennity.

We have in a few short pages moved away from our point of departure, the expulsion of natural details in the name of spirituality. The more closely one reads the *Aesthetics*, the more one realizes that in Hegel the problematic of the detail is in large measure divorced from that of representation. Thus it is that architecture—the fundamental art in Hegel's system—provides the most fully realized model of an organic whole. The Gothic cathedral—always enlisted as a foil for the Parthenon in neo-classical aesthetics—functions as the equivalent of Greek sculpture in the Romantic aesthetic Hegel undertakes to present.

No one thing completely exhausts a building like this; everything is lost in the greatness of the whole. It has and displays a definite purpose; but in its grandeur and sublime peace it is lifted above anything purely utilitarian into an infinity in itself. This elevation above the finite, and this simple solidity, is its *one* characteristic aspect. In its other it is precisely where particularization [*Partikularisation*], diversity, and variety gain the fullest scope, but without letting the whole fall apart into mere trifles [*Besonderheiten*] and accidental details [*Einzelheiten*]. On the contrary, here the majesty of art brings back into simple unity everything thus divided up and partitioned. The substance of the whole is dismembered and shattered into the endless divisions of a world of individual variegations, but this incalculable multiplicity is divided in a simple way, articulated regularly, dispersed symmetrically, both moved and firmly set in the most satisfying eurhythmy, and this length and breadth of varied details [*Einzelheiten*] is gripped together unhindered into the most secure unity and clearest independence. (2:685/635)

Whatever the art form considered, the stake of synecdoche remains the same; whether one goes from the detail to the fragment (centrifugal movement of Greek statuary), or from the detail to the whole (centripetal movement of the Gothic cathedral), it is always a question of insuring the delicate balance between the autonomy of the part and the unity of the whole. Autonomy, unity . . . The choice of these words testifies to the profound complicity of the aesthetic and the political, since both are informed by the corporeal metaphor: thus the cathedral presents itself as a confederation of *definalized* details. By definalized I mean not having a finality, a goal, a telos. Sublimated by the totality into which they are absorbed, the ornamental details of the Gothic cathedral become, to borrow from Kant's aesthetic vocabulary, purposeless. It is as though under the aegis of Christianity, the ornamental can rise. In short, as long as the clauses of a certain *aesthetic contract* are respected—avoidance of the contingent, maintenance of the guarantors of classical order (simplicity, regularity, symmetry)—the proliferation of details is authorized, even encouraged. Even if by his reinscription of a certain number of rules and constraints Hegel remains the prisoner of aesthetic principles of a bygone era—though neo-classicism never really dies—by his praise of dispersion and recognition of the beauty of the parcellary—the particular in the etymological sense of the word—he announces the dawn of a new aesthetic age.

It would seem then that once one has eliminated the problem of the naturalistic detail, the no less troublesome problem of the degree of freedom and autonomy to be granted the detail remains. Nowhere is this difficulty more apparent than in Hegel's remarks on music, the second Romantic art. Music, as Hegel candidly admits, is not his strong suit: "I am little versed in this sphere" (2:893) he writes at the outset. Whereas in the fields of painting and literature, for example, Hegel could claim expertise and a substantial degree of first-hand knowledge, in the field of music he is a rank amateur or dilettante and according to him there is a major difference in the music appreciation of the amateur and the connoisseur: "What the layman likes most in music is the intelligible expression of feelings and ideas, something tangible, a topic, and therefore turns in preference to music as an accompaniment: whereas the expert who has at his fingers' ends the inner musical relations between notes and instruments, loves instrumental music in its artistic use of harmonies and melodious interactings and changing forms: he is entirely satisfied by the music itself . . ." (2:953–54).

The layman eagerly clutching at the content a text lends to music is Hegel, Hegel whose logocentrism[14] leads him to center his chapter on music on the relationship of words and music, on music as accompaniment and not on instrumental music, on music itself. For, unlike its sister arts, music, a nonobjective art of memory, is deficient in regard to content:

> This object-free inwardness in respect of music's content and mode of expression constitutes its formal aspect. It does have a content too but not in the sense that the visual arts and poetry have one; for what it lacks is giving to itself an objective configuration whether in the forms of actual external phenomena or in the objectivity of spiritual views and ideas. (2:892)

A text acts as a sort of substitute for music's missing objective correlative; "the determinate sphere of words" (2:952) supplies or supplements the content music lacks: "The details of the content are precisely what the *libretto* provides" (2:941). The specific lack of unaccompanied music is then specificity itself. Why does music need specificity? Because in the listener—Hegel's concern here is reception—decontextualized melody, however moving, produces a specular "self-apprehension" that is "in the last resort merely a mood" (2:940) and thus at risk of trivialization. In the interpenetration of text and melody, the text gains the particularization necessary to heighten the affective response of the auditor: "But if grief, joy, longing, etc. are to resound in the melody, the actual concrete soul in the seriousness of actual life has such moods only in an actual context, in specific circumstances, particular situations, events, and actions . . . the more the heart flings itself with all its might into some particular experience, the more are its emotions intensified" (2:940–41).

There is then an inner necessity in music that calls for the supplement of the text and its wealth of details. But Hegel would not be Hegel if he were content to leave matters there. For, at the same time as the libretto grounds the melody in the particular, enhancing the listener's emotional response, it introduces a dangerous scissure between the *melody* and *characterization*, reproducing *within* music the differences that oppose the Italian (melodic) and the German (characteristic) schools of music on the one hand, sculpture and painting on the other.

Hegel is then in turn both the layman and the expert. Having first argued the case for the combination of words and music, he proceeds to warn against the great risk inherent in this alliance: the overpowering of the melody by the characterization and the ensuing loss of musicality itself: "So soon as music commits itself to the abstraction of characterization in detail, it is inevitably led almost astray into sharpness and harshness, into what is thoroughly unmelodious and unmusical . . ." (2:948). So grave is the threat posed by the dispersive forces of characterization, that Hegel avows: "In this matter the chief demand seems to me to be that the victory shall always be given to the melody as the all-embracing unity and not to the disunion of characteristic passages scattered and separated individually from one another" (2:947).

Finally, music is the locus of the emergence of the tension always present throughout the *Aesthetics* between a drive toward unity, articulation, and wholeness and an equally strong countervailing drive toward fragmentation, disjunction, and particularization. Where architecture succeeds, one might say, music fails:

> . . . truly musical beauty lies in the fact that, while an advance is made from pure melody to characterization, still within this particularization melody is always preserved as the carrying and unifying soul just as, for example, within the characteristic detail of a Raphael painting the note of beauty is always still retained. Further, melody is meaningful, but in all definition of its meaning it is the animation which permeates and holds together the whole, and the characteristic particulars appear only as an emergence of specific aspects which are always led back by the inner life to this unity and animation. But in this matter to hit the happy medium is of greater difficulty in music than in the other arts because music more easily breaks up into these opposed modes of expression. (2:948)

If music is particularly prone to the conflicting pulls of melody and characterization, because of the successivity of reading, poetry and especially the descriptive poetry that would emulate painting, the art of simultaneity, is at constant risk of disintegration:

> . . . it can bring before our minds only in isolated traits one after another what we can see at one glance in the real world, and therefore in its treatment of an individual occurrence it cannot so far spread itself that the total view of it is necessarily disturbed, confused, or altogether lost. (2:982)

And yet, according to Hegel, unlike lyric poetry which by virtue of its inwardness is by definition antidescriptive, epic poetry can and even must indulge in minute descriptions; it constitutes, then, an exception to the rule. To what is this exceptional status of the detail under the epic regime due? There is first what one might call the "psychological realism" of epic, that is of Homeric epic, which enjoys paradigmatic status in the *Aesthetics*:

> . . . Homer's circumstantial descriptions of things of this sort must not seem to us to be a poetic addition to rather dry material; on the contrary, this

detailed [*ausführlicher*] attention is the very spirit of the men and situations described . . . (2:1055/950)

Hence, to cite the most celebrated example of epic ekphrasis, "the shield of Achilles" is, according to Hegel's very Kantian formulation, "a description not to be regarded as an external parergon" (2:1055). The habilitation of the detail is always bound up with a breakdown of hierarchies: whereas in our day, Hegel writes, "we have an extensive hierarchy of grades of distinction in clothing, furnishings, etc. . . . the world of the heroes was not like this . . . it was possible to linger over their descriptions because all things rank alike" (2:1054). There is further what one might call the "argument according to Lessing," the fact that in epic poetry there is no break between description and diegesis. Not only, as Lessing demonstrates, are epic descriptions active, but, as Hegel insists, the action is in turn informed by the descriptive details. What makes the epic detail so special is that, as both these arguments suggest, it is the product of a human praxis. In contradistinction to the natural detail, embodied by the dermal blemishes to be expunged from portraiture, the epic detail, typified by the crafted embellishments of homely objects, attests to the power of human agency to transform the brute given of nature and to inspirit the inert facticity of matter. Finally, and this is the most surprising, there is the fact that epic poetry being— unlike dramatic poetry which is entirely oriented by a telos, a crisis to resolve— a poetry with a slow and regular tempo, there is no reason to hurry through it. On the contrary. The epic is a text which by virtue of its definalization offers the reader the leisure to take pleasure in the grain of the text which is the detail. It is quite literally in Hegel a text of pleasure, if not of *jouissance:*

> . . . such a total world, which nevertheless is concentrated into individual lives, must proceed tranquilly in the course of its realization, without hurrying on practically and dramatically towards some mark and the result of aiming at it, so that we can linger by what goes on, immerse ourselves in the individual pictures in the story and enjoy [*geniessen*] them in all their details [*Ausführlichkeit*]. (2:1044/941)

Let us not hasten to conclude this deliberately anachronistic reading of the *Aesthetics* on the triumphant note that often accompanies modernist appropriations of classical texts. If there is as much Barthes in Hegel as there is Hegel in Barthes (and that at least is the hypothesis that has guided me in this study), there is no question but that a chasm separates the author of the *Aesthetics* from the author of *Mythologies*, that aesthetic of everyday life. The contempt Hegel flaunts for "the little stories of everyday domestic existence" and the "multiform particularities of everyday life"—in short, for all that he lumps under the dismissive heading "the prose of the world" (1:150)—goes along with his famously limited interest in the art of his time. Thus at the very moment when Balzac undertakes to write what was to become the *Comédie humaine,* Hegel elaborates an aesthetic where the novel is not recognized as a major genre. Lukács, as we shall see later, will attempt to correct this oversight by writing what is virtually a supplement to the *Aesthetics,* his *The Theory of the Novel,* but no belated supplement can mask this striking absence. Absence or displacement? If one reads Hegel on painting—the Romantic art par excellence, in Hegel's idiosyncratic use of that word—it would appear that one has but to transpose (with all the precautions and adjustments necessary) Hegel's analysis of the origins of Romantic painting, and especially of the beauties of Dutch painting, to the field of writing in order to find the "theory of the novel" one seeks in vain under the rubric of poetry, even epic. There is nothing particularly surprising about this displacement when one considers the "preeminence of the pictorial code over literary *mimesis*" which characterizes representation in the nineteenth century and from which Barthes, in a section of *S/Z,* entitled precisely, "Painting as a Model," derives the following consequences:

> Thus, realism (badly named, at any rate often badly interpreted) consists not in copying the real but in copying a (depicted) copy of the real: this famous *reality,* as though suffering from a fearfulness which keeps it from being touched directly, is *set farther away,* postponed, or at least captured through the pictorial matrix in which it has been steeped before being put into words: code upon code, known as realism.[15]

Let us note that Barthes's Platonic analysis of the painting-novel relationship in the nineteenth century does not go far enough in its demystification of the referential illusion, since it seems to suggest that, unlike mediated fiction, painting enjoys an immediate proximity to the real, whereas, as Gombrich has shown, painting itself is never directly in touch with the real: it too is always already a copy of a copy. But in the end what matters is not the degree of difference that separates painting and literature from the real: for anyone who wants to understand anything about the controversies provoked by the French realist novel—which are to a large extent controversies of the detail—the principal consequence of the primacy of *pictoria* over *poesis* in nineteenth-century representation is the primacy of the *theory of painting* over the *theory of the novel.* Whereas from the Renaissance up to the late eighteenth century, literature and its rhetoric held sway over painting, nineteenth-century fictional prose was governed by aesthetic norms derived from painting, and from Academic painting at that. It is then in the light of this relationship of the pictorial and the literary that one must read Hegel's remarks on painting.

The question arises: how does painting—the art of the detail—succeed in smuggling particularities, even naturalistic details, into the field of representation? Let us return, however briefly, to the "myth of origins" of Romantic art, to Hegel's conception of the evolution of Classical into Romantic art. This passage, it would appear, constitutes a chapter in the history of religions, in particular of the advent of Christianity, the religion of the human God. The humanization of the divine, which is the achievement of classical art, is replaced by the divinization of the human, which defines Christianity and the art it produced. This reversal entails the irresistible return of what classical art repressed:

> But in so far as in this appearance the accent is laid on the fact that God is essentially an individual person, exclusive of others, and displays the unity of divine and human subjectivity not simply in general but as *this* man, there enter here again, in art, on account of the subject-matter itself, all the aspects of the contingency and particularity of external finite existence from which beauty at the height of the classical Ideal had been purified. (1:536)

In fact it is a question of more than the return of the repressed; what is involved is the promotion of the circumstantial, a radical rearrangement of the hierarchical ordering that underpins the composition of the classical painting:

> . . . painting must go beyond this immersion in the rich content of subjectivity and its infinity. On the contrary it must free, and release into independence, particular detail [*Besonderheit*], i.e. what constitutes as it were something otherwise incidental, i.e. the environment and the background. (2:812/741)

The content of romantic painting—for unlike classical art, romantic art is characterized by the inadequation of form and content—would then be the refuse of the Ideal, that collection of insignificant materials left by the wayside in classical art:

> Thereby art becomes not only what romantic art is more or less throughout, i.e. portrait-like, but it completely dissolves into the presentation of a portrait, whether in plastic art, painting, or descriptive poetry; and it reverts to the imitation of nature, i.e. to an intentional approach to the contingency of immediate existence which, taken by itself, is unbeautiful and prosaic (1:596)

> In the presentations of romantic art, therefore, everything has a place, every sphere of life, all phenomena, the greatest and the least, the supreme and the trivial . . . (1:594)

"If heart and thought remains dissatisfied," Hegel says, "close inspection reconciles us to them" (1:598). Where then does the pleasure these works provide come from? Such is the question posed most urgently by Dutch genre painting, a *locus criticus* in the history of the detail as aesthetic category.[16] Entirely devoted to the representation of the hidden side of the classical ideal, hyperbole of painting, Dutch art seems a priori to go against Hegel's stated preferences. How then does Hegel go about reconciling his ideal of the Ideal with his very favorable appreciation of this school of art, a school generally looked down upon by Reynolds and other Academic aestheticians, notably Hegel's most illustrious predecessors and contemporaries, Winckelmann, A. W. Schlegel, Schelling? The myth of origins of painting we have just rehearsed in highly schematic fashion provides the elements of an answer in the form of an already familiar scenario:

> In general terms, the essence of painting's progress is this: a start is made with *religious* subjects, still *typically* treated . . . Next there enter more and more into the religious situations the present, the individual, the living beauty of the figures . . . until painting turns towards the world; it takes possession of nature, the everyday experiences of human life, or historically important national events, whether past or present, portraits and the like, all down to the tiniest and most insignificant detail [*Unbedeutendsten*], and it does this with the same love that had been lavished on the ideal content of religion. And in this sphere above all it attains not only the supreme perfection of painting but also the greatest liveliness of conception and the greatest individuality in the mode of execution. (2:870–71/790)

There is then according to Hegel a sort of *transference* onto profane subjects of the love initially lavished exclusively on sacred subjects.[17] If we admit that the detail is, as it were, sponsored by the religious, it follows that whatever the degree of secularization attained by a given civilization, the detail will never completely liquidate its debt to the sacred. In other words: to the extent that the profane detail (with its cluster of negative connotations: the everyday, naturalism, prosiness, smallness, insignificance) is shaped in the mold of the sacred detail, it will forever bear the stamp of its religious origins. Even camouflaged by the fetishism peculiar to our dechristianized consumer society, the detail entertains a relationship—however degraded—to the sacred. God, as Mies van der Rohe, Aby Warburg and others are credited with saying, dwells in the details.

But there is more. There is in Hegel—and it is in this sense that his conception of Romantic art can be qualified as romantic (in the restricted sense)—the possibility of conceiving of a *sublimation* of the detail, a new transcendence which would sublate "what is itself without significance" (1:596).[18] This *Aufhebung* of the prosaic detail is bodied forth by Dutch painting:

> Here the subject-matter may be quite indifferent to us or may interest us, apart from the artistic presentation, only incidentally, for example, or momentarily. In this way Dutch painting, for example, has recreated, in thousands and thousands of effects, the existent and fleeting appearance of nature as something generated afresh by man. Velvet, metallic lustre, light, horses, servants, old women, peasants blowing smoke from cutty pipes, the glitter of wine in a transparent glass, chaps in dirty jackets playing with old cards—these and hundreds of other things are brought before our eyes in these pictures, things that we scarcely bother about in our daily life, for even if we play cards, drink wine, and chat about this and that, we are still engrossed by quite different interests. But what at once claims our attention in matter

of this kind, when art displays it to us, is precisely this pure shining and appearing of objects as something produced by the *spirit* which transforms in its inmost being the external and sensuous side of all this material. For instead of real wool and silk, instead of real hair, glass, flesh, and metal, we see only colours; instead of all the dimensions requisite for appearance in nature, we have just a surface, and yet we get the same impression which reality affords. (1:162–63)

How is this "marvel of ideality" (1:163) produced, how is this "artistic phenomenalization" which succeeds in spiritualizing an initially vulgar matter arrived at? How are scenes and objects of everyday life—and in this perspective the shiny and the slimy are equivalent—invested with a transcendent aesthetic value? Hegel provides two answers: answers of a purely local sort, which take into account the specificities (ecological, economic, historical, and religious) of the Dutch situation, and philosophical answers which engage the very foundations of the *Aesthetics*. From the first series of explanations I will retain only the religious argument which Hegel privileges, writing: "the Dutch were Protestants, an important matter, and to Protestantism alone the important thing is to get a sure footing in the prose of life, to make it absolutely valid in itself independently of religious associations, and to let it develop in unrestricted freedom" (1:598). If, as Hegel would have it, Protestantism is singularly receptive to profane details, that would explain the early rise of realism in Protestant countries such as Holland (painting) and England (novel). This hypothesis also raises a difficult question: is there any difference between Protestant and Catholic varieties of realism?

It would not be exaggerated to claim that the transformation of the so-called insignificant object into an art-object engages the entire *Aesthetics*, in that this transformation relies on the superiority of the spiritual to the natural which serves as the axiom of Hegel's lectures, and, more generally, his philosophical writings. Announcing from the start the differences between his approach and Kant's, Hegel excludes natural beauty from his field of inquiry, by virtue of the following principle: "spirit and its artistic beauty stands *higher* than natural beauty" (1:2). The insignificant object is then but an extreme example of the object in its natural state, before it has been informed and transformed by the creative spirit. What Dutch genre paintings make manifest—hence their exemplary status in the *Aesthetics*—is the equivalence, not to say the irrelevance, of the content, and by extension of the faithful imitation of the real. What is finally at stake in the sublimation of the prosaic (which covers both "insignificant objects" and "the scenes of life which may seem to us not only contingent, but vulgar and common"), is the subject-object relationship. In order for the "sum of insignificances" which constitute the décor of everyday life to have access to the world of art, they must acquire "the look of independent and total life and freedom which lies at the root of the essence of beauty" (1:149); and, by the same token, for us to derive pleasure from their representation, "we must pull ourselves together and concentrate" (2:835). In other words, the object relation must be characterized on both sides by independence and autonomy: a *double detachment* is required. In order for this relationship of mutual independence to be instituted, there must be a passage from a subject-object relationship of *appropriation* to one of *identification*. A complex process. This passage can be broken down into two stages: first there must be what Hegel calls a "withdrawal" of the "desire" which links man to his environment, for, the indifference or repulsion inspired in us by the prosaic result from our tendency to view objects in a purposive fashion, in short, from our egocentrism:

> Further, if we allow our pleasure to be trivialized by accepting the supercilious intellectual reflection that we should regard such objects as vulgar and unworthy of our loftier consideration, we are taking the subject-matter of painting in a way quite different from that in which art really presents it to us. For in that case we are bringing with us only the relation we take up to such objects when we need them or take pleasure in them or regard them from the point of view of the rest of our culture and our other aims; i.e. we are treating them only according to their external purpose, with the result that it is our needs which become the chief thing, a living end in itself . . . (2:834)

The withdrawal of desire corresponds to a definalization of the disdained object or scene, a *definalization* which cannot but provoke a *defamiliarization*, because once the object or the other is freed from the practical bonds tying it to what we might call, borrowing from Freud, "his Majesty the Ego," they appear in a new and altogether different light.

At the second stage, the complementary movement of withdrawal of the object is accomplished, paradoxically favored by the interest which the subject bears or attributes to it:

> Man always lives in the immediate present; what he does at every moment is something particular, and the right thing is simply to fulfil every task, no matter how trivial, with heart and soul. In that event the man is at one with such an individual matter for which alone he seems to exist, because he has put his whole self and all his energy into it. This cohesion [between the man and his work] produces that harmony between the subject and the particular character of his activity in his nearest circumstances which is also a spiritual depth and which is the attractiveness of the independence of an explicitly total, rounded, and perfect existence. Consequently, the interest we may take in pictures of objects like those mentioned does not lie in the objects themselves but in this soul of life which in itself, apart altogether from the thing

in which it proves to be living, speaks to every uncorrupt mind and free heart and is to it an object in which it participates and takes joy. (2:833)

This somewhat difficult passage is illuminated by another in which Hegel attempts to lay bare the mechanism of the "irresistible attraction" exerted on the spectator by the representation of vulgar subjects. It emerges that pushed to the limit, the deconstruction of the insignificant (vulgar) / significant (noble) paradigm calls into question the very notion of insignificance-vulgarity. It is then that the concept of independence takes on its full meaning, for the independence of the subject represented confers upon the most vulgar scenes and characters a title to nobility that likens them to the Gods of Olympus, those paradigms of the classical ideal. Here is Hegel at the moment when he is expanding on his praise of Dutch painting by praising Murillo's canvases:

> In the like sense the beggar boys of Murillo . . . are excellent too . . . the mother picks lice out of the head of one of the boys while he quietly munches his bread; on a similar picture two other boys, ragged and poor, are eating melon and grapes. But in this poverty and semi-nakedness what precisely shines forth within and without is nothing but complete absence of care and concern—a Dervish could not have less—in the full feeling of their well-being and delight in life. This freedom from care for external things and the inner freedom made visible outwardly is what the Concept of the Ideal requires . . . We see that they [the boys of Murillo] have no wider interests and aims, yet not at all because of stupidity; rather do they squat on the ground content and serene, almost like the gods of Olympus. (1:170)

What does all this mean? It seems to me that Hegel is not far from proposing here the same analysis of the "irresistible attraction" exerted by the representation of inner freedom that Freud will propose nearly a century later to account for the magnetic effects of narcissism:

> It seems very evident that another person's narcissism has a great attraction for those who have renounced part of their own narcissism and are in search of object-love. The charm of a child lies to a great extent in his narcissism, his self-contentment and inaccessibility, just as does the charm of certain animals which seem not to concern themselves about us, such as cats and the large beasts of prey.[19]

Juxtaposed, these passages from Hegel's *Aesthetics* and Freud's "On Narcissism: An Introduction" (1913) disclose the aesthetics of narcissism, if not the narcissism of aesthetics. The fascinating freedom of Murillo's beggar boys and the seductive autarchy of Freud's children, animals (and, of course, women) display the same mechanism, as evidenced by the centrality of the child in both texts. In both instances, desire is mediated by the object's sui-referentiality. What is perceived as beautiful in Hegel's example is what Freud refers to as the object's

Figure 4.  Brouwer, *The Smokers*

"blissful state of mind" and the "unassailable libidinal position" it constitutes
and with which the subject identifies.

But, finally, the reason why the subject-matter is indifferent and the signif-
icant/insignificant paradigm impertinent, is that in their representation the formal aspect overrides the content to the point where it becomes an end in itself.
As the profane invades the universe of representation, form is sacralized: "apart

Figure 5.   Murillo, *The Melon Eaters*

from the things depicted, the means of the portrayal also becomes an end in itself, so that the artist's subjective skill and his application of the means of artistic production are raised to the status of an objective matter in works of art" (1:599). Now the "illusion of reality" is closely bound up with the representation of the/in detail:

> In supreme art we see fixed the most fleeting appearance of the sky, the time of day, the lighting of the trees; the appearances and reflections of clouds, waves, lochs, streams; the shimmering and glittering of wine in a glass, a flash of the eye, a momentary look or smile, etc. Here painting leaves the ideal for the reality of life; the effect of appearance it achieves here especially by the exactitude with which every tiniest individual part is executed. (2:812)

Artistic phenomenalization constitutes in some sense the *apotheosis of the detail*, so much so that as long as the imperatives of the organicist model are respected, realist art defies the ideal:

> Yet this is achieved by no mere assiduity of composition but by a spiritually rich industry which perfects each detail [*Besonderheit*] independently and yet retains the whole connected and flowing together; to achieve this, supreme skill is required. (2:812–13/741)

Seen close up, pictorial details turn out to be insignificant signs that become meaningful only in the differential play which opposes light and darkness; the "reality-effect" (Barthes) depends then on maintaining a "proper distance": if a spectator comes up too close to a painting, the mimetic detail dissolves into a swirl of points and incoherent strokes:

> If we look closely at the play of colour, which glints like gold and glitters like braid under the light, we see perhaps only white or yellow strokes, points of colour, coloured surfaces; the single colour as such does not have this gleam which it produces; it is the juxtaposition *alone* which makes this glistening and gleaming. (1:600)

This pulverulence is the final stage in the sublimation of the prosaic detail, for it is as though the prosaic could not make its debut on the scene of representation except reduced to pure facticity, filtered through a myopic gaze for which all things resolve themselves into a haze of indistinct and dull color. Compared to Hegel's myopic vision, Proust's celebrated "little patch of yellow wall"—that fragment of Vermeer's "View of Delft" that arrests Bergotte's dying gaze[20]— looms as monumental. If, as I suggested above, Hegel's theory of painting also serves as a theory of the novel, the novel Hegel theorizes is neither Balzac's nor Proust's, but rather Flaubert's. For Flaubert, who had read Hegel's *Aesthetics*, is similarly myopic in his gaze. His descriptions are notable for their juxtaposition of heterogeneous details which, in extreme cases, work to reduce the objects of referential reality to inert and stupid matter.

# 3.
# DECADENCE:
## Wey, Loos, Lukács

A gradual progress from simplicity to complex forms and profuse
ornament seems to be the fate of all the fine arts.
Lord Kames, *Elements of Criticism*

The rise of realism did not still criticism of the detail. On the contrary: it amplified
it and made it more shrill. Even as or rather because the detail continued to
expand its empire over the field of representation, it remained throughout the
nineteenth century and, more important, well into the twentieth, the focus of
a virulent controversy, putting in the same bed such unlikely companions as
Sir Joshua Reynolds and Georg Lukács. Nor did the invention of photography,
widely hailed as the art of the detail, immediately change this attitude for, as
we shall soon see, the theory of photography in statu nascendi came, like the
novel, under the aesthetic sway of Academic painting. Of all the arguments
enlisted against the detail, none was to receive more attention in the mid-nine-
teenth century than the ancient association of details and decadence, which runs
in an unbroken continuity from the critique of realism to the critique of modernism. It is the posterity of this classical association that I would like to trace
here, following a somewhat meandering course spanning two centuries and
crisscrossing national boundaries.

Francis Wey

> Francis Wey: (1812–82), born in Besançon, man of
> letters. Author of scholarly works: *Histoire des Rév-
> olutions du Langage en France*, and of novels: *Les En-
> fants du marquis de Gange*, a work which inaugurated
> the genre of the serialized novel (*roman feuilleton*).
>
> Quillet

Hostility to the detail pervades the texts which constitute the "reception" of
realism in nineteenth-century France.[1] It features as prominently in the critical
writings of the greats—Sainte-Beuve, Taine and Brunetière—as in the writings
of a host of journalists whose names (Emile Daurand Forgues, Hippolyte Babour,

Armand de Pontmartin, to name but a few) are known today, if at all, only by a handful of scholars. From this dense journalistic activity, a remarkably coherent discourse on the detail emerges, repeating in degraded form the main tenets of an idealist aesthetics which survives a century of revolution and change with astonishing resilience: the totalizing ambitions of realism that claims to account for the entire domain of the visible are deplored; the privilege accorded the "horrible" detail is decried; the loss of difference between the insignificant and the significant, when it is not the outright promotion of the insignificant, is lamented; the possibility of reconciling the respect for the whole of classicism with the attention to minutiae which characterizes realism is duly debated; and, finally, the invasion of the arts by an anarchic mass of details is pronounced the unmistakeable sign of cultural dissolution. In short, the detail had a bad press.

From this chorus of protest against the imperialist detail, one voice gradually emerges as deserving an especially attentive hearing. Francis Wey, the author on the one hand of "Of the Cult of Details" ("De la Recherche des Détails"), and on the other hand "Theory of the Portrait," an article which appeared in *La Lumière*, the first French weekly entirely devoted to photography and to which Wey was, at least at the outset, a regular contributor. Posterity has dealt selectively with Wey: his important contributions to the theory of photography are well known to historians of photography, but his contributions to rhetoric and fiction have sunk into oblivion.[2] My purpose here is not to dispute literary history's assessment of his contribution to literature and its theory; rather I would like to suggest that it is precisely because Wey bridged two artistic media that his aesthetic texts should be of interest to literary as well as photographic historians.

### Of the Cult of Details

Wey quickly stakes out his position: "The taste for and the close attention to details characterizes young and strong literatures; the abuse, the profusion of details signals decadent literatures . . ."[3] As we have already noted, the equation of an excess of details and decadence is an essential tenet of neo-classical doxa. It will receive its final consecration in the still unsurpassed definition of "decadent style" given by Paul Bourget at the turn of the century:

> A decadent style is one where the unity of the book decomposes to give way to the independence of the page, where the page decomposes to give way to the independence of the word.[4]

Decadence in literature signifies a disintegration of the textual whole, the increasing autonomy of the parts, and in the end a generalized synecdoche. The decadent style is inherently ornamental.[5] Decadence is a pathology of the detail: either metastasis or hypertrophy or both. For Wey the equation between details and decadence serves above all as a diagnostic tool, allowing him to discriminate between the healthy and the sick literary body, the good use of the detail and the bad. Thus he opposes Greek literature (rich in details) to Roman literature (chary of details), just as some one hundred years later, Lukács will oppose realism (rich in essential details) to naturalism (rich in inessential details). The benefit Wey derives from the opposition of the Greek and the Latin use of the detail is that it allows him to rewrite the literary history of France from a novel vantage point, producing a new literary history organized around and by the detail:

> These clearly distinguished schools resulted in France in two very different types of literature: the sixteenth century which drew its inspiration from the Greeks delighted in the detail, in stylistic arabesques; the seventeenth century which fell under the banner of the Latins, is like them, severe and stripped of those fancies one calls details. (375)

According to Wey, his contemporaries have joined the ranks of the Atticists, and—crowning touch of decadence—their detailism is third-hand, mediated by the "century of Henry II:" a degraded decadence, a decadence of decadence. Wey concludes: "the detail has become among us the object of an exclusive cult, that is an abuse, in prose as in verse" (376).

But just as Wey seems to have pronounced his final sentence on his Atticizing contemporaries, he infuses new life into the discussion by giving his argument an unexpected turn. He recognizes that the proliferation of details among those whose writings exert the greatest influence on the young—Hugo and Balzac— is precisely their main claim to fame: "if one took away from their style this shower of flowers, this mass of ornaments, one would rob them of a part of their attraction and their novelty." The flowers turn out to be, to mix metaphors, "feathers" in their caps, the ornaments, ornaments. It is then a question of reorienting the article, of abandoning polemics in favor of a simple statement of facts, but hardly has Wey started down this path, than he enlists an analogy borrowed from classical rhetoric. The immediate effect is to bring his argument back to its starting point:

> The object of this article is then less to criticize a tendency characteristic of the contemporary literary period, than to signal one of those transformations which the arts undergo in a society which is past its prime; when, *like women* who have passed the stage when the simple beauty of youth sufficed to make them beautiful . . . they seek new charms in the artifice of ornament and the glitter of adornments. (376–77; emphasis added)

Wey does nothing more than reinscribe a venerable metaphorics equating rhetorical ornaments with the artifices of painted women: an ornamental style is an effeminate style. As Quintilian writes: "But such ornament must, as I have already said, be bold, manly and chaste, free from all effeminate smoothness and the false hues derived from artificial dyes, and must glow with health and vigour."[6] Cicero, on the other hand, contrasts the Asiatic (degraded, effeminate, ornamented) style with the Attic (virile, noble, unadorned) by opposing two types of women: one who is made-up, the other sporting the "natural look":

> Just as some women are said to be handsomer when unadorned—this very lack of ornament becomes them—so this plain style gives pleasure even when unembellished: there is something in both cases which lends greater charm, but without showing itself. Also all noticeable ornament, pearls as it were, will be excluded; not even curling-irons will be used; all cosmetics, artificial white and red, will be rejected; only elegance and neatness will remain. The language will be pure Latin, plain and clear; propriety will always be the chief aim. Only one quality will be lacking, which Theophrastus mentions fourth among the qualities of style—the charm and richness of figurative ornament.[7]

For the archaeology of the detail, the sexism of rhetoric is of crucial significance. Neo-classical aesthetics is imbued with the residues of the rhetorical imaginary, a sexist imaginary where the ornamental is inevitably bound up with the feminine, when it is not the pathological—two notions Western culture has throughout its history had a great deal of trouble distinguishing. This imaginary femininity weighs heavily on the fate of the detail as well as of the ornament in aesthetics, burdening them with the negative connotations of the feminine: the decorative, the natural, the impure, and the monstrous. Wey's apparently innocuous analogy demonstrates the durability of a century-old metaphorical system, a scheme associating the ornamental with feminine duplicity or degradation, as though the ornament-femininity equation were an established fact. As though it were, in a word, natural.

There is then nothing less spontaneous, nothing less innocent than Wey's threadbare analogy: by inscribing himself in the tradition of classical rhetoric, by borrowing its language, Wey accredits the system of values this highly figurative language conveys. It is the hold exerted on Wey by this language, by this chain of equivalencies, that will prevent him from progressing, from abandoning an aesthetic he himself considers obsolete. Indeed what is ultimately most curious, most symptomatic about this text is the way Wey hesitates between an enlightened modernism and a bloodless neo-classicism. Thus, acting on the principle that "il faut être de son temps" and not "submit in any absolute fashion the arts of one century to the ideas of another century" (378), Wey praises the Hugolian detail in these rather surprising terms:

> The profusion of details, the importance they are accorded, the brilliance with which they are presented, the manner in which they are interlaced with the principal idea, which often takes up little space and seems to be only a pretext, a canvas for images, all constitute a new manner, one which is very bold, extremely brilliant . . . No one makes use of this manner with more daring and success than M. Victor Hugo. (381–82)

This passage marks a distinct departure from classical discourse and reveals the inroads of another aesthetics; Wey is completely ready to praise the proliferation of details and the overwhelming of the main subject that it entails, even the installation of a self-authorized writing, a texture which reduces the signified to a mere prop. That is no small thing. But there are limits to Wey's tolerance. Its threshold is reached at the moment when the cultivation of the detail turns to a cult, hence the title of Wey's article. The line of demarcation between "lovingly cultivated details" (308) and "vicious" details is quickly crossed, for the difference between the good and the bad detail is first a quantitative difference, a difference of degree. The bad detail is a good detail which has gone bad by completely detaching itself from its support to become an end in itself, a detail for detail's sake:

> But I don't think the love of the detail is without danger, and abuse cannot be far distant from this great success. As soon as effort appears, the limit has been transgressed; as soon as a detail adds nothing to the image, no color to the idea, does not seem to be naturally led up to, or is not in harmony with the general polish of the work, the detail becomes vicious. (384)

And Wey goes on to cite the exemplary case of Balzac, whose prose "positively signals a decadent literature" (384). The Balzac/Hugo opposition—a commonplace in nineteenth-century French literary criticism—is here placed in the service of a certain ideal of the metaphor which is natural, thus adequate. The importance of the notion of the "natural" stands out clearly in the following passage where Wey argues, somewhat paradoxically, that Balzac's artificiality results from his lack of artifice:

> His taste is impure, and he lacks certain turns, certain artifices of the noble style, he compensates for the lack of acquired skill with a natural skill, when he is led to express ideas which are finer than and superior to the means of execution with which his knowledge provides him. But these improvised forms, these particular touches which ordinarily have the detail as their goal, mislead it and force it to seek complicated effects which are too far from the natural. (384–85)

If Balzac serves as a foil to Hugo, it is because where Hugo's pursuit of details yields successful metaphors, Balzac's leads only to failed comparisons. In other words, in Wey the fate of the detail in literature is closely linked to that of analogy. Consequently he is less interested in the nature of the objects connected by a comparison or metaphor than in the nature of the relationship itself. There is strain when the gap between the tenor and the vehicle is too great, when there is "baroquism"; thus Wey's Balzac is, curiously, a precious Balzac. Here is the hyperbolic example of Balzac's studied detail, a "deliberate and calculated effort" according to Wey, complete with typography and a commentary which leave little doubt as to the target of the rhetorician's barbs:

*The breath* of her soul deployed itself *in the folds of* the syllables, AS SOUND DIVIDES ITSELF UNDER THE KEYS OF THE FLUTE, it died out *in waves* to the ear, *from which it hastened the action of the blood*. Her way of pronouncing the endings in I evoked some bird's song; *pronounced by her the* CH *was like a caress.* AND THE MANNER IN WHICH SHE ATTACKED the Ts BETRAYED THE DESPOTISM OF HER HEART.

You see here the detail of the most quintessential, the vainest, the most burlesque of details. (386)

The play of the type faces selected by Wey makes abundantly clear the hierarchy of offenses committed by Balzac against literary proprieties. Beyond the italicized metaphoric language, which already constitutes a deviation from the norm represented by the words in Roman type face, two syntagms stand out in bold face. In the first, it is a matter of a partition, a dispersion of the signifying substance. The comparison is thus foregrounded, functioning as a *mise en abyme* of the very act of detailing: it really is a detail of a detail. The second and last syntagm illustrates yet another negative aspect of the Balzacian detail: the deviation, indeed the disproportion between the detail (isolated, minute, arbitrary) and the univocal and globalizing interpretation to which it gives rise. Balzac's decadence consists then in the extenuation and extrapolation to which he subjects detail in his texts. Realism—a word that appears nowhere in this text—turns out to be an avatar of the baroque (another absent word), the school of the studied detail par excellence.

## "Theory of the Portrait"

Well before the twentieth century, and the writings of Benjamin, Sontag, and Barthes, photography was hailed as a remarkable technical invention allowing for the first time in the history of representation the monumentalization of details either invisible to the naked eye, or neglected in everyday life, or reputed to be unrepresentable. An anecdote Wey repeats practically verbatim in two different newspapers testifies to the contemporary awareness of the way photography decisively extended the field of the detail:

Thanks to so many efforts, heliography arrived at an ideal perfection. Such even is the almost fantastic power of the process that it permits the person examining an architectural design to explore the nature, the quality, the grain, the flaws in the stone and to make observations unnoticed in the field. This assertion calls to mind a singular occurrence.

Three and a half years ago, M. Baron Gros, then minister plenipotentiary in Greece, fixed by means of a daguerreotype, a point of view taken at the Acropolis in Athens. There were disseminated ruins, sculpted stones, all manner of fragments. Back in Paris, M. Baron Gros relived his travel memories and, as he contemplated with the help of a strong magnifying glass the fragments piled up in the foreground of his picture, all of a sudden he discovered on one of the stones an ancient figure which had escaped his attention. It was a lion devouring a serpent incised in the stone . . . The microscope allowed to bring into relief this precious document, revealed by the daguerreotype alone, and to restore to it proportions accessible to study.

Thus, this prodigious instrument renders that which the eye sees and what it cannot distinguish; so that, just as in nature, the spectator, coming up more or less close thanks to graduated lenses, perceives an infinity of details, when objects in their totality no longer satisfy his curiosity.[8]

Let us stop for a moment to develop some of the implications of Wey's "Blow-Up" anecdote. In contrast with earlier modes of recording travel impressions—paintings, sketches, engravings—photography operates by morcellization. It is a detailing technique, in the etymological sense of the verb *détailler:* to cut in pieces. To the jaded eye, bored with pictorial overviews, the new technique opens up the vast unexplored territory of luxuriant, inexhaustible detail—colonial metaphor intended.[9] Not only does photography extend space, it dilates time. For the details brought into sharp relief by the daguerreotype and revealed by magnification are by definition *delayed details*. It is interesting to contrast Baudelaire's mnemonic art, an anti-photographic art where difference serves to filter out superfluous detail and bring to light the essential form, with Wey's daguerreotype, where temporal delay acts to develop (pun intended) and enhance detail. In both instances, detail and difference are closely bound up with each other.

Photography transforms tourism into a privative activity; the Baron Gros[10] examines his daguerreotype much the same way today's tourist views his vacation slides. One does not relive a touristic visit through photography, one lives it otherwise for the first time. The advent of the new technique ushers in an era of armchair archaeology which will in due time become a "couch-archaeology," the recollection in tranquility of traumatic details of the past that is psychoanalysis: the "blow-up" in Wey's anecdote, as well as in Antonioni's film by the same name, is a perfect illustration of the workings of *Nachträglichkeit*. Finally, according to Wey, photography has a particular aptitude for reproducing inanimate subjects, ancient ruins as well as minerological landscapes whose profuse ornamental detail painting is incapable of rendering; it is in the inhuman realm of the dead city and the winter woods that photography's affinity for the minute makes its superiority to painting most acutely felt:

Subjects crawling with details, monuments laden with arabesques, the crossroads of ancient cities, place it above any competition. We have seen landscape painters lost in admiration before prints taken in winter in the woods, prints where the planes were a prodigious tangle of bare bramble, twigs, tree trunks, grounds bristling with grass and small branches . . .[11]

What one tends to forget today is that when it was applied to the representation of the human face, when it invaded the sacred precincts of the portrait, photographic detailism aroused something less than enthusiasm on the part of both clients and critics. As Gisèle Freund notes, the invention of photography and the widespread popularization of the photographic portrait were almost immediately followed by the inauguration of new techniques of idealization, making it possible to erase unsightly physiognomic blemishes that the camera could not help but register: "New technological advances generally developed in response to contemporary social needs. The bourgeois insistence on a 'pleasant' prettified self-image led to the practice of retouching."[12] Wey, however, is opposed to retouching, all the while deploring in the field of the portrait that which constitutes for him the interest of photography in the field of the landscape, namely its uncanny capacity to capture details:

Risky details, the more they are scintillating and minute, the more it accentuates them, the more it reproduces them vivaciously. With the result that the head, the chief subject is erased, becomes tarnished, loses its interest, its unity, and everything shimmers, without one's attention being concentrated anywhere.[13]

If Wey is opposed to retouching it is because for him circumstantial rather than physiognomic details constitute the greatest threat to the ideality of the photographic portrait; it is "the indiscreet prolixity of the detail" that all too often prevents photography from rivaling the "style" of the work of art. Consequently, to palliate the unfortunate dispersal of the spectator's attention, Wey recommends the simple transfer to the field of photography of the "theory of sacrifices" that holds sway in pictorial representation. Baudelaire elegantly articulates the basic economy of this sacrificial theory: "an art is nothing but an abstraction and a sacrifice of detail to the whole."[14] Wey's "theory of the portrait" is then nothing but an appropriation of idealist portrait painting theory to the realm of photography:

This primordial law of the theory of the portrait, which painters depart from the less is their talent, has been transgressed by the majority of heliographers and that is why their portraits offended by god knows what vulgarity, by the absence of impression, and excited curiosity, without providing the satisfaction one expects from works of art.[15]

Thus we see reappearing in the very midst of these pioneering theoretical writings on photography the old Academic conventions, for if the question of the aesthetic status of photography was hotly debated at the time, the legitimacy of the influence exerted by the theory of painting on the theory of photography seemed to go unquestioned. For Wey—and Wey was a "modern" in the controversies over photography—truth cannot reside in the vulgar immediacy of realistic details; the photographic portrait must conform to the Ideal or risk falling prey to teratology; caricature is there to serve as a warning against the excesses of realism:

> Truth in art is never a matter of a pitiless, unintelligent trace of nature, but of a spiritual interpretation. From the point of view of scurrilous reality, the Daguerrian portraits can be said to have proclaimed loud and clear the superiority of thought and the necessity of inspiration. The streets and quais were strewn with horrific portraiture, conscientiously exact, but poor likenesses. Thanks to the interpretation of painting, one could never have suspected that bourgeois ugliness could attain such high levels. Everyone saw with horror entire families, arranged in bunches like packets of onions, display without taste or discernment, the most antipathetic costumes, attitudes, and expressions [. . .] It's enough to make Traviès and Daumier recoil. Are these then portraits? In truth no! For they do not correspond to the image the model has etched in our memory. One cannot repeat it often enough: truth in the arts is ideal and results from a subtle interpretation.[16]

Finally it would appear that in the field of portraiture the advent of photography breathed new life into the ideal of the ideal.

It is no accident that the reaffirmation of the primacy of the spiritual and the subjective in the field of the arts goes hand in hand with an aristocratic contempt for bourgeois ugliness. For the question of the detail is also a social, indeed an economic question.

## Adolf Loos

> Ornament: That which ornaments, which serves
> to ornament: any detail or object with practical use-
> fulness which is added to a whole to embellish it
> or to give it a certain character.
>
> Le Robert

The controversy over the ornament that arose in response to art nouveau was an aspect of the detail polemic. "Ornament and Crime" (1908), the sensational and widely read article by Adolf Loos, the Viennese architect and art critic, remains one of its central documents. But before dealing with this text— surely one of the great manifestoes of modernity—let us return for a moment to Hegel's *Aesthetics*, in order to confront his analysis of the ornament with Loos's. Hegel's remarks occur in a passage demonstrating that art is inherent in man's reflexive nature. In fact, man, "a *thinking* consciousness" can "take pleasure in himself" only by exteriorizing himself, finding his imprint on the outside world, indeed on himself to the extent that he participates in that world. In other words for Hegel, corporeal ornamentation derives its justification and meaning from the ontological need man experiences to annex *physis* to the domain of culture, to infuse brute nature with spirituality:

> And it is not only with external things that man proceeds in this way, but no less with himself, with his own natural figure which he does not leave as he finds it but deliberately alters. This is the cause of all dressing up and adornment, even if it be barbaric, tasteless, completely disfiguring, or even pernicious like crushing the feet of Chinese ladies, or slitting the ears or lips.[17]

Loos's point of view on this question is quite different, Loos who as we know read Lombroso and sanctioned a sort of aesthetic Darwinism, according to which corporeal adornment, which is the prerogative of savages, constitutes in civilized society the seal of criminality, the irrefutable sign of racial degeneracy:

> The Papuan tattoos his skin, his boat, his oars, in short, everything he can get his hands on. He is no criminal. The modern man who tattoos himself is a criminal or a degenerate. There are prisons in which eighty percent of the prisoners are tattooed. Tattooed men who are not behind bars are either latent criminals or degenerate aristocrats.[18]

Let us note that if on a certain level, Hegel and Loos agree—both exhibit the same tolerance with regard to primitive practices which are considered to be the matrix of civilization—on another level, there is profound disagreement: in bringing into play the case of the tattooed civilized man, Loos decisively displaces the question of the ornament. For if there is tattooing in contemporary society for Loos it has to do less with an ontological need, than with a need he qualifies as "erotic." Thus, whereas in the Hegelian perspective, "it is only among civilized people that alteration of figure, behaviour, and every sort and mode of external expression proceeds from spiritual development" (1:31), for Loos (who is much closer to Freud, his contemporary in fin de siècle Vienna) primitive, indeed infantile erotic instincts can subsist in "modern and adult man" in the form of "pathological symptoms" (248). What constitutes for Hegel a sign of spiritual advancement signals for Loos a pathological regression. For modern man to distinguish himself from the Papuans, the erotic instinct must be ruthlessly repressed.[19]

Loos's most telling illustration of the erotic properties of adornment occur in his piece on "Ladies' Fashion" (1902). Not surprisingly, Loos scores the prevalence of the ornamental in ladies' fashion:

> The clothing of the woman is distinguished externally from that of the man by the preference for the ornamental and colorful effects and by the long skirt that covers the legs completely. These two factors demonstrate to us that woman has fallen behind sharply in her development in recent centuries.

Figure 6.  Loos, Advertisement

No period of culture has known as great differences as our own between the clothing of the free man and the free woman. In earlier eras, men also wore clothing that was colorful and richly adorned and whose hem reached the floor. Happily, the grandiose development in which our culture has taken part this century has overcome ornament.[20]

Though the ladies' fashion system is ruled by the coquette, Loos was no believer in inborn female narcissism. If woman covers her body with rich adornments it is because in turn-of-the-century society she must attract and keep a "big, strong man" if she is to hold her own in the "battle of the sexes," and man is repelled by the naked female body. Woman is forced to fetishize herself because of the inherent perversion of male desire. Female mystery is a male construct: "Woman covered herself, she became a riddle to man, in order to implant in his heart the desire for the riddle's solution."[21] Loos's demystification of the riddle of woman contrasts sharply with Freud's celebrated remystification in his essay on "Femininity." So foreign to woman are her adornments, that Loos foresees the day when a liberated woman will shed her man-catching accoutre-ments; that day, however, will come not when man forswears his perverse sen-suality, but rather when woman achieves equal economic status with men. Loos always insists on the economic dimension of ornament:

That which is noble in a woman knows only one desire: that she hold on to her place by the side of the big, strong man. At present that desire can only be fulfilled if the woman wins the love of the man. But we are approaching a new and greater time. No longer by an appeal to sensuality, but rather by economic independence earned through work will the woman bring about her equal status with the man. The woman's value or lack of value will no longer fall or die according to the fluctuation of sensuality. Then velvet and silk, flowers and ribbons, feathers and paint will fail to have their effect. They will disappear.[22]

Where Loos distinguishes himself from Hegel is not in his ultimately elementary psychoanalysis of the "decorative instinct," but rather in his very notion of modern man, in his affirmation of modernity. It is worth noting that for Loos espousing modernity does not mean forsaking the classical ideal. Absolute modernity, enlightened, rational modernity, is in fact a return to the principles of an earlier aesthetic:

[the ancient Greeks] created only that which was practical, without concerning themselves in the least with that which was beautiful, without worrying about complying with an aesthetic imperative . . . The English and the engineers are our Greeks . . .[23]

When he enunciates what we might call the "modernist corollary" to the ornament/decadence association, Loos gives it a radical new twist, turning his gaze away from an idealized past and directing it instead toward a bright new future of functionalism: *"cultural evolution is equivalent to the removal of ornament from articles in daily use"* (226–27). Coming after and reacting to art nouveau and the Viennese Secession movement, presided over by Gustav Klimt, the goldsmith's son, Loos writes in a beyond of ornamentalism, announcing in apocalyptic tones the coming of a golden age of functionalism, a golden age which will be a white age, white being the modern color par excellence.

But I said, "Don't weep. Don't you see that the greatness of our age lies in its inability to produce a new form of decoration? We have conquered ornament; we have won through to lack of ornamentation. Look: the time is nigh, fulfillment awaits us. Soon the streets of the town will glisten like white walls. Like Zion, the holy city, the metropolis of heaven. (227)

Self-proclaimed prophet of modernism, Loos complained of preaching in the desert, since he saw a powerful minority of his contemporaries suffering from an ornamental nostalgia, a retrograde and thoroughly conservative aesthetic useful to the State. To reinflate the "ornamental style," argues Loos, is to condemn Austria to take its place as the last of the industrialized nations, while Great Britain and the United States have both grasped the usefulness, even the profitability, of a functionalist aesthetic. This is perhaps the most modern aspect of this astonishing manifesto: the pride of place accorded economic considerations. What Loos understood—and it seems to me to be a fundamental insight—is that at the dawn of the twentieth century, at the height of bourgeois capitalism, the ornament controversy is nothing less than purely rhetorical, or to put the matter otherwise: rhetoric has invaded the market place. The real crime constituted by the cult of the ornament is then less of an aesthetic than an economic order. "But it is a crime against the national economy that [in fashioning ornaments] human labour, money, and material should thereby be ruined" (228). Consequently, ugliness depends not on aesthetic canons, but on economic, not to say ecological criteria; ugliness is pegged to waste: "The most unaesthetic decorated objects are those made of the best materials with the greatest care, those that have demanded hours of work" (230).

If Hegel's *Aesthetics* bears witness to the first great turning point in the modern history of the detail, its secularization, Loos's manifesto bears witness to its second: its commercialization, or commodification. If Hegel deplores the invasion of the domain of the sacred by the profane "prose of life," Loos rails against another desecration: the invasion of the market place by Junk. What Loos describes—and deplores—is the way in which the capitalist system has succeeded in placing the ornament in the service of consumption. Loos makes readily apparent the setting into place and the functioning of what Barthes calls the "fashion system." Ornament, it turns out, is the mainspring of that rapid and planned obsolescence we know to be essential to the smooth functioning of the industrial machine:

> I have coined an aphorism: The form of an object should last (i.e., should be bearable) as long as the object lasts physically. I shall try to clarify this: A suit will change in fashion more often than a valuable fur. A ball gown, for a lady, only meant for one night, will change its form more speedily than a desk. But woe to the desk that has to be changed quickly as a ball gown, because its shape has become unbearable, for then the money spent on the desk will have been wasted.
>
> This is well-known to the ornamentalists, and Austrian ornamentalists try to make the most of it. They say: "A consumer who has his furniture for ten years and then can't stand it any more and has to re-furnish from scratch every ten years, is more popular with us than someone who only buys an item when the old one is worn out. Industry thrives on it. Millions are employed due to rapid changes." This seems to be the secret of the Austrian national economy. (229–30)[24]

But to take Loos's masterful demystification of the mechanisms of consumer society for a Marxist analysis would, however, constitute a serious misunderstanding. Although he denounced the exploitation of the workers who produce ornaments, Loos is hardly a man of the Left. On the contrary, by his own admission: "Modern man is still in our society an isolated man, a forward sentinel, an aristocrat" (286). The persona created by Loos's discourse is that of a dandy—

despite or because of his harsh words about German dandies. As Loos remarks, "No dandy will admit to being one. One dandy mocks the other."[25] At least from Baudelaire on, a certain kind of modernism has always been bound up with elitism. In a society where the proliferation of ornaments prevents ornaments from fulfilling their primary function, which is to serve as distinctive signs of belonging to a caste—that is the precise function of the ancient *Kosmos*—the rejection of ornament becomes the ultimate strategy for the Happy Few.[26] As Hubert Damisch notes with great finesse a propos of Loos: "in a class society, the absence of ornament can still be an ornament."[27]

It is not completely accidental that the pleasure of the ornament repressed by Loos breaks through in an incongruous passage devoted to his shoes. Indeed the only exception Loos allows in his merciless rejection of personal adornment, his refusal of any mark of social distinction concerns his shoes. Fetishism, the perversion par excellence of an ornamentalist society, lurks not surprisingly in Loos's footwear. The following passage deserves to be quoted in its entirety:

> My shoes are covered over and over with decoration, the kind made up of pinking and perforations. Work done by the shoemaker but not paid for. I go to the shoemaker and say: "You want thirty kronen for a pair of shoes. I'll pay you forty." In this way I have raised the man to a level of happiness which he will repay me for by work and material of a quality absolutely out of proportion to the extra cost. He is happy. Good fortune rarely comes his way. Here is a man who understands him and appreciates his work and does not doubt his honesty. In his imagination he can see the finished shoes before him. He knows where the best leather is to be had at present, he knows which of his workers he can entrust the shoes to. And the shoes will boast perforations and scallops, as many as can possibly be fitted on an elegant shoe. And then I add: "But there is one condition. The shoe must be quite plain." With that I have toppled him from the heights of contentment into Tartarus. He has less work, but I have robbed him of all his pleasure. (230–31)

There is something almost Baudelairean about this cruel anecdote: the narrator would offer a poor craftsman a supplement in pay *not to do* that which gives him the most pleasure, to cover the shoes he has been commissioned to make with a profusion of ornaments. The pleasure of sadism masks here another pleasure, the always masked gratifications of fetishism. Just as Hegel dwells lovingly on those very corporeal details he would cancel out, Loos takes delight in imagining the production of the very ornaments he would pay to do away with. What I am suggesting is that despite its explicit message—the pleasure of ornamentation is the poor benighted shoemaker's—this passage conveys a delight in ornament that is Loos's alone.

*After Loos*

The irresistible development of consumer society in the twentieth century has completely confirmed Loos's connection between the proliferation of ornamental details and mass production. In France Loos's posterity is double: there is the strain represented by Barthes on the one hand, and by Baudrillard on the other. But whatever the differences between their analyses, on one crucial point there is agreement between the authors of *Système de la mode* and of *Système des objets:* the ornamental detail serves to discriminate between mass-produced objects, a fact one can either deplore, as will Baudrillard, or applaud, as will Barthes, but which one cannot in any case deny.

For Baudrillard, as for Loos, the role of the ornamental detail is essentially negative. The detail which adorns a mass produced object—and the mass-produced object is always ornamented—is designed to mask its "mass-produced reality," to convince the consumer that the mass-produced object is in fact a "model-object." Nothing could be further from the truth.

> In the model-object, there are neither details nor play of details: Rolls-Royces are black and only black. . . . The model has harmony, unity, homogeneousness, a coherence of space, form, substance, function—it is a syntax. The serial object is nothing but juxtaposition, accidental combination, inarticulate discourse. Detotalized, it is but a sum of details which are mechanically inscribed in parallel series.[28]

Baudrillard's vocabulary is revealing. All the qualifiers he applies to the model-object (harmony, unity, homogeneity, coherence) are not only meliorative, they derive from the lexicon of the classical ideal. The model-object figures ideality. It follows that the mass-produced object is the concretization of all that the classical ideal opposes. The serial object is paratactic, heterogeneous, without organic links. Note the primacy of the linguistic model: Baudrillard's aesthetic is structured like a language. On the one side there is the model object clearly articulated and ruled by a syntax, on the other, the disarticulated serial object afflicted with a sort of aphasic disturbance.

Much of Baudrillard's work is tinged with a scarcely veiled nostalgia for a lost or unattainable object that would not be disfigured by the industrial ornamental detail. Within a traditional imagery and system of values, Baudrillard's detail of the "inessential difference" is an always parasitic element, invading the good object and reproducing itself in a pathological mode. But, at the same time, Baudrillard is forced to recognize that the detail is anything but inessential:

> There is a cancer of the object: this proliferation of astructural elements which makes for the triumphalism of the object is a sort of cancer. Now, it is on these astructural elements (automatism, accessories, inessential differences) that the entire social circuit of fashion and of directed consumption is organized. (175–76).

The question then arises: why is it that the detail, which is both dysfunctional and astructural, plays a central role in the circulation of the serial object? Baudrillard proposes two answers that operate on two very different levels. First—this would be the argument of the merchants and consumers of detail—the superfluous structural element serves to "personalize" the industrial object, to make of it, as we have just seen, a pseudo-unique object. "Optional" features provide the individual consumer with the illusion that the mass-produced object he has purchased is molded to his specifications and his alone. Second—and this would be the semiotician's analysis—the marginal element serves to *naturalize* the industrially produced object, to deny not so much its seriality as its very status as an industrial object:

The astructural, inessential element, such as the car's tail-fin, always connotes the technical object *naturally*. By the same token, therefore, it connotes it allegorically. When the fixed structure is invaded by astructural elements, when the formal detail invades the object, the real function is no longer but an alibi, and *the form does nothing more than signify the idea of the function:* it becomes allegorical. The car's tail-fins are our modern allegory. (85)

The form of the detail is then eminently functional, but in the second power. Instead of improving the "performance" of the car, the tail-fin—and let us note that catachresis is the very figure of the naturalizing detail: it confers an organic necessity on the arbitrariness of the technical object—is an icon of functionality.

The condemnation that Loos and Baudrillard pronounce on the industrial ornamental detail is based on an elitist ideology: In the final analysis what they hold against the formal detail is that it disfigures the ideal object by or while putting it within reach of the masses. Barthes's position is diametrically opposed to that of both Loos and Baudrillard; in *The Fashion System* he enthusiastically praises just the sort of the detail despised by those who yearn after the lost ideal object:

the rhetoric of the detail seems to take on an increasing extension, and the stake it has in doing so is an economic one: by becoming a mass value (through its magazines, if not through its boutiques), Fashion must elaborate meanings whose fabrication does not appear costly; this is the case of the "detail": one detail is enough to transform what is outside meaning, what is unfashionable into Fashion, and yet a "detail" is not expensive; by this particular semantic technique Fashion departs from the luxurious and seems to enter into a clothing practice accessible to modest budgets; but at the same time, sublimated under the name *find*, this same low-priced detail participates in the dignity of the ideal.[29]

For Barthes the "detail" offers an attractive, low-budget means of ensuring mass participation in the Fashion System. By virtue of the *metonymic contagion* which enables the addition of a single inexpensive detail (an "accessory," in fashion-code) to (re-)valorize the whole, the detail makes it possible for all consumers, however modest their means, to participate in the Fashion System at minimal cost. Rather than lowering Fashion by vulgarizing it, the recourse to the accessory detail confers on the consumer a new dignity, giving him access to the realm of the ideal. But there is one necessary condition: the detail must be "*sublimated* (my emphasis) under the name *find* [*trouvaille*]." (In Chapter 5 I shall return at greater length to the importance of sublimation/desublimation in Barthes's aesthetic; for the moment, I would just like to remark the significance of this restriction: the detail can only perform its transvaluative operation under another name.) To paraphrase an expression dear to Barthes—Descartes's "larvatus prodeo"—the detail can only advanced masked. It is then of the order of the lure, but an essentially *positive lure*, since it makes it possible to reconcile with elegant economy the commercial dictates of fashion and the aesthetic imperatives of taste.

## Georg Lukács

Inherited from the ancients, revived and amplified throughout the eighteenth and nineteenth centuries, the association of the cult of the decorative detail and decadence has persisted (at least) until the middle of the twentieth century, finding its most consummate elaboration in the work of one of, if not the, major Hegelian aestheticians of our time, Georg Lukács. Lukács, as is well known, sought to extend to the novel, a genre neglected by Hegel, the great principles of Hegelian aesthetics. His most notable success in this project is generally held to be his early (pre-Marxist) *The Theory of the Novel*, which marks, according to Lukács's 1962 preface, his move from Kant to Hegel. Hegel, writes Lukács, serves as the preeminent "methodological guide" to the work, though he is quick to add, "the author of *The Theory of the Novel* was not an exclusive or orthodox Hegelian," borrowing freely as he does from Goethe, Schiller, Friedrich Schlegel and Solger.[30] The Hegelian legacy of the author of *The Theory of the Novel* does not, however, include the privileging of the category of the detail. By Lukács's own admission, *The Theory of the Novel* is an abstract work, notable for its *lack* of detail: one searches in vain here for any move toward specification. Though largely discredited by Lukács's Marxist followers, *Studies in European Realism*, on the other hand, does enlist the detail in its enterprise of historicization. By bringing to bear on the detail a new orientation derived from Marx, *Studies in European Realism* situates the detail for the first time in History and precisely dates its decadence.

### Details and Revolution

Read or reread in the light of our preoccupations, Lukács's *Studies in European Realism* turns out to be closely tied to the Hegelian discourse on the detail, but inflected in the direction of the history of the nineteenth century. Thus, in this Marxist version of the history of the detail, 1848 marks—at least in France, because for obvious geopolitical reasons, the Russian realist novel escapes this periodization—the passage from the golden age of the detail to its bronze age; after 1848, "details meticulously observed and depicted with consummate skill are substituted for the portrayal of essential features of social reality and the description of the changes effected in the human personality by social influences."[31]

In Lukács, then, 1848 cleaves the detail, as it does realism. Before 1848, during the period of "revolutionary realism," the "good" detail reigns supreme, the detail that, according to Hegel's organicist ideal, scrupulously respects all the clauses of the aesthetic contract binding the part and the whole. A good detail is any detail said to be dramatic and essential that serves as a mainspring of the plot. The good details are: "sensually visible and vehemently experienced objectivations of decisive emotional turning points in the lives of people" (174). The opposite of these details situated on the border between the descriptive and the diegetic, Balzacian or Tolstoyan details, are the "bad" details of a Flaubert or a Zola. Thus, according to Lukács, "bourgeois" or "trivial" or "petty" Western realism is characterized by a predilection for, and inflation of details variously described as "inessential" (157), "isolated" (62), "superficial and unconnected" (177), or "superfluous" (197).

It is perhaps no accident that to dramatize the difference between the decadent and revolutionary uses of the detail Lukács compares the descriptions of death in *Madame Bovary* and *The Death of Ivan Ilyich*. Consider two passages, first Sainte-Beuve, then Lukács. As the juxtaposition indicates, the scene of Emma's death enjoys paradigmatic status in the debate on the detail, linking an excess of particularization to the themes of death and decay, as well as to femininity:

> although it was certainly not the author's deliberate intention, his very method, describing everything and leaving nothing out, leads him to include many too vividly suggestive details, which come close to appealing to the reader's erotic sensuality. He should definitely not have gone so far. After all, a book is not and could never be reality itself.[32]

> The meticulous details with which the death of Ivan Ilyich is described, is not the naturalist description of a process of physical decay—as in the suicide of Madame Bovary—but a great internal drama in which approaching death, precisely through all its horrible details, tears the veils one after the other from the meaningless life of Ivan Ilyich and exposes this life in its appalling blankness.[33]

At first sight, these two critiques appear rather different: one scores the gratuitousness of Flaubert's decadent details; the other, their exhaustiveness. At bottom, however, it is the same reproach: lack of selectivity, a lack of what Lukács calls *perspective*.

### Details and Allegory

Although Lukács borrows the very terms of criticisms levelled against realism in the nineteenth century, it would nevertheless be wrong to conclude that Western nineteenth-century literature constitutes his sole or even real target. In fact, for Lukács, the category of the detail serves two purposes: to make it possible to separate out realism and naturalism—naturalism being defined precisely as a realism whose details have gone bad—as well as to bring to light the unsuspected complicity of naturalism and modernism. For Lukács, there is no break between naturalism and modernism, since under both regimes the descriptive detail breaks the organicist contract, entailing the loss of the "hierarchy of signification" constitutive of the realist masterpiece. In other words: the target aimed at through the critique of naturalism is actually modernism. And the author who, better than any other, exhibits the status of the detail in modernism is Kafka.

Not surprisingly, however, the case of Kafka is complex. Indeed, Lukács is obliged to recognize that by the scarcity of his details, Kafka does respect the criterion of selectivity. But, he adds, despite their "immediate sensuality," these rare or rarefied details are no less decadent than those of naturalism, for they create a trompe l'oeil reality, haunted by the God of Nothingness whose presence is inscribed in this "spectral reality." This is tantamount to saying—and let us note in passing Lukács's explicitly acknowledged debt to Benjamin—that Kafka's fiction is on the order of allegory. Allegory would then be *the* modern art of the detail:

> In realistic literature each descriptive detail is both *individual* and *typical*. Modern allegory, and modernist ideology, however, deny the *typical*. By destroying the coherence of the world, they reduce detail to the level of mere particularity (once again, the connection between modernism and naturalism is plain). Detail, in its allegorical transferability, though brought into a direct, if paradoxical connection with transcendence, becomes an abstract function of the transcendence to which it points. Modernist literature thus replaces concrete typicality with abstract particularity.[34]

By underscoring the affinity of allegorism and detailism—and despite his own rejection of modern allegory—Lukács made an important contribution to the modern understanding of allegory. Throughout the twentieth century—and this current seems to be gaining ground constantly—other aestheticians and critics more receptive to modernity (notably Fletcher, de Man, Baudrillard) have insisted on the preeminence of the detail, indeed of the hypertrophied and detotalized detail in allegory, at the same time as they have promoted allegory to the status of exemplary narrative or art form.[35] Indeed, the detail with an allegorical vocation is distinguished by its "oversignification" (Baudrillard); this is not a matter of realism, but of surrealism, if not hyperrealism. Finally, the allegorical detail is a disproportionately enlarged ornamental detail; bearing the seal of transcendence, it testifes to the loss of all transcendental signifieds in the modern period. In short, the modern allegorical detail is a parody of the traditional theological detail. It is the detail deserted by God.

With what, then, does Lukács reproach modern allegory and by the same token naturalism and modernism? What is for him the difference between "concrete typicality" (positively valorized) and "abstract particularity" (negatively valorized)? The critique of modern allegory is, it would appear, centered on the notion of the typical, a key word, as we know, in Lukács's aesthetic lexicon. By foreclosing the typical, which serves to mediate between the particular and the universal, the modern allegorist, such as Kafka, severs the ties which link the detail to concrete existence while at the same time putting it into contact with a totality that gives it meaning. By eliminating the typical, by skipping the stage of generalization, Kafka condemns his details—which are, it should be emphasized, meticulously observed and seized in all their phenomenal density—to be nothing but details, pure hypostases of a transcendence which is very much in doubt. The allegorical detail is a disembodied and destabilized detail.

### Speciality: Lukács's aesthetics of difference

Lukács's lifelong engagement with Hegel, Marx, and the realm of art culminated in his late systematic aesthetic, *Die Eigenart des Ästhetischen* [The Specific Nature of the Aesthetic]. Originally conceived of as the first of a tripartite work, the 1,700-page volume stands alone, for the other two projected parts were never written. On the other hand, a spin-off of what was to be the second part of the aesthetic but which took on a life of its own was published separately under the significant title *Über die Besonderheit als Kategorie der Aesthetik* [On Speciality as a Category of Aesthetics]. For as Lukács makes clear in the closely related twelfth chapter of *Die Eigenart* ("Die Besonderheit als ästhetische Kategorie") and the fifth chapter of *Über die Besonderheit* ("Das Besondere als zentrale Kategorie der Ästhetik"), speciality is not *a*, but *the* central category of his late aesthetics. What then is speciality and what bearing does it have on the detail?

Speciality—the accepted translation among Lukácsians of *Besonderheit*—is more familiarly known as the Hegelian particularity. Particularity, it will be recalled, is the mediating term in the triadic "Concept-structure" Hegel elaborates in the final section of his *Logic*, the other two being universality (*Allgemeinheit*) and individuality (*Einzelheit*). The concept is *at once* universal, particular, and individual for, as Hegel is at great pains to emphasize, the three categories are indissolubly linked. The Augustan distinction between the general and the particular is in a Hegelian perspective inconceivable, for the universal is no "abstract generality": ". . . the universal of the notion is not a mere sum of features common to several things, confronted by a particular which enjoys an existence of its own. It is, on the contrary, self-particularizing or self-specifying, and with undimmed clearness finds itself at home in its antithesis."[36] Hegel's triad informs the *Aesthetics*, of course, but only at the level of the overarching design. Overriding certain linguistic inconsistencies which seem to present "the art forms as particular and the arts as individual"—when it is not precisely the opposite—Stephen Bungay proposes the following tripartite division of the *Aesthetics*:

*universality:* the Ideal, the determination of art

*particularity:* the arts, as spatio-temporally different

*individuality:* the socio-historical factors involved in the actual works of art, with real examples[37]

In what is to my mind his most inspired appropriation of Hegel in the realm of aesthetics, Lukács, on the other hand, brings to bear on the problematic of the detail (*Einzelheit*, individuality)—a central category of Hegel's aesthetics—the full force of Hegel's *Logic*. In the guise of speciality, Hegel's particularity becomes the keystone of Lukács's system, the middle or meeting point (*Sammelpunkt*) where all the centrifugal forces innervating the work of art are reconciled: "There is then . . . a movement going from speciality to universality (and back), and, at the same time, a movement going from speciality to individuality (and back); in both cases, it is the movement toward speciality that brings the process to closure."[38]

Lukács goes on to say: "the individual on the one hand, the universal on the other always appear both abolished and preserved (*aufgehoben*) in the special" (79/210). The promotion of speciality to a position of centrality rests on the *Aufhebung* or sublation of the universal and above all the individual. For as Lukács emphasizes: "The relationship of particularity to individuality consists in an eternal process of cancellation (*Aufhebung*), wherein the moment of preservation (*Aufbewahrung*) is in a certain sense more strongly emphasized" (82/213). The notion of the *Aufhebung* of the individual constitutes without a doubt Lukács's most promising contribution to a theory of the detail; it allows us to begin to detect the presence of the detail even there where it appears absent, indeed to find the *trace* of the detail in the totality with which it has merged, into which it has vanished, been absorbed, rather than remaining obsessively fixated on the manifest detail, in its intractable thereness. The tendency of the detail to persist and to inform in absence is precisely what that other great neo-Hegelian aesthetican of the twentieth century so critical of Lukács, Adorno, describes when he writes: "In major art works the details do not just vanish in the totality."[39]

In short, the sublation of the individual in the special signifies a vertiginous extension of the field of the detail which no longer needs to be made manifest to produce its effects. The vaunted "reality-effect" (about which more in chapter 5) is not necessarily produced by details duly inscribed in the text; it may spring from a set of cancelled particularities whose non-representation subliminally conditions the reader's response. Thus, during the genesis of *Madame Bovary*, Flaubert writes to Taine: "there are many details I don't write. Thus Homais is slightly pockmarked."[40] The trace of a trace, Homais's pockmarks are for Flaubert essential details that would continue to haunt the text of *Madame Bovary*, ensuring its verisimilitude even while unwritten. My point remains, despite the fact that reversing himself, Flaubert did finally chose to write out this detail. In the definitive text of the novel the initial description of Homais reads:" A slightly pockmarked man in green leather slippers . . ."[41] Invisible to the naked eye, inscribed in relief, the detail sublated both by and in the special is a phantom detail. Detail of the trace, trace of the detail, the phantom detail is in some sense the modern or postmodern detail par excellence, to the extent that it participates in what we are now in a position to call an *aesthetic of difference*.

But let us not dream. The theory of the phantom detail we have teased out of Lukács's text is, in context, placed in service of a reflection theory long since discredited. After having formulated this insight with "long resonances" (to paraphrase Borges's evocative characterization of the realistic detail), Lukács returns to his attack on the detotalized detail dear to the naturalists; decadence would be precisely that artistic regime which privileges the individual at the expense of the special, where sublation fails: "the theory and the practice of decadence always emphasize the individual which they fetishize by presenting it as incomparable, unique, impossible to repeat or analyze" (83–84).

Constantly in danger of becoming mired in the detail—situated of course at the base of the vertical axis onto which Lukács projects his schema (individual—special—universal)—the novel, just like the epic, would be opposed to drama, whose "general tendency . . . consists in determining the center of cristallization in the particular at a point closer to the universal" (88). Of all the literary genres, the novel would be the one most threatened by an escape into the individual.

But at this point Lukács stumbles onto a sticky aporia built into the relationship which links the individual to the special and vice versa. Just as in Hegel the Idea can appear only in the form of particularized materiality, the special, which is after all only a meta-category, depends for its apprehension on highly visible concrete details. It is because the individual and the special are soldered together and can be separated only by a heuristic artifice that the detail must be fully realized; a strong particularity requires a strongly detailed individuality:

it [speciality] is, without a doubt, present in all the guises under which the immediate individuality appears, without ever being separable from it. Consequently . . . the raising of the individual to the level of the special can only be accomplished if it is rendered more directly perceptible; it is only on this condition that the manifest presence of the special in every detail and in the totality of details which constitutes the work itself can be realized; it is only thus that the work can incarnate—and transform into experience—the speciality of a fashioned "universe." (96–97/229)

What I have attempted to make visible, or better audible, in this chapter is what Foucault calls a discursive formation, which by definition violates disciplinary boundaries. By juxtaposing the discourses produced by an obscure nineteenth-century French polymath, a high priest of Viennese Modernism, and the major twentieth-century exponent of Marxist aesthetics, I have wanted to show both the persistence of an aesthetic thematics and its contextual modulations. But that is not all: to approach the history of an idea from a genealogical perspective is to reject the linear model and instead to give full play to discontinuities, overlaps, the disordered ebb and flow of intellectual events. Thus instead of going from Lukács to Barthes, following strict chronology, in the following chapter we will go back once again to the nineteenth-century. For even as the main tenets of Academic aesthetics continued to cast their baleful shadow over the detail, the decorative, the domestic, and the feminine, an epistemological break was taking shape that would at last bring the detail into the epistemological and aesthetic spotlight.

# 4.

# DISPLACEMENT:
## The Case of Sigmund Freud

> The old woman fetched a clean basin which was used as a footbath,
> poured plenty of cold water in and added warm. Odysseus was sitting at
> the hearth, but now he swung abruptly round to face the dark, for it had
> struck him suddenly that in handling him she might notice a certain scar
> he had, and his secret would be out. Indeed, when Eurycleia came up to
> her master and began to wash him, she recognized the scar at once.
> Homer, *The Odyssey*

The scene is Freud's study in Vienna, the interlocutors, those two great sleuths,
Sigmund Freud and Sherlock Holmes. Holmes is saying:

> You know, Doctor, I shouldn't be surprised if your application of my methods
> proves in the long run far more important than the mechanical uses I make
> of them. *But always remember the physical details.* No matter how far into the
> mind you may travel, they are of supreme importance.[1]

I begin with this episode from Nicholas Meyer's best-seller of several seasons
back, *The Seven-Per-Cent Solution*, because the apocryphal but altogether plausible encounter between the master of Baker Street and the sage of Berggasse
seems surprisingly rich in implications for our study. This imaginary and imaginative dialogue assumes: one, that the boundaries between sciences (psychoanalysis and criminology) and, more important, between science and fiction
are not impermeable; two, that both share a common epistemological framework, linking heightened attention to details with the quest for truth.

All that is merely implicit in Meyer's text is made quite explicit in Foucault's
*Discipline and Punish: The Birth of the Prison*, which constitutes a veritable genealogy of the detail. Indeed, as I have noted, Foucault remarks that one might
profitably undertake to write a "History of the Detail," with special emphasis
on the eighteenth century, since it was during that critical transitional period
that the detail went from being a theological category to a secular and political
instrument of both power and knowledge:

> A meticulous observation of detail, and at the same time a political aware-
> ness of these small things, for the control and use of men, merge through

65

the classical age bearing with them a whole set of techniques, a whole corpus of methods and knowledge, descriptions, plans and data. And from such trifles, no doubt, the man of modern humanism is born.[2]

I would argue, however, basing myself in part on Foucault's own evidence, that if one were to undertake such a monumental study, then the nineteenth rather than the eighteenth century is the more promising period to investigate. At the risk of what might be described as naive periodization—a self-serving teleological view of history endemic to nineteenth-century historians—I would go so far as to call the nineteenth century the Golden Age of the Detail. Whether one considers the very diverse material adduced by Foucault in his attempt to correlate the birth of such detail-oriented disciplines as the social sciences and the penal system, or the rise of realism with its well-known predilection for what Roman Jakobson has termed "synecdochic details," or the elaboration by Morelli of that form of art expertise Edgar Wind calls "connoisseurship," where an artist's signature can be deciphered in his distinctive depiction of an ear lobe or a finger nail or, more recently, Edward Said's characterization of Orientalism as a "theory of Oriental detail," all these disparate and apparently unrelated phenomena point to the existence of a *Zeitgeist* which gives the detail pride of place.[3]

The question then becomes: where do Freud and psychoanalysis fit into this projected history? We can respond at least provisionally with the help of Foucault, who remarks that a history of the detail in the eighteenth century would inevitably conclude with Napoleon. Freud is, as it were, the Napoleon of the psychic detail. Or, to parody Freud's celebrated if unfortunate parody of Napoleon: for Freud, detail is destiny.

What then constitutes a detail for Freud? At the outset I would like to suggest that the detail in Freud functions in opposition to the fragment, that other form of synecdoche operative in Freud's tropological system. Though the two terms are occasionally used interchangeably, generally they are clearly distinguished. Freud differs in this respect from Hegel, for whom detail and fragment are located on the same continuum and enjoy a mutually reinforcing relationship: the detail ensures the self-sufficiency of the fragment, while the fragment as virtuality justifies the proliferation of details. As a first step toward determining the specificity of the detail in Freud, I would propose the following series of binary oppositions between the detail and the fragment: the fragment is to the detail as the ancient is to the modern, as depth is to surface, as scarcity is to surplus, and as construction is to interpretation. In other words, whether implicitly or explicitly, in Freud the fragment always refers to an archaeological model, while the detail is directly linked to the psychopathology of everyday life. But perhaps the most significant opposition between the detail and the fragment in Freud—and here he diverges totally from Hegel—is sexual: the fragment, a solid and detachable part-object, is, however subtly, connoted as masculine, while the detail is, as I hope to show, connoted as feminine, because

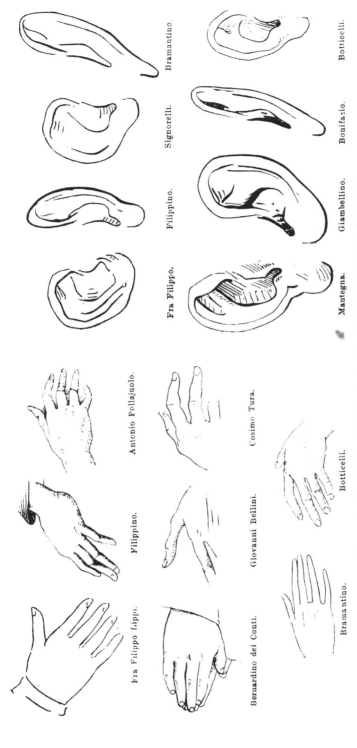

Figure 7. Morelli. *Kunstkritische Studien über Italienische Malerei.* Vol. 1, 98–99

it is in the detail that Freud's own femininity is encoded. Finally, whereas Freud's often extended archaeological metaphors remain easily localized, the detail is everywhere in Freud's texts, constantly gaining new semantic ground to the point of being co-extensive with the vast field of insignificance which Freud undertook to reclaim. It is this network that I would like to uncover and explore, before going on to a detailed study of Freud's text on screen-memories.

If Freud deserves a prominent place in a future History of the Detail, the detail in Freud has no history: its privileged and problematic status is inscribed from the birth of psychoanalysis. The formulation of what was to become the "fundamental rule" of psychoanalysis, what I would prefer to call the first law of the detail—"to say everything that comes into [one's] head"—results from a discovery that Breuer and Freud made while treating their hysterical patients: the effectiveness of the "talking cure" is bound up with a "talking out": "*each individual hysterical symptom immediately and permanently disappeared when we had succeeded in bringing clearly to light the memory of the event by which it was provoked and in arousing its accompanying affect, and when the patient had described that event in the greatest possible detail (im möglichst ausführlicher Weise) and had put the affect into words.*"[4] Catharsis, just like the psychoanalytic treatment to which it gave rise must then pass through the straight gate of the detail, a passage which facilitates both the patient's abreaction and the therapist's interpretation. However, to put these trivial events of everyday life into, or rather back into circulation, to articulate the specificities of the symptoms are steps not taken lightly on either side of the couch: the iron-clad say-all rule provokes resistances on the part of the patients, and reticence on Freud's part, as we shall soon see.

Indeed, resistance is often a reaction to the inquisitorial constraint-to-confess placed upon the patient by Freud. Witness the Rat Man's panic, when he is on the verge of revealing his "great obsessive fear": "Here the patient broke off, got up from the sofa, and begged me to spare him the recital of the details [*die Schilderung der Details*]. I assured him that I myself had no taste whatever for cruelty . . . but that naturally I could not grant him something which was beyond my power. He might as well ask me to give him the moon. The overcoming of resistances was a law of the treatment, and on no consideration could it be dispensed with" (*S. E.*, 10:166; *G. W.*, 7:391). Freud's self-assurance, not to say insistence, in this episode is noteworthy, for if the enforcement of the first law of the detail in the course of the analytic session admits of no exceptions, Freud is a good deal less truculent when the scene shifts from the field of speech to that of writing. I wish to stress that what is problematic for Freud is the status of the *written detail*, in contrast to the *spoken detail*. Thus he remarks at the end of one of his studies on hysteria: "it still strikes me myself as strange that the case histories I write should read like short stories and that, as one might say, they lack the serious stamp of science" (*S. E.*, 2:160). It would appear that for Freud fiction is characterized by a proliferation of details; thus he goes on to speak of a "detailed description of mental processes such as we are accustomed to find in the works of imaginative writers . . ." (ibid.).

The problem posed by the written detail now stands out quite clearly: due to its apparent lack of seriousness it threatens the scientificity, not to say the veracity, of the text it invades. In other words: the detail belongs to the domain of *Dichtung* and seems out of place in scientific texts. Subsequently, in writing of Dora, Freud will liken his detailed case histories not merely to short stories, but to a far more suspect genre, the *"roman à clef"* (*S. E.*, 7:9; in French in the text). There are then details which are fit to be uttered, but not to be written down. We are here confronted with a paradox: a disseminator of fiction on the one hand, the detail is a purveyor of truth on the other. When applied to the field of writing, the law of the detail which obtains in the field of speech comes up against the equally compelling imperatives of the doctor-patient relationship. The analytic pact pledges the patient to say all, the analyst to hear all, but not to transcribe all. Thus the beautiful symmetry of free association and "evenly poised attention" is shattered in the act of writing. And, let us note, the analyst shares the patient's dissatisfaction with the terms of the contract; he too balks at the oath he has taken:

> I cannot give a complete history of the treatment, because that would involve my entering in detail into the circumstances of my patient's [the patient is the Rat Man] life [*weil sie ein Eingehen auf die Lebensverhältnisse meines Patienten im einzelnen erfordern würde*]. The importunate interest of a capital city . . . forbids my giving a faithful picture of the case. On the other hand I have come more and more to regard the distortions usually resorted to in such circumstances as useless and objectionable. If the distortions are slight, they fail in their object of protecting the patient from indiscreet curiosity; while if they go beyond this they require too great a sacrifice, for they destroy the intelligibility of the material, which depends for its coherence precisely on the small details of real life [*kleinen Realien des Lebens*]. (*S. E.*, 10:155–56; *G. W.*, 7:381–82).

The impossibility of ever capturing or recapturing in writing the full course of an analysis will oblige Freud to resign himself to a considerable loss of detail, a necessity he will get round by a sort of compromise solution: making his ellipses explicit.

What happens then in the borderline case of a self-analysis, for after all no Hippocratic oath governs the relationship of Freud the writer-analyst and Freud the analysand? The answer is forthcoming: in *The Interpretation of Dreams*, Freud blithely breaks what I call the second law of the detail—every detail must be interpreted—which he enunciates in a note to his case history of the Wolf Man: "it is always a strict law of dream interpretation that an explanation must be found for every detail" (*S. E.*, 17:42). Indeed, beginning with the analysis of the Irma dream, Freud is careful to stress the limits of his interpretation: "I had a feeling that the interpretation of this part of the dream was not carried far enough to make it possible to follow the whole of its concealed meaning. If I had pursued my comparison between the three women, it would have taken me far afield.—There is at least one spot in every dream at which it is unplumbable—a navel, as it were, that is its point of contact with the unknown" (*S. E.*, 4:111). That the details Freud chooses to leave in the dark have to do with his sexuality no longer needs to be demonstrated, this quotation only serves to underscore another contradiction between Freud's theory of the detail and his practice. On the basis of these brief remarks, we can draw a preliminary conclusion: for Freud, the laws of the detail obtain in an utopia where interpretation encounters no resistance, where there is adequation of speech and writing, and where, of course, the economy of words presents no problem, in short a utopia of transparency and exhaustiveness. Rather than speaking of laws of the detail, it would be more accurate to speak of a *detail ideal,* an ideal that psychoanalysis strives in vain to reach.

If psychoanalysis's threefold totalizing aim—to say all, to hear all, to interpret all—is doomed to failure from the outset, then why doesn't Freud give it up? Quite simply because his clinical data leaves him with no other choice. Thus in the passage from the *Studies in Hysteria* quoted above, Freud invokes what I would call the "mimetic alibi" to justify the literary minuteness of his case histories. "I must console myself with the reflection that the nature of the subject is evidently responsible for this, rather than any preference of my own" (*S. E.*, 2:160). Like hysteria, paranoia and obsessional neurosis take the form of pathologies of the detail, reflecting a society sick with the detail, so to speak. The example of obsessional neurosis is particularly instructive: one might even speak of another law, the *Zwang,* which compels the obsessional to perform pathological ceremonials as though, Freud remarks, fulfilling "a series of unwritten rules" (*S. E.*, 3:118). The attention to detail with which these neurotic ceremonies are carried out brings to mind religious rites, with this difference: "while the minutiae of religious ceremonial are full of significance and have a symbolic meaning, those of neurotics seem foolish and senseless" (*S. E.*, 9:119). The key word here is, of course, *seem:* for, according to Freud, "when, with the help of psychoanalytic technique of investigation, one penetrates to the true meaning of obsessive actions" (*S. E.*, 9:119–20), each one of these apparently absurd and enigmatic gestures turns out to be meaningful. The question then becomes: how does psychoanalysis work this transvaluation, this alchemy of the detail? Or to phrase the question in less magical terms, since the decoding process does nothing but retrace in reverse the encoding process, how does the detail come to be inflated with meaning?

It is in seeking to understand the remarkable preference which the manifest content of dreams exhibits for "unimportant details of waking life," the refuse of the day's residues, a refuse of refuse, that Freud removes the paradox:

A psychological process by which, according to our account, indifferent experiences take the place of psychically significant ones, cannot fail to arouse suspicion and bewilderment . . . What takes place would seem to be something in the nature of a "displacement"—of psychical emphasis, shall we say?—by means of intermediate links; in this way, ideas which originally had only a *weak* charge of intensity take over the charge from ideas which were originally *intensely* cathected and at last attain enough strength to enable them to force an entry into consciousness. (*S. E.*, 4:177)

Displacement is then a sort of strategy devised by the unconscious to evade censorship, and the hypersemanticized detail, in turn, becomes a camouflage allowing repressed contents to surface. This then is Freud's great innovation in the field of the detail: the detail owes its privileged status in pathological as well as normal states to the primary process of displacement. As long as one persists in viewing the minute as an autonomous, self-sufficient element, it appears to be a usurper of signification, but once the mechanism of displacement has been discovered, once the detail has been connected with the whole which it represents, it becomes the royal way to the unconscious.

Now, to speak of displacement, at least in the contemporary French context, is not a matter of course. Among the rhetoricians of the unconscious, opinions seem evenly divided between those like Jakobson and Lacan, who assimilate displacement and metonymy and those like Tzvetan Todorov who asserts that this assimilation is improper: "displacement is not a metonymy, is not a trope, for it is not a substitution of meaning, but a linking up of two equally present meanings. But the ambiguity is, admittedly, in the Freudian text itself."[5] Without wishing to get involved in this controversy, I would like to take up again the question of the rhetorical status of displacement, which is to say of the detail, through a close study of Freud's essay on screen-memories.

This essay's starting point is a paradoxical phenomenon analogous to the one already noted in dreams, the apparently aberrant selection principle of childhood memories, the lack of logic of infantile amnesia or anamnesis, which amounts to the same thing: ". . . there are some people whose earliest recollections of childhood are concerned with everyday and indifferent events which could not produce any emotional effect even in children, but which are recollected (*too* clearly [*überscharf*], one is inclined to say) in every detail [*mit allen Details*], while approximately contemporary events, even if, on the evidence of their parents, they moved them intensely at the time, have not been retained in their memory" (*S. E.*, 3:305–6; *G. W.*, 1:534). Of course, memory's remarkable preference for unimportant childhood recollections can, like the dream's marked preference for the refuse of the day's residues, be explained by the process of displacement. But in the case of screen-memories, Freud distinguishes three categories of displacement, depending on "the *chronological* relation between the screen-memory and the content which is screened off by it": "*retrogressive*," "*displaced forward*," and "contemporary or *contiguous*" (*S. E.*, 6:44). This taxonomy allows us to assert that there is metonymic displacement only in the case of the so-called contemporary or contiguous screen-memory, and that is precisely the first case which Freud considers in our text: "the case, that is, where the essential elements of experience are represented in memory by the inessential elements of the same experience. It is a case of displacement on to something associated by contiguity [*eine Verschiebung auf der Kontiguitätsassoziation*] or, looking at the process as a whole, a case of repression accompanied by the substitution of something in the neighbourhood (whether in space or time)" (*S. E.*, 3:307–8; *G. W.*, 1:537).

Strangely enough, however, the screen-memory Freud choses to analyze in this text is an atypical case, a case of retroactive or retrogressive displacement. How then does Freud negotiate the transition from the typical to the atypical? By means of an analogy whose "seduction" operates at such a deep level that at first reading it appears absurd, inexplicable: "The assertion that a psychical intensity can be displaced from one presentation (which is then abandoned) on to another (which thenceforward plays the psychological part of the former one) is as bewildering to us as certain features of Greek mythology—as, for instance, when the gods are said to clothe someone with beauty as though it were with a veil, whereas *we* think only of a face transfigured by a change of expression" (*S. E.*, 3:308–9).[6]

What does this mean if not that the oddity of the process of displacement is comparable to the oddity of figures of speech, in this instance a metaphor? Moreover a metaphor of disguise neither gratuitous nor innocent. It would appear that Freud uses this comparison precisely to shift our attention to metaphor, for the example of a screen-memory which he cites brings into play metaphoric displacement, that is, a form of displacement which verges on condensation. The functioning of this type of displacement will become clear in what follows; let us simply state at this juncture the hypothesis that there exists a metaphoric displacement, or rather a displacement which is predominantly metaphoric—for it goes without saying that metaphor and metonymy, just like displacement and condensation, are inextricably linked. Such a hypothesis would ground a revisionist reading of Freud: for, if the detail is not seen as referring metonymically back to a whole from which it has become detached, but rather as substituting metaphorically for another detail which it resembles, then we move from the typically Freudian valorization of totalization—which anchors Freud in the nineteenth century—to the notion of a detotalized detail, which would make of Freud a precursor of modernity, even of the post-modern.

The case which Freud presents is that of a "man of university education, aged thirty-eight" (*S. E.*, 3:309), whom he treated for a phobia. This patient recounts the following childhood memory:

> I see a rectangular, rather steeply sloping piece of meadow-land, green and thickly grown; in the green there are a great number of yellow flowers— evidently common dandelions. At the top end of the meadow there is a cot-

tage and in front of the cottage door two women are standing chatting busily, a peasant-woman with a handkerchief on her head and a children's nurse. Three children are playing in the grass. One of them is myself (between the ages of two and three); the two others are my boy cousin, who is a year older than me, and his sister, who is almost exactly the same age as I am. We are picking the yellow flowers and each of us is holding a bunch of flowers we have already picked. The little girl has the best bunch; and, as though by mutual agreement, we—the two boys—fall on her and snatch away her flowers. She runs up the meadow in tears and as a consolation the peasant-woman gives her a big piece of black bread. Hardly have we seen this then we throw the flowers away, hurry to the cottage and ask to be given some bread too. And we are in fact given some; the peasant woman cuts the loaf with a long knife. In my memory the bread tastes quite delicious—and at that point the scene breaks off. (*S. E.*, 3:311)

A first gloss of this memory-text is provided by the patient himself who, as Freud remarks, "was no novice at jobs of this kind" (*S. E.*, 3:312): "Altogether, there seems to me something not quite right about this scene. The yellow of the flowers is a disproportionately prominent element in the situation as a whole, and the nice taste of the bread seems to me exaggerated in an almost hallucinatory fashion" (*S. E.*, 3:311–12). The juxtaposition of these two quotations leads me to describe screen-memories as mnemonic fragments featuring heightened details, the locus of the articulation of two parts which here enter into a hierarchical relationship, the fragment subsuming the detail.

In the course of the analysis of this fragment—an analysis transcribed in an unusual dialogue form—it is precisely these salient details which offer a hold for associations, in keeping with that other law of the detail repeatedly stated by Freud in *The Interpretation of Dreams*. the fragmenting of dreams is the necessary prerequisite for any interpretation, for the interpretation of dreams is always carried out "en détail" and not "en masse" (in French in the original German text). It is not possible here to follow the movement of this session; thus I will confine myself to a brief summary of the results of the interpretation: by going back over his memories, the patient brings out two fantasies whose interpenetration produced the screen-memory. If he had married either the young heiress dressed in yellow whom he fell in love with on a trip back to his hometown (at the age of 17), or the cousin represented in the screen-memory, the daughter of a rich uncle he visited some three years later, then his life would have become far more pleasant. In other words: had he deflowered one of these maidens, he wouldn't have had such a hard time winning his bread. "I see that by producing a phantasy like this I was providing, as it were, a fulfilment of the two suppressed wishes—for deflowering a girl and for material comfort" (*S. E.*, 3:318).

If this "dandelion fantasy" is invented out of whole cloth—the analyst compares its make-up to that of a work of fiction—then the patient begins to doubt the authenticity of his memory. Is this childhood memory true or false? That becomes the question. It is at this critical juncture that, resuming the direction of the dialogue, the analyst puts forth a defense of the authenticity of the suspect memory, and this defense is a variant of the theory of anaclisis (leaning on) developed by Jean Laplanche in *Life and Death in Psychoanalysis*. Indeed the phantasy cannot be accommodated by the memory, "unless there is a memory-trace the content of which offers the phantasy a point of contact—comes, as it were, half way to meet it" (*S. E.*, 3:318). In the example under discussion this point of contact (*Berührungspunkt*) would be defloration, literally in the childhood memory, figuratively in the erotic fantasies of adolescence. (The point of contact is thus a play on words and, I would add, not just any word, but we shall return to the language of flowers.) Freud, however, does not stop there, he adds (and I am paraphrasing): what pleads in favor of the authenticity of the childhood memory is not only the existence of points of contact, but also and equally, the fact that there exist points of non-contact, that is mnesic details which find *no* correspondent or analogue in the adolescent fantasies:

> there is another thing that speaks in favour of the genuineness of your dandelion memory. It contains elements which have not been solved by what you have told me and which do not in fact fit with the sense required by the phantasy. For instance, your boy cousin helping you to rob the little girl of her flowers—can you make any sense of the idea of being helped in deflowering someone? or of the peasant-woman and the nurse in front of the cottage?
>
> "Not that I can see."
>
> So the phantasy does not coincide completely with the childhood scene. It is only based upon it at certain points. That argues in favor of the childhood memory being genuine. (*S. E.*, 3:318–19).

In the final analysis, it is the supernumerary detail, the *floating detail* (to speak structuralese) which stamps the memory with the seal of genuineness. At this point it becomes necessary to go back to the German text, for it is only in German that the relationship between the theory of anaclisis and our subject becomes manifest: "*Die Phantasie deckt sich also nicht ganz mit der Kindheitsszene, sie lehnt sich nur in einigen Punkten an sie an. Das spricht für die Echtheit der Kindheitserinnerung*" (*G. W.*, 1:549). Let us note the clear parallelism of the two expressions, *sich decken mit* and *sich anlehnen*, that is: to coincide and to lean upon, and let us recall, at the same time, the German title of this essay, *Über Deckerinnerungen*, a title inaccurately rendered by current translations, because as Wladimir Granoff has pointed out in *La Pensée et le féminin*: "the word *Deckerinnerung* means what the verb *decken* expresses, which is to say not to occult simply by means of a non-specific interposition, but to cover as with a *Deckel*, a lid, thus: covering memory, or better yet, 'cover-memory'."[7] If I am indebted to Granoff for having drawn my attention to the literal meaning of the title, I must part ways with him when he goes on to say: "And there exists between that which covers and that which is covered a relationship different from that which exists between that which screens off and veils, and that which is thus hidden. There is a relationship of total adequation . . . a neat, strict, coincident superimposition."[8] On the contrary, it seems quite obvious that what constitutes the specificity as well as the authenticity of the cover-memory is precisely the play, indeed the play of words between the *Deckende* (the cover) and the *Gedeckte* (the covered); the hermeneutic gap determines a hermetic one, the anaclisis is only partial, and condensation, failed.

If in the case of the childhood memory, Freud takes an *excess* of details to be the guarantee of truth, in the analogous case of the childhood seduction scene, it is the *repetition* of identical details which testifies to the authenticity of the implausible: "There are, however, a whole number of other things that vouches for the reality of infantile sexual scenes. In the first place there is the uniformity which they exhibit in certain details [*in gewissen Einzelheiten*], which is a necessary consequence if the preconditions of these experiences are always of the same kind, but would lead us to believe that there were secret understandings between the various patients" (*S. E.*, 3:205; *G. W.*, 1:441). The homology of the cover-memory and the so-called *proton pseudos* (first lie) does not stop there; both will suffer the same fate. Just as Freud was obliged to give up defending the reality of the seduction scene, in an unexpected tactical reversal, in the third part of his text, Freud drops his plea in favor of the genuineness of the cover-memory. The ground of the truth-bearing detail gives way when, coming at the question from a very different angle, that of "the origin of conscious memories in general," Freud arrives at the following far-reaching conclusion: no childhood recollection can enter consciousness without undergoing some reworking along the way in the service of repression: "the raw material of memory-traces out of which it was forged remains unknown to us in its original form" (*S. E.*, 3:323). And we must give the word *forge* full play here, for what Freud is in effect saying in that any memory—and this conclusion breaks down the difference between cover-memories and other childhood memories—is always already a forgery, a falsification, or even a fantasy. It calls to mind Derrida's definition of the word *voire*, literally truly: "the undecided suspense of that which remains on the march or in the margin of truth, not being false for no longer being reducible to the true."[9]

Freud stops here, but, by way of conclusion, I should like to take up again the question of the relationship of the true, the false, and the detail. In fact the details of the cover-memory recounted by the patient serve a number of purposes: they facilitate interpretation and guarantee authenticity, but they also function as a lure. Because of their hyperclarity and signification, these details—like de Man's "allegorical details"—act to blind the reader, hypnotizing her so as to prevent her from noticing other equally important details, in particular (all) those that might reveal the identity of this talented patient. Indeed it was not until 1946 that the detective work of Dr. Siegfried Bernfeld confirmed what certain members of Freud's inner circle had long suspected (according to Ernest Jones), namely that the patient, "someone who is not at all or very slightly neurotic," was none other than Freud himself. This essay is thus an important document about Freud's self-analysis; Granoff even claims it is the key document, in that it marks the end of the self-analysis and constitutes the "birth-certificate of psychoanalysis."[10] What we have here is a sort of parody of Rousseau's *Dialogues:* Freud as analyst of Sigmund.

Two questions then arise: how did Freud succeed in giving his readers the slip for nearly fifty years, and why? Bernfeld answers the first when he goes over the changes Freud made in the autobiographical data: first there are the out and out lies, such as his description of the patient, "his own profession lies in a very different field"; then there are the distortions, such as the transformation of his nephew John and sister Pauline into cousins. All these wrenches given to truth take the form of disguise. If we now refer back to the German text, we can observe that the semantic component of covering which is in the title, *Deck-* is activated throughout the text. The first example we encounter is the metaphor upon which we had reserved commentary earlier, the one which serves the analogy between displacement and figurative language in Greek myths: "mit Schönheit wie mit einer Hülle *überkleiden*" ("to clothe someone with beauty as though it were with a veil" [*S. E.,* 3:308–9; *G. W.,* 1:538]); there are others: "Die Blumen wegwerfen, um ein Brot dafür einzutauschen, scheint mir keine üble *Verkleidung* für die Absicht, die Ihr Vater mit Ihnen hatte" ("Throwing away the flowers in exchange for bread strikes me as not a bad disguise for the scheme your father had for you" [*S. E.,* 3:315; *G. W.,* 1:545]).[11] It should be pointed out, parenthetically, that the polysemy of the word does not stop there: in both German and English, "to cover" also means "to copulate with a female." Thus Freud makes the most of this polyvalent word, in a text where what is covered up is precisely a covering-fantasy.

What purpose is served by all these disguises, these transformations of "true little facts" dear to nineteenth-century realist novelists into what Alain Robbe-Grillet has termed "the little detail which has a false ring."[12] I would put forth the following hypothesis: what we have here is an object-lesson, demonstrating the final thesis of Freud's essay which is that in memory the overlapping of the true and false is such that in the end there are only *degrees* of falsification. Thus Freud's remarks about the falsification of childhood memories could just as well apply to the fabrication of his own text: "Not that they are complete inventions; they are false in the sense that they have shifted an event to a place where it did not occur . . . or that they have merged two people into one or substituted one for the other, or the scenes as a whole give signs of being combinations of two separate experiences" (*S. E.,* 3:322). Freud's floral disguise, his rhetorical flowers, are a mimesis of the falsification-work which repression carries out on childhood recollections: by a process of *mise en abyme*, Freud has produced a true-false cover-memory, or better yet has re-forged an already counterfeit child-hood memory.

Because the detail is the fulcrum of truth, it must be falsified if there is to be deceit. But then how are we to explain the aspect of the text that Bernfeld finds most astonishing: the fact that with the exception of the few pieces of trickery Bernfeld pinpoints, Freud leaves enough true details in the text to allow Bernfeld and others to unmask him.[13] Of all these clues, there is one whose nature and vicissitudes seem to me of great interest, for they suggest the need for a third category of details; neither false, nor falsified, but "under erasure" (Derrida). In filling in the analyst about his early childhood, the so-called patient empha-sizes one particularly traumatic event: ". . . what should have made most impression on me was an injury to my face which caused a considerable loss of blood and for which I had to have some stitches put in by a surgeon. I can still feel the scar resulting from this accident, but I know of no recollection which points to it, either directly or indirectly" (*S. E.*, 3:310). This is what Jones tells us of the vicissitudes of the publication of *Screen-Memories* which turns out to be intimately bound up with the history of this scar:

> In 1899, when it was written . . . nothing was known of Freud's early personal life, but he did not reprint the essay where it would naturally belong, in either the *Sammlung kleiner Schriften* or the *Psychopathologie des Alltagslebens*. Ten years later he inserted into the second edition of *Traumdeutung*, which contains so many personal allusions, a remark (concerning his facial scar) which would reveal the personality of the so-called patient. When the *Ges-ammelte Schriften* were being arranged, in 1925, Freud could not refuse the editors the permission to include the beautiful little essay in question, "*Über Deckerinnerungen*" ("*On Screen Memories*"). It would have been too pointed and would certainly have aroused their suspicion of a mystery. But at the same time he took care to erase from the *Traumdeutung*, which was also being reprinted for the *Gesammelte Schriften*, the revealing passage—even at the cost of making the context there unintelligible.[14]

If Freud went to such lengths to prevent his readers from closing the lips of this symbolic wound—and we have come full circle here, back to the physical details Sherlock Holmes urged Freud to remember—it is not because, as Jones hy-pothesizes, he was attempting to hid his Oedipus,[15] but rather to hide something on the order of his femininity. Freud's blind spot would then consist in his non-connection of the traumatic episode and the contemporary cover-memory which he juxtaposes to it. The point of contact between the two is, of course, blood: the blood which flows so profusely from the wound on the one hand, the blood of the deflowering on the other. That there exists in Freud's mind an intimate connection between blood and femininity, not to say bleeding and feminization is confirmed by yet another childhood memory which returns to Freud in a dream in the course of the same period of self-analysis which he recounts to his friend Fliess. The dream features his governess, whom he refers to as "his instructress in sexual matters": "she washed me in reddish water in which she had previously washed herself (not very difficult to interpret; I find nothing of the kind in my chain of memories, and so I take it for a genuine rediscovery)."[16]

The chain of associations that allows us to link up Freud's scar to the bath waters bloodied by the governess's menstrual period does more than confirm the persistent polymorphous association in the male imaginary between details and femininity; it also points the way to another association which will come spectacularly to the fore in Barthes's post-modernist aesthetics: that between the corporeal detail and the realm of the senses.

# 5.

# DESUBLIMATION:
## Roland Barthes's Aesthetics

He attempts to compose a discourse which is not uttered in the name of the Law and/or of Violence: whose instance might be neither political nor religious nor scientific; which might be in a sense the remainder and the supplement of all such utterances. What shall we call such discourse? *erotic*, no doubt, for it has to do with pleasure; or even perhaps: *aesthetic*, if we foresee subjecting this old category to a gradual torsion which will alienate it from its regressive, idealist background and bring it closer to the body, to the *drift*.
Roland Barthes, *Roland Barthes by Roland Barthes*

. . . it is of a detail that I asked for the revelatory ecstasy, the instantaneous access to Roland Barthes (himself, he alone), an easy access, foreign to all labor. I expected it of a detail both highly visible and dissimulated (too obvious), rather than from the great themes, the contents, the theorems or the writing strategies that I felt I knew and would easily recognize after a quarter of a century . . . *Like him* I searched . . . like him I searched for the freshness of a reading in one's relationship to the detail . . .
Jacques Derrida, "The Deaths of Roland Barthes"

In his Fourth *Discourse on Art*, delivered to the students of the Royal Academy on the distribution of prizes in December, 1771, Reynolds cautioned against excessive attention to details in the following terms: "The general idea constitutes real excellence. All smaller things, however perfect in their way, are to be sacrificed without mercy to the greater."[1] Commenting on his own painting technique some two centuries later, Barthes writes in *Roland Barthes by Roland Barthes*: "I proceed by addition, not by sketch; I have the antecedent (initial) taste for the detail, the fragment, the *rush*, and the incapacity to lead it toward a 'composition': I cannot reproduce 'the masses'."[2]

Even as Barthes's tongue-in-cheek confession to the inadequacies of his painting technique is couched in terms that attest to the persistence of Academic norms ("composition," "masses"), the mere fact that he feels quite free to own up to a scandalous preference for the partial, a spontaneous privileging of parataxis, dramatizes the major shift away from idealist aesthetics that defines the post-modern. The question arises: what aesthetic system, if any, takes on Barthes's aesthetic practice? Does Barthes have an aesthetics? I mean the subtitle of this chapter, "Roland Barthes's Aesthetics," to be somewhat provocative, to raise, for example, the question: what grounds are there for speaking of Barthes's aesthetics as one does of Hegel's?

At the outset, admittedly, the confrontation seems designed to produce nothing but a keen awareness of unbridgeable differences. Whereas Hegel's aesthetics are set forth in a monumental work called precisely the *Aesthetics*, Barthes's aesthetics take the form of a discourse whose disjointed members are scattered throughout a series of texts, none of which bears the title "Roland Barthes's *Aesthetics*." On the one hand we have a systematic, totalizing aesthetics, on the other, one which is detotalized and fragmentary. And, of course, this initial difference inaugurates a series of differences one could all too easily enumerate. But to do so would simply be to confirm what seems evident. A far more promising though risky enterprise is the discovery of the secret affinities of these two aesthetics which I would ascribe in the broadest terms to Hegel's modernity and to Barthes's classicism. Or, to be more precise, to their common double aesthetic allegiance. For just as Hegel oscillates between Classical and Romantic art, Barthes is poised between the two artistic regimes which in his scheme of things figure the classical and the modern, in his idiolect, the regimes or economies of pleasure and bliss ( *jouissance*). In short, in going from Hegel to Barthes, the double aesthetic allegiance has simply been displaced a notch. Now this double allegiance entails an essentially archaeological attempt to reconstruct the stages of great aesthetic mutations. And, further, in both instances, the detail is the critical aesthetic category ensuring the passage of one age, one regime to another.

Two examples drawn from Barthes's *Mythologies* should serve to lend some weight to my initial hypothesis. *Mythologies*, Barthes's acerbic articles on the semiotics of everyday life in a post-war France rushing headlong into consumerism, may seem a rather peculiar place to begin an inquiry into Barthes's aesthetics. It does not, for example, figure in the *Points* edition under the rubric "aesthetics." And yet I will argue that it is possible to make out in some of its pages degraded but perfectly recognizable topoi of classical idealist aesthetics. Consider the mythologies entitled the "Harcourt Actor" and "The Face of Garbo."

The Harcourt actor, that is the actor photographed by the Harcourt photography studios, is one of the gods in the Barthesian pantheon figured in *Mythologies*. Indeed it is important to note that *Mythologies* is among other things a witty and persuasive refutation of Hegel's conviction that the invasion of everyday life by what he called the "prose" of the world signifies the death of the Gods. What Barthes's *Mythologies*, with its operetta-like cast of unlikely divinities (wrestlers, gangsters, and bicycle racers, to name but a few), shows is that everyday life in the age of consumerism is shot through with residues of the sacred. Thus, it is not difficult to recognize the Harcourt actor with his ageless appearance "fixed forever at the pinnacle of beauty"[3] as a modern avatar of the marble god of high antiquity: a hieratic figure whose idealization is bound up with the absence of any particularity betraying his membership in the human race. All of the elements of this portrait are borrowed from the classical code of representation. But—and it is at this point that I wish to set against the background of their similarities, the difference, or rather one of the differences between Hegel and Barthes—unlike Hegel, when Barthes enlists the topoi of neoclassical aesthetics it is not to exalt the paradigmatic perfection of Fifth-Century Greek statuary, but rather to denounce the mystification of contemporary idealization. If for Hegel the passage from classical to romantic art represents—at least in principle—decadence, for Barthes the passage from what we might call the neo-classical to the modern, or better the avant-garde, constitutes unquestionable progress. Thus, at the end of this mythology, the conventional photographs of the Harcourt studio are contrasted with the de-idealized work of such avant-garde artists as Agnès Varda and Thérèse Le Prat, who show the actor "with exemplary humility, in its social function" (*ET*, 22).

At first glance, the face of Garbo, known as the "divine," appears to be that of a goddess of the classical age, a "deified face."[4] Like the face of the Harcourt actor, Garbo's blinds one by the inhuman perfection of her features, preserved by artful make-up from any mark of specification. Garbo's face is that of a woman of stone. By the absence of any physical detail—always the bearer of contingency and death—the face of Garbo incarnates Essence, the Idea in all of its transcendent universality and immutability:

> The name given to her, *the Divine*, probably aimed to convey less a superlative state of beauty than the essence on her corporeal person, descended from a heaven where all things are formed and perfected in the clearest light. She herself knew this: how many actresses have consented to let the crowd see the ominous maturing of their beauty. Not she, however; the essence was not to be degraded, her face was not to have any reality except that of its perfection, which was intellectual even more than formal. The Essence became gradually obscured, progressively veiled with dark glasses, broad hats and exiles: but it never deteriorated. (*M*, 56–57)

And yet, if one takes a closer look, beneath the plaster mask of the eternally youthful goddess, faint signs of life are stirring. Far from being an icon of high classical art, the face of Garbo is in Barthes's view a transitional work that participates in two aesthetic regimes:

> Garbo's face represents this fragile moment when the cinema is about to draw an existential form from an essential beauty, when the archetype leans toward

Figure 8.    Studio Harcourt, Martine Carol

Figure 9.  Garbo as Queen Christina

the fascination of mortal faces, when the clarity of the flesh as essence yields its place to a lyricism of Woman.

> Viewed as a transition the face of Garbo reconciles two iconographic ages; it assures the passage from awe to charm. (*M*, 57)

Thus the face of Garbo, which epitomizes the waning classical aesthetic is set against the eminently modern and mobile face of Audrey Hepburn. And—just as in Hegel—the passage from the older to the newer aesthetic takes the form of an increased specification, that is of a proliferation of details:

> the face of Audrey Hepburn, for instance, is individualized, not only because of its peculiar thematics (woman as child, woman as kitten) but also because of her person, an almost unique specification of the face, which has nothing of the essence left in it, but is constituted by an infinite complexity of morphological functions. (*M*, 57)

Having argued the case for Barthes's subtle intertextual relationship with Hegel and the tradition he represents, I want now to single out what is from the perspective of the archaeology of the detail the major difference between the two projects. Whereas the Romantics—and I here include Hegel—were forced, in response to pressure from a normative neo-classical aesthetics such as Reynolds's to devise theoretical and rhetorical strategies in order to bring the banned realist detail into the field of representation, the Modernists—and I here include Barthes—took it upon themselves to undo what the Romantics had wrought. Or, to phrase it otherwise, whereas the Romantics were engaged in sublimating—in the sense of elevating—the humble or prosaic detail, revealing as Wordsworth did so spectacularly in England or Balzac in France, "the charismatic power in the trivial and the mean,"[5] the Modernists were or are engaged in undoing the work of sublimation, in restoring realist details to their brute and unsublimated materiality. In short, Barthes's fundamental aesthetic imperative is *desublimation*. When in "The Harcourt Actor" Barthes notes: "The Harcourt iconography sublimates the actor's materiality" (26), he restores to the actor the very materiality of which the idealizing, essentializing Harcourt photograph had robbed him. Similarly, when in the mythology entitled "At the Music Hall" Barthes lays bare the mechanism whereby human sweat and toil is magically transmuted into an airy and delightful ballet, he undoes the work of sublimation—"the music hall is human work memorialized and *sublimated* [emphasis added]":

> Here reign the gleaming balls, the light wands, the tubular furniture, the chemical silks, the grating chalks, and the glittering clubs; here visual luxury parades *facility*, disposed in the brightness of substances and the continuity of gestures: sometimes man is a support planted in the center, a tree along which slides a woman-branch; sometimes the entire hall shares in the coe-

nesthesia of energy, of weight not vanquished but *sublimated* [emphasis added] by rebounds. (*ET*, 125)

Sublimation, as it operates in the Music Hall, fuses essentialization and weightlessness. To desublimate is to refreight the sublime element with the gravity of facticity. And nowhere perhaps is Barthes's project of desublimation more in evidence than in his celebrated essay "The Reality Effect" ("L'effet de réel").

Critics are not done with Barthes's scandalous assertion that there exist in realist texts "useless," totally parasitical details that contribute neither to advancing the plot, nor to enhancing our knowledge of the characters and their physical surroundings. One need only recall that a long critical tradition condemns the superfluous detail as symptomatic of decadence in order to appreciate the importance of the question raised by Barthes: what is at stake is nothing less than the legitimacy of the organic model of literary interpretation, according to which all details—no matter how aberrant their initial appearance—can, indeed must be integrated into the whole, since the work of art is itself organically constituted. To accredit the existence of a truly inessential detail, to make of it a distinctive trait of ordinary Western narrative is tantamount to attacking the foundation of hermeneutics which is constantly engaged in shuttling between the part and the whole. Worse: to privilege the insignificant detail is to practice a sort of decadent criticism, to promote a poor management of linguistic capital, since these notations seem in Barthes's words to "be allied with a kind of narrative *luxury*, profligate to the extent of splurging on 'extravagant' details, and increasing the cost of narrative information."[6]

In order to avert the threat constituted by Barthes's audacious hypothesis, some critics have sought to demonstrate that there are no inessential details, just inadequate readers: viewed in the proper perspective, any prodigal detail can be brought back into the fold of meaning. To venture down this recuperative path is to risk missing the interest this essay presents, which is that in it Barthes once again attempts to reconstruct the stages of a major aesthetic shift, using the detail as his main category. The "reality effect," which is a sort of myth of origins of modernity, recounts the passage of the "concrete detail" from the domain of history, to which Aristotle assigned it, to that of fiction: in other terms, the emergence of a new verisimilitude—realism—from an older one: classicism. Barthes's essay is then an archaeological text where what is being re-staged is realism *in statu nascendi*. The birth of realism is made manifest in the famous description of Rouen in *Madame Bovary* where, in Barthes's words, "the realist imperatives" overtake the "tyrannical constraints of what must be called aesthetic plausibility" (*RE*, 13).

The passage from classicism to realism would then correspond to the invasion of fiction by those "concrete details" of which history has always been so inordinately fond. Now these details, whose function it is to denote reality, always refer to matters deemed of little interest ("casual movements, transitory attitudes, insignificant objects, redundant words" [14]), what we might call the refuse of aesthetic verisimilitude, in keeping with the notion dear to the doxa that the concrete is one with the unintelligible:

> Unvarnished "representation" of "reality," a naked account of "what is" (or was), thus looks like a resistance to meaning, a resistance which confirms the great mythical opposition between the true-to-life (the living) and the intelligible. (*RE*, 14)

It follows that the more a detail is proof against meaning, the more it resists attempts at semantico-structural recuperation, the better it is able to lend to the referential text the full weight of reality.

Implicit in this account of the rise of realism is the problematization of two interrelated notions: one, the conventional equation of the real and the unintelligible; two, a pre-semiotic apprehension of the workings of denotation. For it appears that when submitted to semiotic analysis, the functioning of the concrete detail turns out to be a good deal more complicated than we had been led to believe. "Semiotically," writes Barthes, "the 'concrete detail' is constituted by the *direct* collusion of a referent and a signifier; the signified is expelled from the sign." But—and this is the key point in Barthes's argument—that which is expulsed insists on returning; the so-called "reality effect" is then the return of the repressed signified, with one important difference: it returns in a new guise, as what Barthes calls a "signified of connotation":

> eliminated from the realist utterance as a signified of denotation, the "real" slips back in as a signified of connotation; for at the very moment when these details are supposed to denote reality directly, all that they do, tacitly, is signify it: Flaubert's barometer, Michelet's little door, say, in the last analysis, only this: *we are the real*. It is the category of the "real," and not its various contents, which is being signified. (*RE*, 16)

For Barthes, realism, which is to say realist description, is a lure, an optical illusion, indeed a *"referential illusion."* At the very moment when one thinks one is embracing the real in its concrete materiality—and let us note that throughout the text the word *real* is in quotes, under suspicion—one is in fact in the grip of a "reality effect," where what we are given is a category and not a thing.

Two questions then arise, having to do with the problematic notion of the real, for what is at stake in this essay and to a larger extent in all Barthes's writings on realism, is the nature of the real. What, after all, is the reality produced by the lark's mirror which is the concrete detail, since it is obvious that a "reality effect" and "real-reality" are not coextensive? To expel the signified from the sign is to reduce the referent to its initial facticity. If one evacuates the signified and applies the signifier directly to the referent, one may well produce a powerful reality effect, but the reality in question is a bizarre reality, a desublimated reality, since the signified is the agency of sublimation in the sign.

Thus it is that whereas for the aestheticians of the eighteenth and nineteenth centuries the paradigmatic detail is Diderot's "little wart," for Barthes it becomes Mme Aubain's barometer: the ugly detail is replaced by the brute or stupid detail.

This observation brings us to our second question: what is the notion of the real that Barthes opposes to the discredited notion of the real as the unintelligible which grounds realism? This is not an easy question to answer, for Barthes's answer varied over the years. My answer will be a bit roundabout, but it seems important to me to at least touch upon the main stages in Barthes's trajectory.

The first time, to my knowledge, that Barthes raises the question, "what is the *real*," is in 1961, well before the publication of "The Reality Effect" (1968). He begins by demystifying the notion of a universal, transparent real always identical to itself, a notion that grounds the mimetic enterprise of classical realism. Our knowledge of the real—whose problematic status is signaled here by the use of italics—is always partial, subjective; at best realism cannot copy *the* real, only *some* real:

We never know it except in the form of effects (physical world), functions (social world) or fantasies (cultural world); in short, the *real* is never anything but an inference; when we declare we are copying reality, this means that we choose a certain inference and not certain others: realism is, at its very inception, subject to the responsibility of a choice . . .[7]

What falsifies realism from the very start is the fact that our vision of the *real* is refracted through the prism of language; there exists no relationship to the *real* which is not mediated through the opaque medium of language. "I am in my room, I *see* my room; but already, isn't *seeing* my room *speaking* it to myself?" (*CE*, 160). The gaze one brings to bear on the *real* is structured like and above all by language. Barthes concludes:

Realism, here, cannot then be the copy of things, therefore, but the knowledge of language; the most "realistic" work will not be the one which "paints" reality, but which, using the world as content (this content itself, moreover, is alien to its structure, i.e., to its being), will explore as profoundly as possible the *unreal reality* of language. (*CE*, 160)

Two conceptions of realism clash head-on here: on the one hand, naive mimetic realism—realism in its most conventional sense—on the other, the new linguistic realism Barthes seeks to promote. In the first instance, the degree of a work's realism would be gauged against the standard of its greater or lesser fidelity to the representation of worldly reality; in the other, against the greater or lesser exploration of the irreality of language. The most realistic literature would then be the one which would designate its own irrealism.

The contorted and ultimately unsatisfying nature of Barthes's high structuralist conception of reality and realism should be apparent. However salutary and necessary the emphasis placed by Barthes and others on the primacy of language in literature, a conception of realism which reduces the world to secondary status and views it as "content" made of undifferentiated and interchangeable elements cannot long resist the pressure of the real, for the real, as we have seen above, is precisely that which always returns. If, throughout his career, Barthes never ceased to call "into question, in radical fashion, the age-old aesthetic of representation" (*RE*, 16), in the group of works which constitute what the critics have taken to calling "the last" (Todorov) or "the second" (Compagnon) Barthes, he goes beyond the formalist solution to elaborate an aesthetic that, without relapsing into naive mimeticism, gives its due to referential reality. If, however, in these texts (beginning with *The Pleasure of the Text* and culminating in *Camera Lucida*) the real makes a spectacular comeback, it is a *new real*, not that which *resists* meaning, rather that which *remains* after meaning has been evacuated or, in Barthes's idiolect, "exempted":

> Yet for him, it is not a question of recovering a pre-meaning, an origin of the world, of life, of facts, anterior to meaning, but rather to imagine a post-meaning: one must traverse, as though the length of an initiatic way, the whole meaning in order to be able to extenuate it, to *exempt* it. (*RB*, 27)

Now if in the West the exemption of meaning can only be achieved at the cost of a difficult ascesis, in the Orient, that is in Barthes's imaginary Japan, the situation is different. The new real is an Oriental import, for whereas in the West the concrete real has long been identified with the insignificant, in Japan there is, always according to Barthes, no insignificance. Thus he writes on the back cover of the French edition of *Empire of Signs*: "And above all, the superior quality of this sign, the nobility of its affirmation and the erotic grace of its design are affixed everywhere, on the most trivial objects and actions, those we generally dismiss as insignificant or vulgar."[8]

Consequently, in the empire of signs the detail reigns supreme. In "Japan"— the quotation marks are meant to indicate Japan's fictional status in Barthes's text for, paradoxically, the new real is not referentially anchored—everything is a detail: the hierarchy prevalent in the West which opposes the great and the small, the sublime and the trivial and implicitly valorizes the great and the sublime, does not obtain in "Japan." The very notion of futility is thus rendered impertinent, with this paradoxical result: in "Japan," where everything signifies, nothing is significant. What Barthes says about the haiku can be applied to Japanese life in general; borrowing a neologism from Gérard Genette, we might say that in Japan "haikuization" is generalized:

> What I am saying here about haiku I might also say about everything which *happens* when one travels in that country I am calling Japan. For there, in the street, in a bar, in a shop, in a train, something always *happens*. This something—which is etymologically an adventure—is of an infinitesimal order: it

is an incongruity of clothing, an anachronism of culture, a freedom of behavior, an illogicality of itinerary etc. . . .[9]

What is then the haiku which figures what we might term the "good" relationship to the real? First, unlike Western art which is essentially mimetic, "the
haiku never describes: its art is counterdescriptive" (*EoS*, 77). At the same time—
and this is the tricky part—though non-mimetic, the haiku is not sui-referential,
not cut off from reality.[10] Further, in this universe where the real is meaningless, the real has, so to speak, no sense of the real. Hence: no category of the
real, no reality effect, no connotation. In short, in "Japan" the real is neither
denoted nor connoted, rather it is *designated*:

> Neither describing nor defining, the haiku (as I shall finally name any dis-
> continuous feature, any event of Japanese life as it offers itself to my reading),
> the haiku diminishes to the point of pure and sole designation. *It's that, it's
> thus*, says the haiku, *it's so*. Or better still: *so* it says, with a touch so instan-
> taneous and so brief (without vibration or recurrence) that even the copula
> would seem excessive, a kind of remorse for a forbidden, permanently al-
> ienated definition. (*EoS*, 83)

The difference between European realism and haiku can thus be reduced to
the difference between two expressions: *we are the real* and *so*. On the one hand,
a pseudo-definition enunciated by a small number of personified details, on the
other, a simple exclamation, an accent guaranteed by no subject—for elision of
the copula goes hand in hand with the abolition of the subject—and which can
be renewed ad infinitum. Ultimately, however, the essential difference between
Eastern and Western aesthetics is of a metaphysical order.

> Description, a Western genre, has its spiritual equivalent in contemplation,
> the methodical inventory of the attributive forms of the divinity or of the
> episodes of the evangelical narrative . . . the haiku, on the contrary, artic-
> ulated around a metaphysics without subject and without god, corresponds
> to the Buddhist *Mu*, to the Zen *satori*, which is not at all the illuminative
> descent of God, but "awakening to the fact," apprehension of the thing as
> event and not as substance . . . (*EoS*, 78)

In the Utopia of the detail that is Barthes's Japan, the detail is at last freed from
the close ties that bind it to the sacred of Christian metaphysics and is deployed
in a beyond of the sublime. It is because oriental metaphysics does not recognize
any form of transcendence that haiku is a purely deictic form, designating an
unencumbered real.

The question then becomes: is there any Western artistic practice on the model
of haiku? One has only to read Barthes's last work, *Camera Lucida*, to discover
that the answer is very definitely yes: photography enjoys the same deictic relationship to material reality as does haiku; it too is an art of pure designation:

In the Photograph, the event is never transcended for the sake of something else: the Photograph always leads the corpus I need back to the body I see; it is the absolute Particular, the sovereign Contingency, matte and somehow stupid, the *This* . . . what Lacan calls the *Tuché*, the Occasion, the Encounter, the Real, in its indefatigable expression. In order to designate reality, Buddhism says *sunya*, the void; but better still: *tatahta*, as Alan Watts has it, the fact of being this, of being thus, of being so; *tat* means *that* in Sanskrit and suggests the gesture of the child pointing his finger at something and saying: *That, there it is, lo!*[11]

Barthes's last detail, what he calls the *punctum*, is then bound up with a notion of the Real—and the Real is spelled here with a capital R—which stresses its pragmatic aspect, in the etymological sense of the word *pragma*: fact and event. Consequently, the *punctum* can only be the object of a double encounter. Like Proust's *madeleine*—and *Camera Lucida* is Barthes's *Recherche*—the *punctum* does not come under the sway of the will. It escapes the intentionality of both the photographer and the spectator:

> Hence the detail which interests me is not, or at least is not strictly, intentional, and probably must not be so; it occurs in the field of the photographed thing like a supplement that is at once inevitable and delightful; it does not necessarily attest to the photographer's art; it says only that the photographer was there, or else still more simply, that he could not *not* photograph the partial object at the same time as the total object . . . (*CL*, 47)

> In order to perceive the *punctum*, no analysis would be of any use to me (but perhaps memory sometimes would) . . . it suffices that the image be large enough, that I do not have to study it (this would be of no help at all), that, given right there on the page, I should receive it right here in my eyes. (*CL*, 42–43)

Significantly, in keeping with the Proustian thematics of *Camera Lucida*, the devalorization of the will corresponds to the valorization of involuntary memory. The punctum is often a deferred detail, subject to "a certain latency" (*CL*, 53). There is a great deal to say about the punctum—and much has already been said—but I would like instead to proceed to a somewhat more systematic comparison of several theories of the detail in Barthes, for it should be obvious by now that, for example, the concrete detail and the punctum do not function in the same manner or according to the same rules. I should like to sketch a comparison of Barthes's three main texts on the detail, "The Reality Effect," "The Third Meaning," and *Camera Lucida*, before going on to consider a detail *in* Barthes.

From the outset, a certain category of details, what I would call the "false little Barthesian detail" must be identified and eliminated. These are the details which participate in the economy of meaning, such as Eisenstein's decorative details, or the studious details in certain photographs:

> the Eisensteinian meaning devastates ambiguity. How? By the addition of an aesthetic value, emphasis. Eisenstein's "decorativism" has an economic function: it proffers the truth. Look at III [see figure 10]:in extremely classical fashion, grief comes from the bowed heads, the expression of suffering, the hand over the mouth stifling a sob, but when once all this has been said, very adequately, a decorative trait says it again . . . Within the general detail . . . another detail is mirroringly inscribed; derived from a pictorial order as a quotation of the gestures to be found in icons and *pietà*, it does not distract but accentuates the meaning.[12]

Detail within the detail, detail of the detail, the decorative detail is entirely in the service of the message, indeed of the truth of the film. Similarly there exists in photography a category of details Barthes ranges under the rubric *studium*, details "which constitute the very raw material of ethnological science." "When William Klein photographs 'Mayday, 1959' in Moscow, he teaches me how Russians dress . . . I *note* a boy's big cloth cap, another's necktie, an old woman's scarf around her head, a youth's haircut . . . I can enter still further into such details . . ." (*CL*, 28–30). These details—to which one might add the celebrated "biographemes" of which Barthes speaks in *Sade/Fourier/Loyola*—are not in the restricted sense, Barthesian details. They belong to the voice of Science.

What then is a Barthesian detail, regardless of the artistic medium involved? It is marked, as we noted above in our reading of "The Reality Effect," by its participation in an economy of excess. It always enjoys the status of supplement, a luxurious extra. Thus, in "The Third Meaning," Barthes opposes obtuse meaning to obvious meaning in terms of a by now familiar economic metaphor and one which owes much to Bataille: "obtuse meaning appears necessarily as a luxury, an expenditure with no exchange" (*I-M-T*, 62). The Barthesian detail is always supplementary, marginal, decentered. Whether it is Mme Aubain's barometer, the disguise of a character in an Eisenstein film, or the gold chain worn by one of the black women in a photograph by James Van DerZee, the detail which draws and holds Barthes's attention is like the fetishist's fetish, a detail which, camouflaged by its perfect banality, goes unnoticed by others.

But almost immediately, a preliminary distinction must be introduced between Barthes's supplementary details: whereas the obtuse meaning and the *punctum* are details which "prick" the spectator with their fine points, the same cannot be said for the concrete detail. Unless the reader has a special passion for barometers, Mme Aubain's barometer does not touch her: on the contrary, the concrete detail produces its characteristic effect by its very lack of pathos, its affective neutrality. It does not appeal to the reader's emotions, as does for example, the obtuse meaning. Glossing a still from Eisenstein's *Potemkin* [see Figure 11], Barthes writes:

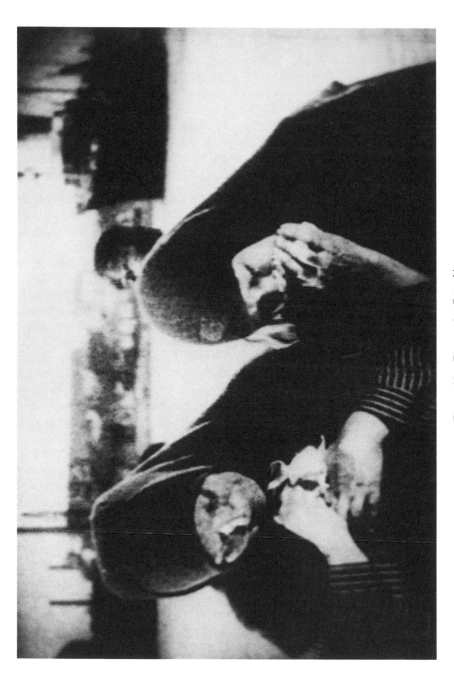

Figure 10.    Eisenstein, *Potemkin*

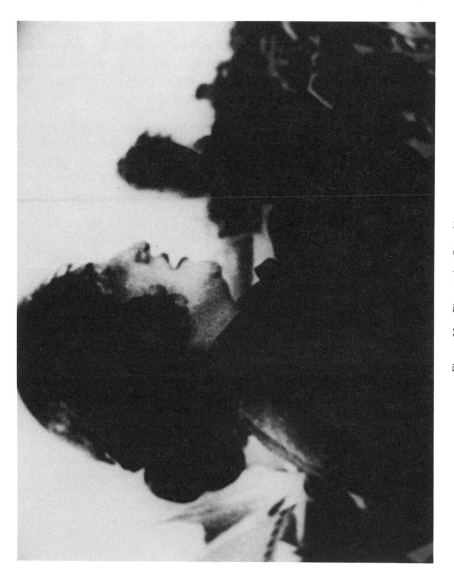

Figure 11.  Eisenstein, *Potemkin*

Look at another bun . . . it contradicts the tiny raised fist, atrophies it without the reduction having the slightest symbolic (intellectual) value; prolonged by small curls, pulling the face in towards an ovine model, it gives the woman something *touching* . . . I believe that the obtuse meaning carries a certain *emotion*. (*I-M-T*, 58–59)

The affective criterion allows us to distinguish the concrete from the punctual detail. And that distinction in turn leads to another. For, if we compare Barthes's remarks on obtuse meaning and the punctum, we find that all punctual details are not identical. In fact, for Barthes, as for Hegel, to each artistic medium there corresponds a particular use or status of the detail. Not only, for example, is the obtuse meaning a specifically filmic detail, it is the very locus of the emergence of the filmic. Similarly, the punctum is the photographic detail par excellence as well as the point of inscription of the photographic.

Finally the question arises: if every system of representation is endowed with a specific modality of the detail, if indeed the detail is the royal way to an artistic medium's specificity, is there in Barthes a literary detail on the order of the punctum, a textual detail which pierces the reader and which, unlike the concrete detail which refers only to the *category* of the real, refers to a duly authentified reality, one of which it can unequivocally be stated: *it has been*, "ça a été."

Two passages drawn from *The Pleasure of the Text* would suggest that such textual details do indeed exist. Whether it is a question of the food mentioned by Stendhal in one of his Chronicles of clerical life, or the weather noted by Amiel in his *Journal*, these details make manifest reality at its most unsurpassable: "the *final state* of reality, its intractability."[13] The observation that such a category of what we might call hyperrealist details exists in certain texts leads Barthes to distinguish between two sorts of realism: "there are two realisms: the first deciphers the 'real' (what is demonstrated but not seen); the second speaks 'reality' (what is seen but not demonstrated); the novel, which can mix these two realisms, adds to the unintelligible of the 'real' the hallucinatory tail of 'reality'" (*PoT*, 45–46).

It would seem, then, that contrary to what we had been earlier led to believe, there do exist in Western textuality details on the order of the ideal details evoked in both *The Empire of Signs* and *Camera Lucida*: non-mimetic realist details. In a sense, for Barthes, who never throughout his work ceased to pursue the phantom of reality, the classical realist text is an aggregate of details enjoying different orders of relationships with reality: a relationship of denotation (the real is the insignificant); a relationship of connotation ("we are the real"), and a relationship of designation ("so"). Only the deictic details have the ring of truth; if they do not necessarily move us, they do procure a distinct form of text pleasure, a pleasure of/in identity patterned on the pleasure of the metaphor in Proust: "astonishment that in 1791 one could eat 'a salad of oranges and rum,' as one does in restaurants today: the onset of historical intelligibility and the persistence of the thing (orange, rum) in *being there*" (*PoT*, 46).

If I return now to my question—are there textual equivalents of the obtuse meaning and the punctum?—I would have to qualify my answer. If by textual one means literary or fictional, then the answer would have to be no. For though Barthes claims to find these minute details of everyday life "in certain novels, biographies, and historical works" (*PoT*, 53), I think it is no accident that the two examples he provides are both drawn from non-fictional prose works: an episode of clerical life recounted by Stendhal and a weather report noted by Amiel in his *Journal*. The discursive *punctum* draws its force from its indexation on a referent guaranteed by a subject, apprehended in his or her most intimate specificity. Therefore it is not in the least surprising that it should be in one of Barthes's most generically heterogeneous texts—where scenes drawn from Barthes's life are explicitly intermingled with literary allusions—that I came upon or was pricked by a textual detail. I am referring to *A Lover's Discourse*.

In one of the rare critical studies devoted, at least in part, to this text, *Fowles/Irving/Barthes* by Randolph Runyon, I learned that *A Lover's Discourse* is one of the modern variations on a theme from the Apocrypha, the story of Tobias, the eighth and final husband of Sarah.[14] As evidence Runyon cites the fact that the enigmatic detail featured in color on the cover of the book is a fragment of *Tobias and the Angel*, attributed to Verrocchio's studio and on display in the National Gallery in London. Surely this choice of iconographic accompaniment is not "innocent." I will not rehearse here Runyon's ingenious analysis of a *A Lover's Discourse*, in the double light of the story of Tobias and the detail of the painting representing it. If I allude here to this study it is not merely out of professional scruple—one must always cite one's sources—but rather to insist upon the fact than once alerted by Runyon, my eye was constantly drawn back to this iconographic detail, but to no avail: I could not pierce the source of its mystery . . .

That was the state of affairs until upon rereading the text I was suddenly and forcibly struck by the insistence of a bizarre detail. Here are the passages in question:

Why is it I desire so-and-so? . . . Is it the whole of so-and-so I desire (. . .)? And, in that case, what is it in this loved body which has the vocation of a fetish for me? What perhaps incredibly tenuous portion—what accident? The way a nail is cut, a tooth broken slightly aslant, a lock of hair, a way of spreading the fingers while smoking?

(I was looking at everything in the other's face, the other's body, coldly: lashes, toenail, thin eyebrows, thin lips, the luster of the eyes, a mole, a way of holding a cigarette [une façon d'étendre les doigts en fumant] . . .)

there are subtle, evanescent trivialities which swiftly pass over the other's body: a brief (but excessive) way of parting the fingers . . .[15]

Suddenly I saw it: in juxtaposing the cover and the text—and everything hinges, of course, on the very particular relationship of image and text in Barthes, "the text does not 'gloss' the images, which do not 'illustrate' the text" (*EoS*, xi)—the detail which has the vocation of a fetish for Barthes is not the hand—as Runyon implies—or not merely the hand, but rather a particular position of the hand, a certain spread. The corporeal detail on which the speaker of a lover's discourse fastens is in the alphabet of the unconscious—and I refer the reader to Barthes's text on Erté's alphabet for evidence of his fascination with the letters of the alphabet, of which S/Z are the most celebrated—a V.[16] In other words—and here I am purposely going very fast to prevent the quickening of interpretation—the detail Barthes's lover fetishizes in the lover's body—the parting of the fingers—is an erotic gap, a sort of icon of castration.

"To give examples of *punctum* is, in a certain fashion, to *give myself up*," writes Barthes (*CL*, 43). To see in the spread of the fingers a punctum and further a literal inscription of castration is a highly idiosyncratic gesture. I run the risk of provoking resistance, denial: the detail of the gaping V may or may not pierce other readers. No matter. What does matter is that in Barthes the detail becomes the privileged point of contact between reader and text: the discursive punctum is the hook onto which the reader may hitch her own fantasies, fasten his own individual myths. Located at the intersection of the private (Barthes's lover) and the public (the painting of Tobias), Barthes's V figures emblematically his aesthetic project.

What we have in Barthes is an eroticization of aesthetics, or, better, an aesthetics of Eros. And Eros resides in the detail, because the detail is always at least partially sited in a real body. Hence the difference between the theater, home of Eros, and the cinema, the realm of pure representation and phantasm:

> The theatre (the particularized scene) is the very site of what used to be called *venusty*, charm, comeliness of form, i.e. of Eros observed, illuminated (by Psyche and her lamp). Enough that a secondary, episodic character offers some reason to be desired (this reason can be perverse, not attached to beauty but to a detail of the body, to the texture of the voice, to a way of breathing, even to some clumsiness), for a whole performance to be saved. (*RB*, 83)

Whereas at the cinema, "the image is the *irremediable* absence of the represented body" (*RB*, 84), at the theatre the sexy detail that arouses the spectator's perverse desire surfaces on a body which even if it remains by convention inaccessible ("essential") is in reality available to touch, present ("contingent"). If Eros resides in a detail of the body, what of the fragment, does it too participate in the general eroticization of aesthetics we find in Barthes? Yes, in the sense that writing by fragments is for Barthes an intensely pleasurable textual activity and that pleasure is born of the abrupt discontinuity introduced by the fragment: "it is a fantasy of discourse, a gaping of desire" (*RB*, 94). The blank interstices between fragments are to the text what the "intermittences of the skin flashing between two articles of clothing" (*PoT*, 10) are to the body: the portals of desire. Asexual in Hegel, sexually differentiated in Freud, the detail/fragment paradigm comes in Barthes—as do so many others—under the regime of perversion, which subjects sexual difference to a radical and endless oscillation. Though highly sexualized in Barthes, the detail/fragment paradigm is degendered, as the marks of sexual specification are erased from the textual, as well as the referential, contingent body of desire.[17] By bringing his aesthetics, in his own words, "closer to the body" and its "drift," Barthes has struck a decisive blow against idealist aesthetics and its devalorizing gendering of the detail. But it would appear that in transvaluating the detail, the feminine has vanished. Because the masculine/feminine opposition is itself tainted as a metaphysical or ideological construct, Barthes's seeming neutralization of sexual difference might appear to many as a sign of progress. Isn't that what you want, my reader asks? Yes, but. Can one be so certain that degendering is not merely defeminizing, leaving the masculine and its prerogatives intact? Does Barthes's fetishization of all part objects, of all that gapes subvert the orthodox psychoanalytic association of castration with femininity or does it, however subtly, reinscribe the primacy of the phallus? Within the gaping V of the lover's hand there is a cigarette and this may be one time where, pace Freud, a cigarette is not just a cigarette.

Appearances notwithstanding, my initial question as to the detail's femininity was not rhetorical; it remains open. That the detail has been traditionally connoted as feminine and devalorized and, further, that the modern age has witnessed a remarkable transvaluation of the detail accompanied by its no less significant degendering, I hope to have demonstrated in the previous pages. Whether or not the detail *is* feminine—and I shall come to this much deferred point in a moment—given Western culture's longstanding association of the order of the small, the finely wrought, and the *heimlich* with the feminine sphere, the need to affirm the power and the positivity of the *feminine particular* cannot for the moment be denied. Whether or not the "feminine" is a male construct, a product of a phallocentric culture destined to disappear, in the present order of things we cannot afford not to press its claims even as we dismantle the conceptual systems which support it.

So, again: is the detail feminine? Are women—that is, females socialized as women—as so many thinkers both male and female assert, more firmly grounded than men in the world of immanence? Do the works produced by women artists exhibit a higher density of homey and/or ornamental details than those produced by their male counterparts? Doubtless my answer will disappoint. Despite the extensive and highly sophisticated work carried out in recent years by feminist critics committed to uncovering the specificities of women's artistic productions, there exists no reliable body of evidence to show that women's art is either more or less particularistic than men's. Indeed, further investigation of this question may lead us to formulate a surprising hypothesis, namely that feminine specificity lies in the direction of a specifically feminine form of idealism, one that seeks to transcend not the sticky feminine world of prosaic details, but rather the deadly asperities of male violence and destruction.

# Part 2
*Readings*

# 6.
# DALI'S FREUD

*I have succeeded at the very point at which a paranoiac fails.*
*Sigmund Freud*

In his 1934 lecture "Qu'est-ce que le surréalisme?" André Breton hailed Salvador Dali's unique contribution to Surrealism: "Dali has endowed surrealism with an instrument of primary importance, in particular the paranoiac-critical method, which has immediately shown itself capable of being applied equally to painting, poetry, the cinema, to the construction of typical surrealist objects, to fashion, to sculpture, to history of art and even if necessary, to all manner of exegesis."[1] It is to this last claim of Breton's, the possible application of Dali's method to "all manner of exegesis," but especially a hermeneutics of the detail that I want to address myself, and there is no better starting place for such an inquiry than Dali's own piece of practical paranoia-criticism, *The Tragic Myth of Millet's Angelus*. While many commentators have been tempted to dismiss Dali's psychoanalytic ventures as parodies of scientific discourse, nothing but another clever hoax perpetrated on the public by the master "crétiniseur," I will argue—by reading Freud *after* Dali—that Dali's surrealist "psycho-criticism" ranks as one of those "misprisions" more perceptive and provocative than many a "serious" application of Freud. In the specific realm of "icon-analysis," the gap between the "patron-saint" and the "crank"[2] turns out to be a great deal narrower than might first appear. If there is humor in Dali's encounter with psychoanalysis—and there is—the joke is not so much on *us* as on *him*. The precise locus of this humor is pinpointed with unerring accuracy in the course of Dali's meeting with Lacan, as recounted in *The Secret Life of Salvador Dali*. While awaiting Lacan's arrival, Dali is at work on an etching. In order to see the drawing on the copper plate more clearly, Dali has found it helpful to stick a small white square of paper on the tip of his nose. After Lacan's departure, Dali goes over their discussion, sorting out their agreements and disagreements:

> But I grew increasingly puzzled over the rather alarming manner in which the young psychiatrist had scrutinized my face from time to time. It was almost as if the germ of a strange, curious smile would then pierce through

his expression. Was he intently studying the convulsive effects upon my facial morphology of the ideas that stirred my soul? I found the answer to the enigma when I presently went to wash my hands . . . I had forgotten to remove the square of white paper from the tip of my nose! For two hours I had discussed questions of the most transcendental nature in the most precise, objective and grave tone of voice without being aware of the disconcerting adornment of my nose.[3]

This very Freudian slip-up, this conspicuous "shine on the nose," will serve as a parable for paranoia-criticism and its vicissitudes; but more of this later.

We must now turn our attention to Dali's paranoia-criticism, what it is and how it works. Dali's most succinct definition occurs in his 1935 text, *The Conquest of the Irrational*.

> Paranoia: a delusion of interpretative association including a systematic structure. Paranoiac-critical activity: a spontaneous method of irrational knowledge based on the critical-interpretative association of delusionary phenomena.[4]

Almost every word in this two-step definition is significant and merits commentary, but it is Dali's bold restriction of paranoia to one of its principal forms or symptoms, what the French call "le délire d'interprétation," that needs to be noted first. In *The Psychopathology of Everyday Life*, Freud describes paranoiacs suffering from this "delusion of reference" as follows: "they attach the greatest significance to the minor details of other people's behaviour which we ordinarily neglect, interpret them and make them the basis of far-reaching conclusions."[5] In other words, that class of paranoiacs whom Sartre refers to as "les grands interprétants"[6] practice a hermeneutics of saturation, leaving no sign unaccounted for in their rage for systematization. Now to equate paranoia with "le délire d'interprétation" is to take it out of the clinical sphere and into the critical; and the "restricted paranoia" described by Dali thereby becomes applicable and relevant to "all manner of exegesis," including, of course, psychoanalytic interpretation. But, at the same time as Dali restricts the field of paranoia, he also extends it by linking up two key psychoanalytic techniques, forging the term "delusion of interpretative association." This subtle shift of emphasis from delirious *interpretation* to delirious *association* is central to Dali's own practice of paranoia-criticism, for the greater part of *The Tragic Myth* is taken up with Dali's interpretative associations, what he calls "secondary delirious phenomena." Primacy and priority are accorded to the "initial delirious phenomenon," that is, to the "spontaneous method of irrational knowledge" featured in the definition quoted above. Paranoiac-critical activity is then as precipitous and irresistible as Jansenist grace; it can strike one at any moment, with the affective force of a *déjà vu* and without any other recourse than to bring to consciousness the unconscious interpretative-critical associations underlying the delirious phenomenon. Thus Dali's total involvement with *The Angelus*, a widely reproduced painting he had been familiar with since childhood, is a case of "instant obsession."

> In June 1932 the image of Millet's *Angelus* presents itself to my mind, without any recent memory or conscious association allowing for an immediate explanation . . . It produces on me a great impression, in me a great upset for, although in my vision of the said image, everything "corresponds" exactly to the reproductions of the painting I am familiar with, it nevertheless "appears" to me absolutely transformed and charged with such latent intentionality that the *Angelus* of Millet suddenly becomes for me the most troubling, the most enigmatic, the densest, the richest in unconscious thoughts of any pictorial works that ever existed.[7]

Dali's attempt at rationalizing his sudden fascination with this apparently innocuous, insipid, second-rate painting consists in explicating the interpretative associations evoked by its main elements; these associations bring into play a wide range of typically Surrealist phenomena: games, chance encounters, fantasies, childhood memories, popular or even "pop" iconography (in the form of postcards), fairy tales, and, last but not least, the scientific writings of the entomologist Fabre. By the proliferation and the concatenation of these interpretative associations. Dali is led from the "obsessive image" to the "tragic myth," which proves to be, not surprisingly, what Charles Mauron calls a "personal myth."

One element in the painting can be said to command the entire network of "secondary delirious phenomena," and that "global and determining element" (37) is the hour of day, dusk. Ever since childhood, Dali had associated dusk with the Tertiary Age, its flora and fauna, now preserved only in the form of fossils. Dusk calls to mind the passing of an age and fills Dali with a prevailing "feeling of extinction" (39). From the moment the once familiar *Angelus* becomes a strange "obsessive image," it seems that no matter what Dali sees or does, it feeds into his obsession, by relating back to what he terms "the atavisms of dusk" (37–39). Playing with some pebbles on the beach, Dali is directed by "the automatism of play" (19) to place two pebbles in precisely the same face-to-face position as that of the two figures in the painting. This involuntary analogy between human figures and geological forms participates in the "atavisms of dusk," because it implies "the notion of the fossil *Angelus*" (43). Or, struck by the expectant, prayerful position of the female figure, Dali is reminded of the praying mantis, an "atavistic" insect. Or, crossing a meadow rich in "atavistic" vegetation, Dali collides with a fisherman coming at him from the opposite direction; this collision too is to Dali's mind "atavistic": "According to Freud it would be a stereotypical repetition of the ancestral sexual aggression become symbolic; this habit must have assumed a power, an extreme importance among the first human beings" (47).

While all these associations seem to point to some sort of violent sexual en-

Figure 12.   Millet, *The Angelus*

counter between the male and female figures, Dali is unable to account for the effects of extreme anxiety generated by this (presumed) latent scenario. The breakthrough comes with the intervention of *le hasard objectif*, whose functioning is, of course, closely allied to that of paranoiac-critical activity: "systematic association, a product of paranoiac power, would be in a way an activity productive of 'hasard objectif'" (59). Driving at dusk through the town of Port de la Selva, Dali sees in a shop window a set of coffee cups and a coffee pot, all bearing on their sides miniaturized reproductions of *The Angelus*. Of all the bizarre associations this bizarre coincidence inspires, the most significant are those connected with the suggestive shape of the cups and pot, which Dali sees as "surrealist objects with a symbolic function" (61). For Dali this "symbolic function" is always identical and involves a highly eroticized form of cannibalism: "the intervention of the coffee pot meant to fill cups with coffee or café au lait cannot but call forth for us the idea of making the cup itself edible, of devouring it . . ." (63). From this theory of the symbolic function of everyday objects generally acceptable "for people who have been sufficiently perverted poetically," Dali makes a quantum leap forward to a thesis whose arbitrariness he readily acknowledges; thus, he goes on to say, "the symbolic act of pouring coffee into the cup with the coffee pot takes on in our eyes the significance of a disproportionate and brutal copulation . . . of mother and son. The latter was to be devoured by the mother at the conclusion of the sexual act . . ." (63).

This then is the tragedy in the myth; this combined act of incest and maternal cannibalism explains the anxiety attacks caused by all manifestations of "the atavisms of dusk." In sum, according to Dali, Millet's *Angelus* bodies forth "the maternal variant of the tremendous and terrible myth of Saturn, Abraham, the Father Eternal with Jesus and William Tell himself devouring their own sons" (89). The eminently static image of two figures praying in a field at dusk represents in fact a condensation of three successive action-packed sequences, much like Michelangelo's Moses, according to Freud's "reconstructed action"[8]; first there is the "moment of expectation and immobility which heralds the imminent sexual aggression" (79), second, the *coitus a tergo*, displaced onto the two sacks leaning against each other in the wheelbarrow, as well as the fork pitched into the ground. The third and final phase is the consummation by the mother-mantis of her prey-son.

It is at this point that Dali's exposition runs into serious trouble, for, basing himself strictly on the manifest content of the painting, he can offer no concrete evidence in support of his reconstructed all-important third sequence: "Confining myself to the painting, after all that precedes I can only appeal to the reader's poetic intuition" (87). This heuristic breakdown is, in point of fact, the last in a series of weak links in the chain of associations leading up to the formulation of "the tragic myth." I am alluding in particular to the acknowledged arbitrariness of the association of pouring coffee with maternal cannibalism, and the conspicuous omission from the list of cannibalism myths cited of a single Biblical or classical myth featuring a *mother*-son act. The question then arises: if the steps preceding the final construction are arbitrary, unconvincing, or even missing, does that invalidate the construction itself? In other words, what is the relation of validity in interpretation and validity in construction? Despite Dali's delirious chains of interpretative associations, his completed construction stands up very well indeed; after reading his essay, an "innocent" vision of *The Angelus* is no longer possible. Furthermore, as James Thrall Soby remarks:

> Surprisingly enough, since Dali has had no professional training in psycho-analysis, his interpretation is nearly as plausible as Freud's description of the Leonardo. It has been supported in more recent years by the rediscovery of some exceptionally vicious drawings of sexual subjects by the presumably angelic painter of "The Angelus."[9]

Soby's allusion to Freud's *Leonardo da Vinci and a Memory of His Childhood* is not fortuitous; clearly it served as Dali's model in the writing of *The Tragic Myth*. Indeed, I would and will argue that Dali's paranoia-criticism is nothing but a somewhat idiosyncratic extrapolation from Freud's own critical practice, as manifested most spectacularly in Chapter II of his *Leonardo*.

It will be recalled that Freud's entire study is an extensive commentary on a childhood memory of Leonardo's, recounted in his scientific notebooks:

> I recall as one of my very earliest memories that while I was in the cradle a vulture came down to me, and opened my mouth with its tail, and struck me many times with its tail against my lips (*S. E.*, 11:82).

Freud easily establishes that this "memory" is in fact a fantasy and that the vulture's tail represents the mother's breast, thus "what the phantasy conceals is merely a reminiscence of sucking—or being suckled—at his mother's breast" (87). The next step in Freud's exegesis is somewhat more problematic, for an inevitable and difficult question crops up: why is the mother replaced by a vulture? what possible connection exists between the two? Thereupon follow three pages of paranoia-criticism second to none.

Freud's own commentaries on his *modus operandi* attest to his awareness of the tenuousness of some of the associations he must make in order to arrive at the construction he wants to propose. Thus, at the outset he observes, "a thought comes to the mind from such a remote quarter that it would be tempting to set it aside" (88). However, faithful to the "fundamental rule" of treatment that he himself laid down, Freud allows his associations to take him where they will, without censoring them or rejecting them as "nonsensical." He therefore notes that the Egyptians worshipped a "Mother Goddess, who was represented as having a vulture's head, or else several heads, of which at least one was a vulture's. This goddess's name was pronounced *Mut*. Can the similarity to the sound of our word *Mutter* [mother] be merely a coincidence?" (88). This question is, of course, rhetorical, for in paranoia-criticism nothing is ever left to coincidence. Yet even if the similarity between *Mut* and *Mutter* is not coincidental, a knotty problem remains: "There is, then, some real connection between vulture and mother—but what help is that to us? For have we any right to expect Leonardo to know of it, seeing that the first man who succeeded in reading hieroglyphics was François Champollion (1790–1832)?" (88). A lesser man than Freud would no doubt have found this objection insurmountable and abandoned the "Egyptian connection" altogether. Freud, on the other hand, nothing daunted and bringing his vast erudition into play, sets about demonstrating that despite this awkward historical fact, there was another, albeit more circuitous, route by which Leonardo might have learned of the Egyptian myth. The detour takes us down the byways of Greek and Latin works on Egyptian mythology, in particular the writings of Horapollo, where there is an allusion to the belief that vultures (all of whom are females) are impregnated by the wind. Having shown that the Egyptian connection of vultures and motherhood was known to classical antiquity, Freud returns to his original line of inquiry: "We have now unexpectedly reached a position where we can take something as very probable which only a short time before we had to reject as absurd. It is quite possible that Leonardo was familiar with the scientific fable . . . He was a wide reader and his interest embraced all branches of literature and learning" (89; any resemblance to Freud is, of course, purely coincidental). Not content with a mere probability, Freud adduces a final piece of information "which can turn the probability that Leonardo knew the fable of the vulture into a certainty" (89). It seems that the Fathers of the Church seized upon this obscure fable as proof "drawn from natural history" (90) of the possibility of a virgin birth. Now at last Freud is ready to propose his construction of "the origin of Leonardo's vulture phantasy":

> He once happened to read in one of the Fathers or in a book on natural history the statement that all vultures were females and could reproduce their kind without any assistance from a male: and at that point a memory sprang to his mind, which was transformed into the phantasy we have been discussing, but which meant to signify that he also had been such a vulture-child—he had had a mother, but no father (*S. E.*, 11:90).

It is time to return, as promised, to Dali's "shine on the nose." Let it serve as a parable not only for Dali, but for all unwitting paranoia-critics who suddenly find their best-laid constructions upset by a piece of evidence they have neglected or, worse yet, ignored, but which, as the French expression goes, "leur pend au nez."[10] That Freud's discussion of a patient's fetishization of a "certain kind of 'shine on the nose'" (*S. E.*, 21:152) should involve a problem of translation takes on new significance in the context of this text, for if the fetishist's delusion is based on the confusion of the English word "glance" with the German word "*Glanz,*" Freud's construction of the origin of Leonardo's fantasy is based on an error in translation, though not, I hasten to add, his own. In the actual Italian text, the bird in question is not a vulture, but a kite, a bird of the same feather nevertheless not equivalent in terms of its mythological significance. Consequently, as the editor of the Standard Edition remarks, the Egyptian question becomes largely irrelevant. However, and this is the answer to the question we raised earlier, he goes on to conclude: "the main body of Freud's study is unaffected by his mistake" (62).[11]

If neither Dali's nor Freud's constructions suffer irreparable harm from their punctual interpretative lapses, what, finally, is the status of truth in art analysis (as distinguished from patient analysis, where the validity of the construction is guaranteed by the "further course of the analysis"[12])? Are all essays in paranoia-criticism condemned to be avatars of Freud's "psychoanalytic novel" (*S. E.*, 11:134), works of fiction in which verisimilitude substitutes for veracity? I think not. Perhaps paradoxically, paranoia-criticism's roots in "the delusion of interpretation" are what ensure its validity, for in Freud the status of delusion and the status of truth are always closely linked. Thus he writes at the end of the case of *The Psychotic Doctor Schreber*: "It remains for the future to decide whether there is more delusion in my theory than I should like to admit, or whether there is more truth in Schreber's delusion than other people are as yet prepared to believe" (*S. E.*, 12:79).

Whereas the very *existence* of paranoia-criticism is founded on the recognition that there is "delusion in the theory," its *persistence* depends on the recognition that there is truth in the delusion. And Freud repeatedly asserted that "there is a grain of truth concealed in every delusion, there is something in it that really deserves belief" (*S. E.*, 9:80). The explanation Freud offers of the peaceful coexistence, not to say mutual survival pact, of truth and delusion suggests that paranoia-criticism comes equipped with a fail-safe device. The following quotation is (like the one above) from *Delusion and Dreams in Jensen's Gradiva*, a text whose influence on Dali and the other major surrealists can hardly be exaggerated:[13]

> the method described here by which conviction arises in the case of a delusion does not differ fundamentally from the method by which a conviction is formed in normal cases, where repression does not come into the picture. We all attach our conviction to thought-contents in which truth is combined with error, and let it extend from the former over the latter. It becomes diffused, as it were, from the truth over the error associated with it and protects the latter, though not so unalterably as in the case of a delusion, against deserved criticism. In normal psychology, too, being well-connected—"having influence," so to speak—can take the place of true worth. (*S. E.*, 9:80–81)

Freud's insistence on the truth factor in delusion is part of his larger effort at deconstructing the oppositions between the normal and the pathological, dream and delusion, in sum, the repressive "old antinomies,"[14] which, in Breton's words, the Surrealists sought to destroy. Dali's iconoclastic essay in icon analysis is a product of this joint Freudian-Surrealist deconstructive project; in *The Tragic Myth*, the very differences that structure academic discourse are subverted, as subjectivity and objectivity, poetry and exegesis are interfused. So extensive is the breakdown that finally truth is subsumed to beauty. When Dali's thesis seems to be corroborated by X-ray analysis of the canvas, which reveals a dark oblong shape at the foot of the female figure, exactly where Dali had predicted that the son lay buried, Gala is quoted as saying, "if this result serves as proof, that will be quite wonderful, but if the whole book were but a pure mental construct, then it would be sublime!" (9).

Sublime constructions may well be the revival of the future.

# 7.
# THE DELUSION OF INTERPRETATION:
## *The Conquest of Plassans*

Space and its symbolisms have over the years since Bachelard's pioneering studies proved to be an immensely popular field of inquiry. The imaginary topography of Plassans elaborated by Zola in *The Rougon-Macquart* is no exception to the rule. Critics—myself included—have lavished most of their attention on one of the most richly symbolic features of this topography, the immensely fertile Aire Saint-Mittre, a mythical space located outside the *polis*, in the no man's land where all the marginal characters in Zola's fictional universe—orphans, gypsies, insurgents, bastards—rub shoulders. Nonetheless, beyond the city walls there exist other significant spaces, spaces in which History far from being erased is prominently inscribed. I am thinking in particular of the Tulettes, the insane asylum which plays such a crucial role in the family epic of the Rougon-Macquart and which is centrally featured for the first time in *The Conquest of Plassans*, the fourth of the twenty-volume *Rougon-Macquart* series. The appearance of the insane asylum in the novel corresponds to the simultaneous "births" in the nineteenth century of the clinic and the prison, indeed to the setting into place of a disciplinary system which governs all sectors of human activity through the deployment of the detail as an instrument of knowledge and power.[1] The Tulettes conforms perfectly to descriptions of asylums furnished by Foucault; it is not a therapeutic place—only Doctor Pascal dreams of *curing* the insane by means of miraculous injections[2]—but a place of surveillance, a punitive institution whose sinister architecture bodies forth the imbrication of the medical and the carceral: "Its inner courts looked like prison-yards, and the narrow symmetrical windows which streaked its front with black lines gave it the cheerless aspect of a hospital."[3]

Thus we witness the simultaneous birth of the psychiatric and the anti-psychiatric novel, for, while putting into play a nosological vocabulary that betrays the enthusiasm of the neophyte for a rapidly developing science, a trademark of naturalist novels on insanity,[4] *The Conquest of Plassans* strongly calls into ques-

110

tion the psychiatric apparatus. This double step, this ambivalence has important consequences for naturalist discouse, because the *representation* of madness *in* the novel is accompanied by an interrogation of the madness *of* the novel. To anticipate a little: to speak of the status of madness in *The Conquest* will lead us to speak of the status of the detail in the naturalist text, the literarity of madness in the age of naturalism being bound up with a problematic of the detail.

To place the asylum at the center not only of a novel, but of a novelistic cycle, cannot in any way be taken for granted, for this implantation brings with it a certain number of questions, one of which has immediate repercussions at the evenmential level of the narrative: how does one enter an asylum? What are the conditions of the internment of a subject in a madhouse? Let us recall, at this juncture, that in the 1870s this question was topical. Even as Zola was preparing to undertake *The Rougon-Macquart*, a political debate was raging between those who asserted that under the regime of the Law of 1838, which inaugurated the modern institutional system in France, there had been abuses, and those who praised its efficacy. Everything comes down to the question of whether, under the rule of this law, men and women of sound mind might have been locked up. To this question, a writer such as Maxime Du Camp responded by praising not madness, but asylums. According to him, "arbitrary sequestrations" were an invention of the Left, to which the novelists and playwrights had given credence: "Not only have the theater and the novel given us erroneous ideas about real madness, but they have accredited this folly of arbitrary sequestration to the ignorant and credulous crowd."[5] It is to the same subject of debate that Zola alludes in the introduction to his tale of 1868, "Story of a Madman":

> Of late there has been a great deal of interest in lunatics. It would seem that there have been some audacious confinements; men of sound mind were allegedly bound hand and foot and thrown into padded cells for having committed the sole crime of getting in the way of certain people. I think an investigation was ordered. Heaven preserve me from delving into these infamies; but I can safely tell the story of a madman, which current concerns have just recalled to mind. (*R-M*, 1:1641)

Whereupon Zola recounts the story of M. Maurin, a worthy bourgeois husband locked up at Charenton as a result of a plot hatched by his wife and her lover (a young doctor, appropriately enough). Thus, while eliding the political in favor of the erotic, by preterition if you will, Zola only adds credence to the claims of the opposition.

A closer reading of this passage allows one to understand why the question of "arbitrary" or "audacious" sequestrations affects Zola so greatly: it is because it links up with a series of analogous preoccupations which runs through Zola's *oeuvre*, preoccupations so well known that I will cite only two of them: the man buried alive, and the persecution of an "innocent" individual by the community.

The sequestering of a subject who is of sound mind conflates these two obsessions of Zola's; just like Jean Valjean or the Colonel Chabert, the brave Maurin is a hero with a double purpose: at the same time buried alive and sacrificed. In effect, with Zola, confinement always presupposes a sacrificial rite.

No longer having anything to fear from the censor, in *The Conquest* Zola tackles directly the political question that he had approached obliquely in "Story of a Madman." Let us note, in this regard, that in order to disengage the narrative structures characteristic of the anti-psychiatric narrative, one cannot do without a superposition of the text and its *intra-texte*. Unlike Maurin, driven out for the benefit of an amorous liaison, François Mouret, a steady pensioner, will find himself slowly excluded from his family, dispossessed of his house and property, because his presence interferes with the Bonapartist seizure of Plassans, or, more accurately, because his persecution insures it. Like Silvère in *The Fortune of the Rougons*, like Florent in *The Fat and the Thin*, François Mouret is an ideal "scapegoat victim." Double of (first cousin, and very similar in appearance to) his hysterical wife, despised son-in-law of the Rougons, Republican, Mouret perfectly meets the requirements for effecting the "metonymic 'slippage' from the community"[6] to the ritual victim. He will therefore be the victim of a "unanimous violence" which resolves itself in the reconciliation of the two rival political bands, the mimetic doubles that are the Legitimists and the Bonapartists. It is Mouret himself who explains his delicate situation to the Abbé Faujas, his tenant:

> Rightly or wrongly, I myself pass for a republican . . . Well, on my right here, at Monsieur Rastoil's, we have the cream of the Legitimists, and on the left, at the Sub-Prefecture, we have the big-wigs of the Empire. And so, you see, my poor old-fashioned garden, my little happy nook, lies between two hostile camps. I am continually afraid lest they should begin throwing stones at each other, for the stones, you see, might very well fall into my garden.(37)

For Zola, this type of presentiment functions as a narrative prolepsis. Mouret, who threatens to have a Republican elected in the next election, will be booed, *stoned*, then finally confined at the Tulettes. Just as the first conquest of Plassans is marked by the execution of Silvère, the second is guaranteed by the internment of François, his elder brother. Charged with all the sins of the community, outlet for the internal dissensions of Plassans, Mouret appears above all as a political victim and the workers make no mistake about it: "There was a complete reaction in Mouret's favour. He was considered to be a *political victim*, a man whose influence had been feared so much that he had been put out of the way in a cell at The Tulettes" (234, T. M.; emphasis added).

But the internment of François Mouret cannot be reduced to a simple political crime, because the denunciation of an abuse of a legal order is complicated by a calling into question of science, of its inadequacies. Of course, at a certain level, the inadequacies of science can be explained by its politicization. In effect, the role of the doctor, merely sketched in "Story of a Madman," is here made explicit: the doctor, who will draft the declaration "with regard to the mental condition of François Mouret, householder, of Plassans" (246), and who is endowed with the eloquent name of Porquier, is an esteemed member of the Bonapartist clan, acting in collusion with the reactionary forces. Psychiatric medicine is in the service of power.

The questioning of science is not, however, limited to an accusation of its *ideology*; it extends to an interrogation of its *methodology*. In "Story of a Madman," as in *The Conquest*, the character suspected of madness ends up by *becoming* mad, thus his internment is, in the end, perfectly justified. The polemical strategy adopted by Zola is skillful because unexpected: if he lends faith to the rumors circulating about the "audacious" sequestrations, it is not by showing us a sound man interned, but rather a sound man rendered mad by internment. The nuance is essential, for while the forces which motivate the persecution of Mouret are of a political nature, the method put into play in order to carry out this persecution is that of all sciences, including the science advocated by the author of *The Experimental Novel*, and can be stated simply: observation. Thus, Zola writes: "the naturalist novelists observe and experiment."[7] In effect, one could say, without forcing the point, that the persecution of Mouret consists quite simply in his *observation*, giving to this word the strong meaning that it takes on in a clinical context. This very *observation* constitutes, if you will, the experiment carried out by Zola in *The Conquest*, which was to see if a man with a tainted heredity, married to his cousin, hysterical to boot, and submitted to a regime of persecution by his hostile milieu, would end up by becoming mad. From the point of view of the narrative structures, Zola hyperbolizes a sequence, the etiology of Mouret's madness, all the while consigning the precise moment when Mouret succumbs to psychosis to an implicit ellipse.[8]

Once the suspicion that Mouret is mad begins to disseminate itself in the community, a vast, pseudo-scientific, observational apparatus is set into motion in order to bring the observed deeds and gestures into line with the original hypothesis. The interpretation of the delusion is transformed inevitably into the delusion of interpretation. It is time to recall that the delusion of interpretation *stricto sensu* is a form of paranoia characterized by the overinterpretation of details, aiming at confirming an idea that is fundamentally delusive; it is a systematic regulation of all signs; a hermeneutics of saturation. Freud says of paranoiacs: "they attach the greatest significance to the minor details of other people's behaviour which we ordinarily neglect, interpret them and make them the basis of far-reaching conclusions."[9]

Paranoia, in the sense that we are using the term, is a pathology of that which Benvéniste calls, in a completely different context, "interpretative capacity."[10] It follows that the delusion of interpretation is a form of textual madness, rather than a nosographic category. In fact, I would propose the delusion of interpretation as a model of a certain naturalist discourse, not, I hasten to add, as an exclusive model, but one complementary to what one might call the "obsessional" model, which has until recently monopolized the attention of theorists. By obsessional model, I mean a model which places the emphasis on the redundant or "anaphoric" character[11] of naturalist discourse, a character which is finally reassuring, because repetition always has the function of insuring the readability of a text. Now, one cannot, it seems to me, account for the functioning of the naturalist text—and I am thinking especially of descriptive texts—if one does not foresee its disorder, its dysfunction. In other words, what happens when the observation is no longer guaranteed by the objectivity of the observer? when the "inventory" comes to settle on *one* element of the paradigm? when the author refuses to disambiguate the signification of the "true little fact"?

It is, I believe, just such a crisis of naturalist discourse that occurs in *The Conquest*; an "exquisite crisis of language," to echo Mallarmé, a crisis where interpretative activity takes precedence over a mimesis of reference. *The Conquest* is merely the most consummate elaboration of a series of texts by Zola where the telos of observation is neither the acquisition nor the communication of *knowledge*, but the exercise of *power*; and this diversion of the goal has repercussions on the status of the detail: what is at stake is a loss of innocence. Mouret is subjected to an incessant surveillance, where special attention is paid to small facts normally considered insignificant, infra-semantic. Under the influence of Abbé Faujas, Plassans becomes a universe of the sign gone mad; the delusion of interpretation is not an individual, but a collective pathology: what we have is, in sum, a crisis of generalized paranoia:

> Everybody's curiosity was fully awakened, however, and the two sets of guests began to *keep a sharp watch upon Mouret's least act* . . . He could not stand for a moment in front of *one* bed of vegetables, or examine *one* head of lettuce, or even make *one* gesture of any sort, without exciting in the gardens on his right and left the most unfavorable comments. (239–40, T. M.; emphasis added)

The insistence on the significance attached to lowly and minute signs is reinforced by the choice of "one head of lettuce" (une salade), an absurd vegetable in the produce paradigm. The subject Mouret is thus the object cross-sectioned, reduced to the scale of the individual, the victim of an excessive saturation by the gaze of his compatriots. And not only do those who have an avowed political interest in Mouret's disappearing from circulation participate in this type of interpretation-persecution, but even his cronies, the pensioners of Sauvaire Court, join in wholeheartedly. It is in the following episode, during a Sunday stroll taken by Mouret, that we see the pensioners transformed into judges of the mental health of their old friend; in effect, everything happens as if the bench where the pensioners sit were a jury's bench:

> A former hatter of the suburbs who had scrutinised Mouret from the knot in his cravat to the bottom button of his overcoat was now absorbed in the

examination of his boots. The lace of the one on the left foot had come undone, and this seemed to the hatter a most extraordinary circumstance. He nudged his neighbours' elbows, and winked as he called their attention to the loosened lace. Soon the whole bench had eyes for nothing else but the lace. It was the last proof. The men shrugged their shoulders in a way that seemed to imply that they had lost their last spark of hope. (232–33, T. M.)

This passage merits detailed attention. One could read it in two stages, proposing two contradictory readings: allowing oneself first to be caught in the hermeneutic trap that the author sets for us, and then reading it inversely, as a satire of any attempt at exegesis. Thus—and this is surely not by accident, in a novel which simultaneously represents and questions the science of psychiatry—the result is a text which gives rise to interpretation even as it turns it to ridicule, frustrates it.

Let us first consider what an "oneiric" decoding might produce, for, replaced in its immediate context, a Calvary-like walk through Plassans, this text seems to be a variant of a dream that Freud characterizes as common: the embarrassing dream of finding oneself naked, a dream where the desire to exhibit oneself is dissimulated beneath the fear of being seen in the altogether, a dream with multiple entries where the dreamer is in turn spectacle and spectator.[12] In keeping with the laws of rhetoric which govern the language of dreams, in our text madness is displaced along the vertical axis, the untied lace acting as the sign of the disordered mind. To this displacement along the metonymic axis is added a narrative overdetermination, for the hatter is not the only character in the novel to take the vertical axis for the semantic axis of sanity; further on Monsieur de Condamin remarks: "he is cracked from top to bottom, that joker" (240, T. M.). Furthermore, the political banishment of Mouret is explained in part by his repeated threats to have a *shoemaker* elected; after his internment, it is a *hatter* who is finally nominated by the Republicans. The oneiro-text thus conveys the entire fashion system of Plassans, a system marked by the prestige enjoyed by the extremities, and above all by the fetishism of the foot. Moreover, taken as a whole, the scene is only a representation, a rebus of an idiomatic expression: it is *the worker of the hat* (in the literal sense) who scrutinizes *the worker of the hat* (in the figurative sense).[13] Curious meeting between the madman and his specular image.

Nevertheless, the text forbids us to pursue our exegetic exercise, for, in the second reading announced earlier, the text invalidates any interpretative act. In effect, two elements expose the untrustworthiness of the hatter, the delegated interpreter, or as I prefer to call him, the *interpretant*, borrowing the term from Peirce, in order to distinguish the interpreter-character from the interpreter-reader (see below, p. 122). First, the clause "that which seemed exorbitant to the *hatter*" is an expression of the disassociation that marks the distance which separates the *interpretant* from the voice of the author, of authority. Second, and above all, the disproportion between the observed detail and the interpretation that it authorizes is such that the scene becomes a parody of any hermeneutic enterprise based on the enlarging of a detail, that is to say of Zola's enterprise. Let us cite in its entirety the celebrated description that Zola gives of his scriptural process, in a letter to Henri Céard:

> I would have loved simply to demonstrate the mechanism of my eye to you. I exaggerate, that much is certain; but I do not exaggerate like Balzac, any more than Balzac exaggerates like Hugo. Everything is there, the work is in the conditions of the operation. We all lie more or less, but what are the mechanics and the mentality of our Lie? Yet—it is perhaps here that I deceive myself—I still believe, for my part, that I lie in the sense of the truth. I am afflicted with *an overdeveloped sense of true-to-life details*, shooting to the stars on the springboard of exact observation. The truth climbs to the symbol in the beat of a wing.[14]

Hidden in this declaration of principles are the dangers inherent in the privilege accorded to synecdoche, because it does not suffice that the detail *be true*, or more precisely, *appear true*, produce a "reality-effect," for the interpretation which is assigned it to be equally true. What is more, one would have to elaborate the means of verification of a fictive interpretation, if this expression is not already a pleonasm. It is in the hiatus between the detail and its interpretation, the moment of hesitation between the springboard and the stars, that the ideology, the pathology, the inadequacies of the interpreter can insinuate themselves. One must, of course, distinguish the lie of the characters from the truth of the novelist, and, finally, it is precisely in a scene such as the one which we have just analyzed that Zola tells the truth about the "mechanism" of his eye. To unmask the professional biases of his characters is, perhaps, the best and the only means of guaranteeing the reliability of the author. Whence the proliferation of the "concierge," a character-type whose hermeneutic abuses and excesses are the guardians of naturalist discourse. Espionage thus has a prophylactic value.

The stakes are such that Zola does not limit his questioning of interpretation to the scene of the shoelace; not content to stop at the denunciation of the dangers of an overinterpretation of a detail, he shows us as well the results of a double interpretation of a series of actions. After the street scene, we have the garden scene. Thus, in the course of a scene which takes place in Mouret's garden, Zola offers us successively three versions of the same event: the basic facts first of all, followed by two contradictory interpretations of these same facts.

> Mouret had stridden over the box-edging and was kneeling in the midst of the lettuces. He held his candle down, and began searching along the trenches

underneath the spreading leaves of the plants. Every now and then he made a slight examination and seemed to be crushing something and stamping it into the ground. This went on for nearly half an hour. (242)

Mouret's enigmatic movements are observed with the attention we have already noted by the members of the two rival parties, meeting together for the first time on this occasion. The informational gap which results from the indeterminacy of the object in question ("something")—and let us note in this regard that already in this passage that claims to be purely objective, a first interpretation is slipped in under the hypothetic form of the "he seemed"—immediately gives rise to hermeneutic activity on the part of the spectators. A first interpretation is proposed by M. Rastoil:

> It is strange, remarked Monsieur Rastoil, who had been buried in thought for a moment or two; but Mouret looked as if he were searching for slugs amongst his lettuces. The gardens are quite ravaged by them, and I have been told that they can only be satisfactorily exterminated in the nighttime. (243)

This interpretation is seductive because it covers all the observed facts, taking into account everything about this scene that is incomprehensible (the action) or preposterous (the circumstances, e.g., the hour), but for all that it is not satisfying to M. de Condamin, who proposes a counter-interpretation that has the advantage of establishing a link between Mouret's pantomime and his supposed madness:

> Slugs! cried M. de Condamin, do you suppose he troubles himself about slugs? Do people go hunting about for slugs with a candle? No; I agree with Monsieur Maffre in thinking that there is some crime at the bottom of the matter. Did this man Mouret ever have a servant who disappeared mysteriously? There ought to be an inquiry made. (243)

Finally, the scene in the garden only reproduces the scene in the street, for again the excesses of interpretation are indicated on the one hand by the isolation of the interpreter, and on the other by the disproportion between the detail and the significance attached to it. Thus, the narrative voice condemns the words of M. de Condamin: "Monsieur Péqueur des Saulaies thought that his friend the conservator of rivers and forests was theorising a little further than the facts warranted" (243). The last word, then, of the evening is Mme de Condamin's, who concludes: "we really must not let the election be controlled by a man who goes and kneels down in the middle of a bed of lettuces after twelve o'clock at night" (244).

The observation advocated and vaunted by the naturalists comes up against the diagnosis of madness, for Zola insists: there are no univocal signs of madness, there are only collective delusions of interpretation. Maurin in "Story of a Madman," like Aunt Dide in *The Fortune of the Rougons*, are only mad-for-others:

> There is nothing that looks more like a madman than a man of sound mind; everything depends on how you view and judge his actions. (*R-M*, 1:1642–43)

> She was certainly very natural, very consistent with herself; but in the eyes of her neighbours her consistency became pure insanity. (*The Fortune of the Rougons*, 42)

In *The Conquest*, this statement becomes a deed, an "analysis in question" (*R-M*, 1:1667), according to Zola's expression. No intervention on the part of the narrator supplements the dialogues or the descriptive pauses which we have just examined, but in the outlines we find once again the same arguments expressed in the same terms: "to show that there is nothing that appears madder than a man in possession of all his faculties. To multiply the little facts . . . *To show that logic becomes madness* for certain provincial bourgeois" (*R-M*, 1:1667).

The diagnosis of madness is not, however, the only instance where the limits of science are underscored; if we superimpose the story of the sequestered man of sound mind onto that of the man buried alive, their common denominator appears: the failure of medical science, its inability to distinguish between such binary opposites as life and death, sanity and madness. When the doctor is called in to confirm the demise of Olivier Bécaille, he emits this choked cry:

> So he knew nothing, this man! All his science was a lie, then, since he could not at a glance distinguish between life and death![15]

And one might note that, fittingly, in *The Conquest*, it is Dr. Porquier himself who remarks before the deathbed of Marthe Mouret: "Science is very often quite powerless" (317).

In order that a novel may be called "anti-psychiatric," the logic of the ideology, or the *ideo-logic*, requires that the madman, the scapegoat-victim of a sick society, be released from the asylum-prison. The doors of the asylum must be opened and the madman who had been banished from society must be reintegrated. This is exactly what happens at the end of *The Conquest*, and it is at this point that the novel of 1874 separates itself (on the evenmential plane) from its pre-1870 prototype. Believing that the liberation of Mouret would spread confusion in Plassans and create problems for the Rougons, who are once again triumphant, Uncle Macquart arranges with the guardian of the Tulettes to facilitate the madman's escape: "In front of him he saw the door of his cell wide open" (305). The plot hatched by Macquart succeeds too well: Mouret returns home, and, finding the house empty, sets it on fire. The alliance of the marginal characters seems to seriously threaten the conquest of Plassans, since the Abbé Faujas is the principle victim of the disaster. Mouret, the political victim, takes on the role of avenger. But, by a reversal that no one could have foreseen, this anarchic act is easily recuperated by the Rougons, who are thus rid of both the Abbé Faujas and Mouret, all the while keeping their hands clean. With the intervention of Macquart, involuntary collaborator of the Rougons, Mouret's madness is finally placed in the service of repression:

> By god! The Rougons must be up in the heavens. They will inherit the Abbé's conquest. Ah! they would have paid anyone well who would have run the risk of setting the house on fire. (327, T. M.)

Whether the door of the asylum be open or closed, the disciplinary system is so fine-tuned that the madman can never prevail over those who have their eye on him.

Zola does not take the part of madmen any more than he does that of the other minorities and marginals about whom he speaks in his novels. Up until the end of *The Conquest*, the contradictions are maintained; but if the ideological choice remains suspended there, the art of description emerges chastened. Henceforth, interpretation as it is thematized in his novels can only be represented as a type of madness, a sort of delusion. Any observer who is transformed into an interpretant is threatened by the dangers of overinterpretation, of hypersemanticization. Thus, subsequently, certain signs will escape all interpretation other than the purely hypothetical interpretation explicitly coded as fictive. I am thinking above all of the case of Madame Maigrat, witness of her husband's castration in *Germinal*. Hidden by a blurred windowpane, Madame Maigrat resists both interpretation and observation, for the two are, in the end, inseparable:

> Up at the window Madame Maigrat was still motionless, but the last rays of the setting sun caught her pale face, and through the distorting glass it *seemed* to be grinning.[16]

If Zola remains, in spite of or beyond all their "differences," very close to Balzac and his interpretative orgies, the lesson of Flaubert has marked him profoundly, the lesson taught in the classroom of the first chapter of *Madame Bovary*. The celebrated description of Charles's cap inscribes the refusal or the impossibility of all hermeneutic activity at the very threshhold of the novel, a strategic point where Balzac's interpretative machine always functions at a maximum of intensity; in Flaubert, where responsibility for the proliferation of details is never assumed by the interpretation, the detail is reduced to a state of insignificant materiality. Whatever Zola's nostalgia for the Balzacian practice, he has been through the Flaubertian deconstruction. The delusion of interpretation is also the agony of interpretation.

(Translated by Susan C. Fischman)

# 8.
# FICTION AS INTERPRETATION/
# INTERPRETATION AS FICTION

In her 1964 essay, "Against Interpretation," Susan Sontag sounded the keynote of a neoformalism, a new wave of French criticism that was about to sweep over modern language departments, wreaking havoc with the traditional interpretative positions standing in its path, all hermeneutics anchored in significant details. Let me recall very briefly the main points of Sontag's essay, for they retain even today their polemical freshness. What must first be noted is Sontag's definition of interpretation, for her assault on hermeneutics is grounded in this definition: "The task of interpretation is virtually one of translation. The interpreter says, Look, don't you see that X is really—or, really means—A? That Y is really B? That Z is really C?"[1] Having thus reduced interpretation to only one of its meanings, Sontag then proceeds to charge it with reductionism (ironically, the very accusation most frequently leveled at the structuralists and their algebraic equations and algorithms): "To interpret is to impoverish, to deplete the world—in order to set up a shadow world of 'meanings'" (17).

As a prime example of the destructiveness of interpretation, Sontag cites the fate of one of its most spectacular victims, Kafka, whose work "has been subjected to a mass ravishment by no less than three armies of interpreters" (18), and these armies of the night are the Marxists, the Freudians, and the Christians. That Sontag should single out Kafka is almost inevitable, for Kafka is unquestionably the touchstone for any future history or sociology of hermeneutics in the age of criticism. The peculiar solicitations of Kafka's "hysterical" texts (hysterical in the sense that they seem to invite rape, while denying penetration) have led to the critics' wonderment, if not the "commentators' despair"[2]: "Each sentence says 'interpret me'"[3] writes Theodor Adorno; similarly Erich Heller remarks: "In the case of Kafka, and *The Trial* in particular, the compulsion to interpret is at its most compelling, and is as great as the compulsion to continue reading once one has begun . . . There is only one way to save oneself the trouble of interpreting *The Trial*: not to read it."[4] Any account of interpretive strategies today must reckon with the Kafka "case," and this study is no exception.

That interpretation need not be equated with translation, need not result in an impoverishment of the text, has been the position consistently held by Roland Barthes, a position I would qualify as "ecumenical hermeneutics." Thus in *S/Z* he proposes a definition of interpretation at complete odds with the definition quoted above: "To interpret a text is not to give it a (more or less justified, more or less free) meaning, but on the contrary to appreciate what *plural* constitutes it."[5] If polysemy is the relatively simple answer to the reductionist argument, the hermeneutician must still respond to the second and more constructive part of Sontag's essay, which calls for the elaboration of a "poetics of the novel": "The function of criticism should be to show *how it is what it is,* even *that it is what it is,* rather than to *show what it means*" (23). The question then arises: on the basis of what we know now, after the revolution, as it were, are poetics and hermeneutics, description and interpretation, mutually exclusive? Is the pursuit of the "how" irreconcilable with the quest for the "what"? Furthermore, has the structuralists' emphasis on the "literariness" of the text, on the priority of the linguistic model in our apprehension of fiction, spelled the end of hermeneutics? In the face of a constantly growing body of evidence, my answer is unhesitatingly no. Almost paradoxically, a critical orthodoxy whose tenets are anti- or an-interpretive has provided a new impetus for latter-day hermeneutics. This apparent paradox is resolved if one considers the structuralists' praxis, and not merely their *theoria*: in their actual readings of texts, such bona fide poeticians as Gérard Genette and Tzvetan Todorov have repeatedly focused their attention on metalinguistic commentary incorporated in the texts themselves, tending thereby to make the authors they examine (e.g., Proust in Genette's "Proust and Indirect Language" or Constant in Todorov's "Speech According to Constant"[6]) appear to be (Saussurean) linguists before the letter.

Now, there is not such a very far way to go from the notion that fiction is self-conscious and reflects upon its own representation of speech acts, to the notion—which seems to be gaining ground today[7]—that novels also represent and reflect upon interpretation as performance. In short, it has taken the importation of semiotics into the field of literary criticism for us to discover and turn to account a rather simple fact: novels are not only about speaking and writing (*encoding*), but also about reading, and by reading I mean the *decoding* of all manner of signs and signals. If, as I am suggesting, interpretation is viewed not as something that is done *to* fiction but rather as something that is done *in* fiction, then to be against interpretation becomes an untenable position, for it is tantamount to rejecting a considerable body of (modern) fiction that is explicitly, indeed insistently, concerned with interpretation: its scope and its limits, its necessity and its frustration. In dealing with what I call fictions of interpretation, the critic finds himself in somewhat the same situation as Joseph K.: "He hardly had the choice now to accept the trial or reject it, he was in the middle of it, and must fend for himself."[8] Indeed, long before Joseph K. came into the picture, the critic was already "embarked" on the Good Ship *Hermeneutic Enterprise*; according to the French psychoanalyst André Green, the necessity of interpretation is *the* lesson of the Oedipus myth: "interpretation is not merely the field of the possible, but obligation, necessity. The relationship of the subject to his begetter grounds the field of *constraint*."[9]

The shift away from the illusion of an *interpretative option* toward a recognition of the *interpretative constraint* requires the introduction of a term which, while not strictly new (it is used by Charles Sanders Peirce in a very different context), will serve to distinguish between two types of interpreters: the interpreting critic, for whom I reserve the term *interpreter*, and the interpreting character, whom I will refer to henceforth as the *interpretant*.[10] That this term evokes the term *analysand* is not coincidental, for the analytic situation is analogous to the one we have been outlining: both involve (at least) a double interpretative activity, interpretation in the second power or "en abyme." Hierarchically the interpretant "ranks" above the "narratee,"[11] the "fictionalized audience,"[12] or any other variety of "implied reader,"[13] in that he is neither supporting actor, nor theoretical construct, nor intaglio figure, but instead coextensive with the first-person narrator or main protagonist of fiction.[14] If there existed a barometer capable of measuring the narcissistic gratification afforded by literary works, then fictions of interpretation would push the needle way over, for what could comfort and delight the interpreter more than to find the interpretant, his specular image, shimmering on the printed page, mirroring his confusions as well as his triumphs? And yet, the interpreter/interpretant relationship is not an easy one: the lure of narcissistic identification only makes it more difficult for the interpreter to keep his distance from the interpretant. My concern here is not, however, with the (impossible/fatal) coincidence of interpretant and interpreter (the interpreter's "countertransference," to borrow a concept from Serge Doubrovsky[15] and pursue the analytic analogy), but rather with a simple proposition: through the interpretant, the author is trying to tell the interpreter something *about* interpretation, and the interpreter would do well to listen and take note.

Interpretants are so widespread in modern fiction that it is imperative to establish some sort of taxonomy to deal with them; what follows is an attempt in that direction. My approach is diachronic: the three interpretants I propose to examine represent three generations of protagonists, and they have been selected to demonstrate that the vicissitudes of hermeneutics in our time reduplicate, with an inevitable time-lag, the vicissitudes of the interpretant around the turn of the century. Two criteria govern my classification, quantity and quality. In other words, how much or how little interpretation the interpretant engages in, and with what results, what degree of success. For convenience's sake, the authors whose works I will draw upon offer impeccable interpretative credentials: James, Proust, and, of course, Kafka.

James, or the Interpretant as Young Artist

That his central or "focusing-characters"[16] are perpetually, indeed obsessively, involved in interpretative ventures should come as no surprise to even the most casual reader of James's fictions and prefaces. To single out any one novel or short story as representative of James's fictions of interpretation might seem arbitrary; however, I feel my choice of the "minor—but important"[17] novella, *In the Cage*, is warranted by the fact that in it all actions have been reduced to one: interpretation. *In the Cage* is the story of an anonymous young woman who works in a postal-telegraph office in an elegant section of London. In the course of events or nonevents, she becomes particularly interested in one of her clients, Captain Everard; in fact, so great is her involvement in his love affair with Lady Aberdeen that the young woman delays her marriage to the dull Mr. Mudge so that she might be at her post in Captain Everard's hour of need. What makes the heroine of this tale an exemplary interpretant is that her interpretative activities bear solely on the written sign, on high society as inscribed in the messages that pass daily through her cage. Furthermore, the messages she deals with are by definition "coded" and incomplete: "*His* words were mere numbers, they told her nothing whatever; and after he had gone she was in possession of no name, of no address, of no meaning."[18] The heroine's hermeneutic hyperactivity is directly proportionate to the paucity of vital pieces of information: "missing the answers . . . she pressed the romance closer by reason of the very quantity of imagination it demanded" (184–85).

What is significant here is that interpretation is synonymous with imagination, it is a "creative" rather than critical activity; the young woman is not content merely to encode and decode, rather she delights in filling in the gaps, piecing together the fragments, in short, adding something of her own to the faulty, often trivial texts at hand. Her pleasure is not finding "the figure in the carpet," but weaving the whole cloth: "On the clearness therefore what she did retain stood sharply out; she nipped and caught it, turned it over and interwove it" (190). The result of this unbridled imagination are "stories and meanings without end" (189). Indeed, as practiced in *In the Cage*, interpretation is always in danger of giving way to overinterpretation, an inflation and debasing of meaning: "Everything, so far as they chose to consider it so, might mean almost anything" (205). So pervasive is this tendency that even the levelheaded shopkeeper, Mr. Mudge, is affected or infected by it: "Mr. Mudge himself—habitually inclined indeed to a scrutiny of all mysteries and to seeing, as he sometimes admitted, too much in things . . . " (228–29).

James was, of course, intensely aware of the problems inherent in excessive interpretation, both in the specific instance of *In the Cage* and in general. In his preface to *In the Cage*, he acknowledges: "My central spirit, in the anecdote, is, for verisimilitude, I grant, *too* ardent a focus of divination; but without this *excess* the phenomena detailed would have lacked their principle of cohesion."[19] But preternatural gifts of "divination" on the part of a character not only defy the laws of verisimilitude, they also lessen reader interest. Nothing, remarks James in the preface to *The Princess Casamassima*, would be duller than the "annals" of "the all knowing immortals" on Olympus: "Therefore it is that the wary reader for the most part warns the novelist against making his characters too *interpretative* of the muddle of fate, or in other words too divinely, too priggishly clever."[20] James's elaborate strategies for providing his interpretants with just the right dose of "bewilderment" to maintain reader interest are too well-known to be rehearsed here. In the case of the young heroine of *In the Cage*, James tempers the interpretative triumph she scores by having her discover in the end how much had eluded her as to the most essential facts of Captain Everard's affairs. After all her "theories and interpretations,"[21] she finds to her surprise and dismay that her knowledge of her hermeneutic object is mediated by a series of eminently unreliable narrators; there is no interpretation without mediation: "She might hear of him, now forever lost, only through Mrs. Jordan, who touched him through Mr. Drake, who reached him through Lady Bradeen" (263).

## Proust, or Doing It Swann's Way

Any discussion of interpretation in *A la recherche du temps perdu* must begin with some mention of Gilles Deleuze's work, *Proust and Signs*, wherein he states flatly at the outset that his subject is "The Search as interpretation."[22] What strikes me as a particularly fruitful insight on Deleuze's part is his insistence on "the violence of the sign," the mechanism that sets the interpretative machine in motion: "The great theme of Time regained is that the search for truth is the characteristic adventure of the involuntary. Thought is nothing without something which forces and does violence to it"; and elsewhere he remarks: "The accident of encounters, the pressure of constraints are Proust's two most fundamental themes."[23] If Deleuze is justified in arguing that in Proust characters operate under an *interpretative constraint*, rather than being driven, as in James, by an *interpretative instinct*, then Proust's involuntary interpretants lie midway between James's typically nineteenth-century "subjective adventurers," with their "morbid" and "penetrating" imaginations, and Kafka's typically twentieth-century interpretants, with their singular interpretive deficiencies.

To test the validity and utility of Deleuze's thesis, let us consider the case of Swann in *Un amour de Swann*. From the first, Swann is presented to us as suffering from a mental condition inherited from his father; Swann is incapable of going to the bottom of things, especially unpleasant ones. When it occurs to him that Odette might be what is commonly referred to as a "kept woman," he suffers a characteristic seizure of this hereditary disease: "He could not explore the idea further, for a sudden access of that mental lethargy which was, with him, congenital, intermittent and providential, happened at that moment to extinguish every particle of light in his brain, as instantaneously as, at a later period, when electric lighting had been everywhere installed, it became possible to cut off the supply of light from a house."[24]

Throughout the initial, euphoric stages of Swann's love affair with Odette, he continues to display his singular mental incapacity. Whereas James's heroine suffers from a pronounced *horror vacui*, Swann exhibits a remarkable *amor vacui*; while the young woman seeks to fill in the blanks, Swann cultivates them: "For Swann's affection for Odette still preserved the form which had been imposed on it from the beginning by his ignorance of how she spent her days and by the mental lethargy which prevented him from supplementing that ignorance by imagination" (309). The worldly and wealthy bourgeois is most sadly lacking in precisely the attribute the poor young woman possessed in abundance: the *supplement* of imagination.[25] Swann's jealousy marks a decisive turning point in his amorous and mental activities. Driven by an *erotic constraint*, Swann becomes highly attentive to the smallest details in Odette's behavior; he goes from apathy to a veritable paranoia of jealousy, the paranoiac being, of course, the interpretant's psychotic double. Despite this stepped-up hermeneutic activity, however, Swann remains singularly inept at interpretation: he is not only the failed artist he has always been portrayed as being, but a failed critic as well. Swann's congenital laziness could be described in rhetorical terms, as an overreliance on synecdoche (cf. the narrator's predilection for metaphor): "Like many other men, Swann had a naturally lazy mind and lacked imagination. He knew perfectly well as a general truth that human life is full of contrasts, but in the case of each individual human being he imagined all that part of his or her life with which he was not familiar as being identical with the part with which he was" (390).

Unable to imagine the difference between the known (visible) and the unknown (hidden), between the part and the whole, bound by an all-or-nothing rule, Swann oscillates between two equally extreme stances: either the refusal, or the compulsion, to interpret. When he receives a poison-pen letter, recounting Odette's lurid sexual past and proclivities, Swann cannot think who among his friends might have written such a letter: "he had never had any suspicion with regard to the unknown actions of other people, those which had no visible connection with what they said" (387). However, on further reflection, he decides that *all* of his friends are capable of authoring such a letter: "But then, having been unable to suspect anyone, he was forced to suspect everyone" (388).

Finally, however much Swann errs in the direction of overinterpretation, reality always exceeds his interpretations. *Un amour de Swann* is, in effect, divided into two equal parts, and *Swann II* functions largely as a reading of *Swann I*. A single example should suffice to illustrate the connection between structure and exegesis, the incidence of deferred interpretation (*Nachträglichkeit*) on the ordering of narrative sequences. In the early part of Swann's affair (*Swann I*), he receives a letter from Odette, written on the stationary of a café, The Maison Dorée. This letter, which reads in part, "My dear, my hand trembles so that I can scarcely write" (246), is among Swann's most treasured possessions. Much later, in *Swann II*, when the romance is nearly over, Odette tells Swann that she was never at the Maison Dorée that day; not only were her sentiments insincere, but the very letterhead they were written under was a lie or lure (all that glitters . . . ): "So, even in the months of which he had never dared to think again because they had been too happy, in those months when she had loved him, she was already lying to him! Besides that moment . . . when she had told him that she was coming from the Maison Dorée, how many others must there have been, each of them concealing a falsehood of which Swann had had no suspicion" (403). Proust's pairing of the man without suspicion and the woman who cannot but does tell lies only serves to hyperbolize the dilemma of the interpretant.

Paradoxically then, in what has long been considered the most reassuringly traditional section of *La recherche*, Proust has portrayed a strikingly modern character, one of the first in a long line of what I would call *reluctant interpretants*; as bizarre as this genealogy may seem, Swann is the distant ancestor of Meursault, Camus's stranger, whose story is also divided into two equal parts, part II providing *the* or *an* interpretation of the events in part I. Just as Swann's jealousy teaches him suspicion, obliges him to overcome his allergy to interpretation, Meursault's trial forces meaning on actions and observations that he had a particularly strong investment in regarding as meaningless. The obvious differences between Swann's and Meursault's reluctance—differences not only of degree, but also of outcome—can be accounted for, at least in part, by the intervening inscription of the Joseph K. of *The Trial*, that is the *failed interpretant*.

## Kafka, or the Death of an Interpretant

In Kafka's fictional universe, the interpretant finds himself in a far graver situation than either James's young heroine or Proust's aging Lothario, for in Kafka, as Charles Bernheimer has phrased it, "the existential implication of a failed hermeneutic is death."[26] K.'s fatal interpretative failure is not, I hasten to point out, a result of any reluctance to interpret; on the contrary, once embarked on his trial, he makes a determined if not always successful effort to analyze the signs he perceives, the signals he receives. But, and this is what definitely sets K. apart from the other interpretants I have been discussing, the prevailing rule in the world of the Court is the hermeneutic double bind: the absolute necessity to interpret goes hand in hand with the total impossibility to validate interpretation. All signs are irremediably ambiguous; whereas the signs Swann initially misses or misreads do eventually render their correct, that is hidden, meaning, K. is repeatedly confronted with signs suspended between two simultaneously plausible but contradictory meanings: "The Examining Magistrate sitting here beside me has just given one of you a secret sign . . . I do not know whether the sign was meant to evoke applause or hissing, and now that I have divulged the matter prematurely I deliberately give up all hope of ever learning its real significance."[27]

That the inability of Kafka's interpretants to decode sign language should have given rise to feverish activity on the part of his many interpreters is not in the least surprising; it is at this juncture in literary history that the identification between interpretant and interpreter begins to produce diminishing narcissistic returns, and the interpreter feels compelled to work overtime lest he suffer the interpretant's sorry fate. What is surprising is that in their eagerness to rush into the semiotic breach, the interpreters have paid little heed to the veritable "allegory"[28] of interpretation that Kafka's texts constitute. Nowhere would this attention be better invested than in a reading of the penultimate chapter of *The Trial*, "In the Cathedral," where K. is assailed by a barrage of enigmatic signs: a foreign language (Italian), pictorial language (the altarpiece), gestural language (the verger), and finally the parabolic language of the Priest. To each semiology correspond specific modalities of hermeneutic distress and disaster: each sign system comes equipped with its own failure device.

In the instance of the "unintelligible Italian" (201), K. does not meet the first interpretative challenge of the day—interpretation-as-translation—because of the gap between acquired linguistic "competence" and the native speaker's "performance." Despite his knowledge of Italian syntax and vocabulary, K. is unable to decode the Italian's speech: "He could understand him almost completely when he spoke slowly and quietly, but that happened very seldom, the words mostly came pouring out in a flood, and he made lively gestures with his head as if enjoying the rush of talk. Besides, when this happened, he invariably relapsed into a dialect which K. did not recognize as Italian but which the Manager could both speak and understand" (200). The pointed contrast between K.'s confusion and the Manager's ease serves to underscore the fact that there is nothing intrinsically unintelligible about the Italian's discourse; it is not even ambiguous. And yet for K. it is totally opaque, obscured by a *series* of obstacles: "It became clear to K. that there was little chance of communicating with the Italian, for the man's French was difficult to follow and it was no use watching his lips for clues, since their movements were covered by the bushy moustache" (200). What is reemphasized in this scene is K.'s characteristic lack of preparedness: he is always somehow taken by surprise, confounded by an unforeseen gap that appears between what he is ready to interpret and the signs he in fact receives.

The inefficacy of book learning is confirmed by K.'s second interpretative fiasco of the day, his misprision in the Cathedral. Despite his certified expertise in art history, K.'s appreciation of the altarpiece falls short of the mark:

[I] The first thing K. perceived, partly by guess, was a huge armored knight on the outermost verge of the picture. [II] He was leaning on his sword, which was stuck into the bare ground, bare except for a stray blade of grass or two. [III] He seemed to be watching áttentively some event unfolding itself before his eyes. [IV] It was surprising that he should stand so still without approaching nearer to it. [V] Perhaps he had been sent there to stand guard. [VI] K., who had not seen any pictures for a long time, studied this knight for a good while, although the greenish light of the oil-lamp made his eyes blink. [VII] When he played the torch over the rest of the altarpiece he discovered that it was a portrayal of Christ being laid in the tomb, conventional in style and a fairly recent painting. (205)

This passage provides us with a remarkable mimesis of interpretation as practiced by Kafka's interpretants, a process which progresses through the following stages:

1.   The fascinated observation/description of the peripheral (I and II)

2.   The (hypothetical) interpretation of the detail (III)

3.   The metamorphosis of interpretation into fiction (introduction of elements of temporality and motivation) (IV and V)

4.   The retroactive deflation of the entire sequence (stages 1, 2, and 3) (VI and VII)

But if this were all we saw in this passage we would, like K., be "beside the point"; what we have here is not just a *mimesis* of the interpretant's modus operandi, but a *mise en abyme*: we have K. looking at the Knight looking at something which we ultimately discover to be Christ being laid in the tomb. This breathtaking deepening of the visual field recalls the series of obstacles that prevent K. from communicating with the Italian and foreshadows the foliate structure of the parable.

From the overinterpretation of a relatively insignificant detail, K. goes on to the outright misinterpretation of a gesture, generally the least ambiguous of signs in Kafka's fiction: "The old man kept pointing at something, but K. deliberately refrained from looking round to see what he was pointing at, the gesture could have no other purpose than to shake K. off" (206). The gesture's "purpose" is, of course, exactly the opposite of the one K. ascribes to it: it points K. in the direction of the priest in his pulpit. The celebrated encounter with the priest must then be seen in the context of this string of interpretative fiascos, and this microcontextual[29] reading cannot but produce results different from the macro- or extracontextual approaches that have traditionally predominated. The figure of the Priest manifests itself at this strategic point in the text to instruct K., not so much in the ways of the Law, as in those of exegesis. Viewed in this perspective, the possible meaning(s) of the parable, "Before the Law," need not worry us, for what matters is the Talmudic discussion that follows it. The lesson borne in on K. is not the definitive reading of the parable, the "correct" interpretation, but something altogether different: the crucial fact that the parable is one with the commentators' interpretations, there is no separating the gloss from the fiction. Even as the priest is speaking, his performance is an interpretation: "'So the doorkeeper deceived the man,' said K. immediately, strongly attracted by the story. 'Don't be too hasty,' said the priest, 'don't take over someone else's opinion without testing it. I have told you the story in the very words of the scriptures. There's no mention of deception in it.' 'But it's clear enough,' said K., 'and your *first interpretation* of it was quite right'" (215; emphasis added). The interpretant is deluded if he thinks his access to the parable is direct and unmediated, if he fancies himself the "first" interpreter; interpretation has always already begun: "'So you think the man was deceived?' 'Don't misunderstand me,' said the priest, 'I am only showing you the various opinions concerning that point. You must not pay too much attention to them. The scriptures are unalterable and the comments often enough merely express the commentator's despair'" (217).

If we return, in conclusion, to James, we find that he was perhaps the first modern novelist to articulate the existence of what J. Hillis Miller has referred to as a "series of interpreters."[30] In the preface to *The Princess Casamassima*, James writes: "The teller of a story is primarily, none the less, the listener to it, the reader of it, too; and, having needed thus to make it out, distinctly, on the crabbed page of life, to disengage it from the rude human character and the more or less Gothic text in which it has been packed away, the very essence of his affair has been the *imputing* of intelligence."[31] We arrive thus at a three-tiered interpretative process: the "teller of a story" deciphers the "page of life," he then "imputes" his deciphering to interpretants, who in turn become the objects of interpreters. But even this vertiginous interpretative chain does not adequately represent the hermeneutic situation, for in fact the "teller of a story" has as little claim to priority as do either the interpretant or the interpreter; there is no sign on that "crabbed page of life" which is not already inscribed in the Great Chain of Interpretation. Here we come full circle and encounter Peirce when he writes: "The meaning of a representation can be nothing but a representation. In fact, it is nothing but the representation itself conceived as stripped of irrelevant clothing. But this clothing never can be completely stripped off; it is only changed for something more diaphanous. So there is an infinite regression here. Finally, the interpretant is nothing but another representation to which the torch of truth is handed along; and as representation, it has its interpretant again. Lo, another infinite series."[32]

Just as Sontag's attack against interpretation was, so to speak, a sign of her times, my concern with fiction-as-interpretation/interpretation-as-fiction is but an aspect of the preoccupation with infinitely receding origins that pervades structuralist and poststructuralist writings. As Edward Said has summarized this trend: "The problem as seen by all structuralists—Lévi-Strauss, Barthes, Louis Althusser, and Emile Benvéniste among them—is that the authority of a privileged Origin that commands, guarantees, and perpetuates meaning has been removed."[33] To read literature in this gloomy (essentially Derridean) optic is not only to renounce any belief in the author's authority—a form of apostasy dating back to the origins of modern formalism—but to renounce any compensatory belief in the interpreter's omnipotence. In the end, what is perhaps most telling about Sontag's essay is her assimilation of interpretation to (masculine) forms of aggression and mastery: rape and imperialism. She is against interpretation as intellectual machismo. The commentators' despair is only the dysphoric corollary of what Sontag refers to as the interpreters' "arrogance," that is, their hubris. Reading Sontag with Peirce, with his metaphor of (impossible) unveiling, leads me to rephrase her conclusion—"In place of a hermeneutics we need an erotics of art" (23)—by calling instead for an *erotics of hermeneutics*, text-pleasure as striptease instead of rape. The recognition of the interpretant's role and situation should put an end to the interpreter's manic-depressive cycle and promote a "saner" mode or, better yet, mood: the commentator's humility, which is somehow bound up with a recognition of his (or her) femininity.

# 9.

# DUANE HANSON:
## Truth in Sculpture

Faced with an object taken from nature and represented by sculpture—
that is to say, a round, three-dimensional object about which one can
move freely, and, like the natural object itself, enveloped in atmosphere—
the peasant, the savage or the primitive man feels no indecision; whereas
a painting, because of its immense pretensions and its paradoxical and
abstractive nature, will disquiet and upset him.
Charles Baudelaire, *Salon of 1859*

Hanson/Balzac

Duane Hanson is the Balzac of twentieth-century American sculpture, a creator
of types (see figures 13 and 14) rendered in highly particularized and ideally
transparent detail: "not a line around the mouth, wrinkled pouch beneath the
eyes, discolored skin on the neck, stubble on the chin, or frayed cuff is shown
that does not betray its bearer's sex, age, health, social class, diet, occupation,
character, idiosyncrasies and personal habits. From such a compendium social
historians could *reconstruct* a convincing model of the society in which the subject
lived."[1] This total synecdochic plenitude fulfills one of Balzac's most cherished
ambitions, which was not so much to emulate's Cuvier's paleontological
triumphs himself, as to provide an inexhaustible lode for some future social
historian. Balzac wrote always from the posthumous vantage point of the ar-
chaeologist, preventatively packing as much information about his society into
every virtual fragment, so that some day *après le déluge*, one would have only
to unpack the shards of this dead civilization to reconstruct it as a living whole.
Balzac invokes this unassailable scientific concern on more than one occasion
to legitimate his extended architectural descriptions, for there is a definite
though unarticulated connection between (an excess of) descriptive details and
the archaeological stance: if a fragment is to ground a projected reconstruction,
it must exhibit a high density of details, and, at the same time, a plethora of
details ensures the survival of at least some trace of a civilization, always con-
jugated in the future anterior:

It so happens that human life in all its aspects, wide or narrow, is so in-

Figure 13.  Duane Hanson, *Tourists*

Figure 14. Duane Hanson, *Supermarket Shopper*

timately connected with architecture, that with a certain amount of observation we can usually *reconstruct* a bygone society from the remains of its public monuments. From relics of household stuff, we can imagine its owners "in their habit as they lived." Archaeology, in fact, is to the body social somewhat as comparative anatomy is to animal organizations. A complete social system is made clear to us by a bit of mosaic, just as a whole past order of things is implied by the skeleton of an ichthyosaurus. Beholding the cause, we guess the effect, even as we proceed from the effect to the cause, one deduction following another until a chain of evidence is complete, until the man of science raises up a whole bygone world from the dead, and discovers for us not only the features of the past, but even the warts upon those features.[2]

The rhetorical strategy deployed by the art critic in his *éloge* of Hanson—"not a line . . ."—echoes, unwittingly, though not coincidentally, the one adopted by Balzac in his defense of the detail—"*Une* mosaïque révèle *toute* une société . . ."—for hyperbole is the figure of the realists's mimetic, which is also to say hermeneutic hubris. Underlying both Balzac's and Hanson's archaeological enterprises there lies the bedrock of the realist's confidence in man's capacity, indeed duty, to permeate phenomena with meaning: reconstruction implies recuperation. By their investment in transparent, meaningful details, Balzac and Hanson are opposed to artists such as Flaubert, whose opaque, detotalized details serve to produce Barthes's "reality effect,"[3] that extreme form of mimesis which derives from the inscription of details as resistant to hermeneutic recuperation as nature itself. And yet unlike Balzac's, Hanson's use of details provokes another effect, a "shock" effect remarked upon by nearly all of his critics. I quote from the jacket of the widely disseminated monograph that served as catalogue for the first major exhibition of Hanson's works to travel across the United States: "Encountering a Hanson . . . is shocking; it violates our sense of reality"; "Hanson's sculptures cause one shock after another. They are so realistic that they are thrilling, almost frightening."[4]

The shock effect created by Hanson's lifelike sculptures is one we know better under a different name: the uncanny, *das Unheimliche*. Indeed, it would appear that if one is to account somehow for the thrilling terror, the *frisson* universally produced by Hanson's "sharp-focus" realism, one must (re)read Freud's classical essay of 1919, "The 'Uncanny.'"

Freud/Jentsch/Cixous

As often in his writings on aesthetics, Freud is from the outset of this essay at great pains to position himself very modestly in the field. In this instance he begins by qualifying his "claim to priority" by a double disclaimer: "As good as nothing is to be found upon this subject in comprehensive treatises on aesthetics . . . I know of only one attempt in medico-psychological literature, a fertile but not exhaustive paper by Ernst Jentsch (1906). But I must confess that I have not made a very thorough examination of the literature . . . so that my paper is presented to the reader without any claim of priority."[5]

Jentsch, it turns out, serves not merely as a bibliographical alibi, but also as a psychological foil for Freud's psychoanalytic investigation. Once one becomes aware of the polemical thrust of Freud's essay, Jentsch appears to haunt the text, creating an uncanny effect of his own, what I will call the *Jentsch-effect*. Transcoded into the idiom of "The 'Uncanny'," Jentsch functions as a sort of double—the archdouble in a text crowded with doubles—or, better yet, as a repressed that insists upon returning. In Hélène Cixous's words: "When the *Unheimliche* forces back the Jentschian motif, is there not, in fact, *a repression of the repressed? Does not Jentsch say more than what Freud wishes to read?"[6]

(Here I must interrupt myself, expose the fictive linearity of my expository narrative, and repeat Freud's inaugural gesture; my writing too is presented to the reader without any claims of priority, for what I have just described as the Jentsch-effect—that form of the uncanny peculiar to the scholarly enterprise— surprised me in the very act of composing this text, in which I, like Freud, have ventured outside my own field of expertise [literature] into an unfamiliar branch of aesthetics [sculpture]. No sooner had I uncovered what I assumed to be the heretofore unsuspected significance of the Freud/Jentsch relationship, than I discovered with a dismay tempered by a perverse delight in the wondrous work- ings of the uncanny, that my claim to priority was rendered null and void by Cixous's remarkable gloss of Freud's text, "Fiction and Its Phantoms: A Reading of Freud's *Das Unheimliche* [The 'uncanny']." Inevitably then, given the logic of the uncanny, in what follows, a Cixous-effect reduplicates the Jentsch-effect itself.)

Two questions now arise: what exactly is the Jentsch-effect, and what bearing does it have on our attempt to explain the uncanny effect produced by Hanson's sculptures? The Jentsch-effect is the uncanny impression evoked in the reader by the insistent recurrence throughout Freud's text of allusions to his prede- cessor's theory—a theory which Freud does everything in his power to discredit, but which exhibits a remarkable resistance to analytical annihilation. That theory assigns privileged status to lifelike three-dimensional figures.

Although the Jentsch-effect relies on repetition, rather than note all of Freud's explicit and implicit references to Jentsch, I shall confine myself to Part 2 of "The 'Uncanny'," because it is there that Freud's engagement with his double is most clearly bodied forth.

Having devoted an inordinate amount of space and effort in Part 1 to de- molishing Jentsch's equation of the uncanny with the unfamiliar, by decon- structing the very opposition between the unfamiliar and the familiar on which Jentsch's equation is posited, Freud surprises the naive reader who had given Jentsch up for dead by opening Part 2 with a passage praising Jentsch for his choice of a particularly suitable example of the uncanny as a starting point for his investigation: "Jentsch has taken as a very good instance 'doubts whether an apparently animate being is really alive; or conversely, whether a lifeless object might not be in fact animate'; and he refers in this connection to the impression made by waxwork figures, ingeniously constructed dolls and automata" (*S. E.*, 17:226). This praise is, however, mere puff; in an ambivalent gesture which characterizes Freud's relationship to Jentsch, as Cixous (para)phrases it:

> Scarcely does he appropriate Jentsch's example (in the manner of children: this doll belongs to me) when he declares himself the true master of the method since his predecessor did not know how to make proper use of it. The way in which he misappropriates betrays a stinging boldness and the ploy of a fox! On the one hand, Freud quotes the Jentsch citation about the Sand-Man beginning with the character of the automaton, the doll Olympia. At the same time, he discards Jentsch's interpretation. The latter links the *Unheimliche* to the psychological manipulation of Hoffmann, which consists in producing and preserving uncertainty with respect to the true nature of Olympia. Is she animate or inanimate? Does Freud regret the psychological argument? So be it. He takes advantage of it to displace the *Unheimliche* of the doll with the Sand-Man. Thus, under the cover of analytical criticism and uncertainty, the doll which had been relegated to the background is already, in effect, in the trap. (Cixous, 532)

Cixous's analysis is compelling and convincing, but nonetheless misleading; by relying on Freud's paraphrase of and selective quotations from Jentsch, she compounds his already skewed reading of Jentsch with her own, leaving the reader with the erroneous impression that Jentsch explicitly cites "The Sand-Man," and specifically the doll Olympia, in support of his theory of intellectual uncertainty. If, however, one rereads the relevant passage from Jentsch as quoted by and then commented upon by Freud, it quickly becomes apparent that Jentsch never mentions "The Sand-Man," or, a fortiori, the doll Olympia. Freud's misappropriation of Jentsch's example is then even craftier than Cixous suggests; in order to set his predecessor/rival up as a straw man, Freud fraudulently attributes to him an interpretation of a text he never even cites by name. Or, to complicate this already complicated scenario even further: because Freud wants to propose an interpretation of "The Sand-Man," and because he cannot get around (or over) the fact that Jentsch had already made the connection between Hoffmann and the uncanny, Freud takes advantage of the brief break between paragraphs to transform a general statement into a pointed reference:

Jentsch writes:

> In telling a story, one of the most successful devices for easily creating uncanny effects is to leave the reader in uncertainty whether a particular figure in the story is a human being or an automaton, and to do it in such

a way that his attention is not focused directly upon his uncertainty, so that he may not be led to go into the matter and clear it up immediately. That, as we have said, would quickly dissipate the peculiar emotional effect of the thing. E. T. A. Hoffmann has repeatedly employed this psychological artifice with success in his fantastic narratives.

This observation, undoubtedly a correct one, refers primarily to the story of "The Sand-Man" in Hoffmann's *Nachtstücken*, which contains the original of Olympia, the doll that appears in the first act of Offenbach's opera, *Tales of Hoffmann*. But I cannot think—and I hope most readers of the story will agree with me—that the theme of the doll Olympia, who is to all appearances a living being, is by any means the only, or indeed the most important, element that must be held responsible for the quite unparalleled atmosphere of uncanniness evoked by the story . . . The main theme of the story is, on the contrary, something different, something which gives it its name, and which is always re-introduced at critical moments: it is the theme of the "Sand-Man" who tears out children's eyes. (*S. E.*, 17:227)

To return to Jentsch's text is not only to become aware of the tendentiousness of Freud's reading, it is to discover the extent of his misreading, and to understand better the uncanny resistance of the Jentschian text to Freud's incursions. For if Jentsch is not, as Freud would have it, primarily concerned with The Sand-Man and Olympia, one might well ask: what is his prime concern? And the answer seems forthcoming: he is concerned with a particularly effective technique Hoffmann uses, an "artifice," to distract the reader's attention from the source of his uncertainty, and thereby maintain it as long as possible. In his eagerness to set Jentsch up, Freud neatly sidesteps the issue of decentering that Jentsch is raising, and directs our attention to the doubt-producing automaton, only to say that the real source of the uncanny lies elsewhere. In other words, by deliberately misreading Jentsch, Freud seems to have fallen precisely into the trap Hoffmann had set for him; instead of focusing on his uncertainty, he focuses on the Sand-Man. It has, of course, not gone unnoticed by Cixous that the theme of "The Sand-Man" is blinding as well as blindness. Now, according to Cixous, it is we the readers who are blinded by Freud: "We get sand thrown in our eyes, no doubt about it" (532). But, what if the sand were in Freud's eyes, Freud who at the very beginning of the essay—indeed in one of his initial references to Jentsch—confesses to a "special obtuseness" (17:220) in the matter of the uncanny, Freud who either forecloses Olympia where she is present (see Cixous), or hallucinates her presence, where she is in fact absent (see above).

Here I must part company with Cixous, who attempts to explain what I would call Freud's "Olympia complex" psychoanalytically, not because of any fundamental disagreement, but simply because in my perspective her analysis is not complete. It seems to me quite possible that Freud's conspicuous inability to successfully integrate Jentsch's work into his own can be attributed in large measure to his failure to make the same critical distinctions between media that he makes between literary genres (the fairy tale and the realistic narrative) or, for that matter, between fiction and real life. One of the reasons why "the theme of the doll" is never dealt with adequately is that Freud consistently occults its specificity, not only its sex (see Cixous, 538), but more importantly its three-dimensional form. By overemphasizing Jentsch's interest in Hoffmann, Freud does more than displace Olympia in favor of the Sand-Man; he displaces sculpture in favor of literature.[7] If we are to further our inquiry into the differences between the uncanny in these two domains, we must *return to the repressed*, which is to say Jentsch's text, and in particular to the passage pertaining to "wax-work figures, ingeniously constructed dolls and automata" which Freud alludes to but does not quote:

> The disagreeable impression easily aroused in many people upon visiting wax-museums, wax-works, and panoramas is well-known. It is often difficult, especially in the half-darkness, to distinguish a life-size wax figure or similar figure from a person. Such a figure, for some impressionable individuals, has the power to prolong their discomfort, even after they have decided whether or not the figure is animated. It is probably a matter here of a half-conscious secondary doubt, automatically and repeatedly provoked by the renewed examination and observation of the finer details, or perhaps it is only a vivid after-vibration of the recollection of the initial painful impression. The fact that such wax-figures do often represent anatomical details may indeed contribute to the intensification of the intended emotional effect, that is, however, by no means the main thing: a genuine anatomical cadaver does not have to look remotely as disgusting as the corresponding wax-figure.[8]

Jentsch's integral text provides valuable confirmation of our initial hypothesis, namely that realistic sculptural details play a significant role in producing and protracting uncanny effects. The "finer details" which catch and hold the spectator's gaze are the plastic equivalents of the psychological artifice so successfully employed by Hoffmann: the fascination they exert on the spectator prevents him from focusing on his doubt. But Jentsch takes us a step further by introducing an important qualification: anatomical details are not the privileged purveyors of the uncanny. The question then becomes: if anatomical details are not primarily responsible for enhancing the disagreeable uncanny impression, is there another category of details which is? One has only to turn to some of the most thoughtful criticism written about Hanson's works to discover the answer: the shock effect produced by Hanson's sculptures is due not to their anatomical verisimilitude, but rather to their vestimentary realism. In an article comparing Hanson to John de Andrea, whose plastic figures are naked, Joseph Mashek states: "Duane Hanson's people are clothed. The nature of their dress, in fact, grants them a truly realistic quality of exemplarity";[9] similarly, in his review of the "Sharp-Focus Realism" exhibition, held at the Sidney Janis Gallery in 1972, Harold Rosenberg writes: "Of the sculpture in the show, Hanson's *Businessman* comes closest to fooling the eye, no doubt through the assistance of authentic posture and clothing; de Andrea's *Sitting Black Boy* is, by being naked, unable to rise to this level of deception."[10]

## Derrida/Kant

Clothed statues are, as Jacques Derrida emphasizes in his translation and gloss of Kant's third *Critique*, the paragon of *parerga*:

> Even what is called *ornamentation* [*Zierathen*: decoration, ornamentation, adornment] (*parerga*), i.e. what is only an adjunct, and not an intrinsic constituent in the complete representation of an object (*was nicht in die ganze Vorstellung des Gegenstandes als Bestandstück innerlich, sondern nur äusserlich als Zuthat gehört*), in augmenting the delight of taste does so solely by means of its form. Thus it is with the frames [*Einfassungen*] of pictures or the drapery on statues, or the colonnades of palaces.[11]

Now for Derrida the *parergon* in general and in particular the example of examples, "the drapery on statues (*Gewänder an Statuen*)" (Derrida, 18), is highly problematic because in point of fact it is not nearly so simple a matter to know the clothing from the statue as Kant's formulation implies: "We may ask as well where the drapery begins. Where a *parergon* begins and where it ends. Whether all drapery is *parergon*—G-strings and the like. What to do with absolutely transparent veils" (Derrida, 22). At this juncture Derrida swerves away from his paradigmatic example, the clothing adorning sculptures, and shifts to an example more germane to his subject, truth in painting:

> And how to transpose the statement to painting. For example, Cranach's Lucretia holds nothing but a flimsy transparent veil over her sex: where is the *parergon*? Must we also consider a *parergon*—not part of her nude body, *au naturel*—the dagger which she points at herself and which touches her skin (only the point of the *parergon* touches her body, in the middle of a triangle formed by her two breasts and her navel)? Is her necklace also a *parergon*? (Derrida, 22)

Hanson's clothed figures stand at the opposite end of the spectrum: it is the opacity of their apparel (rather than their transparency), the excess of their accoutrements (rather than their scarcity), that make it impossible to distinguish the ornamental from the essential. Or rather: in Hanson's works, the ornamental has become the essential: the accessory, which is to say the detail, has been promoted to a radical centrality. The uncanny effect in sculpture arises from a generalization of the supplement, a reversal of the traditional drapery-statue relationship; in a word, it is a frame-effect, to borrow once again from Derrida.

But, one might well ask: is it art? Are the disagreeable impressions provoked by these clothed statues and aesthetic pleasure compatible? What, after all— Freud never does say—is the pleasure of the uncanny? If we return to Jentsch, we find that he concludes his remarks regarding wax-figures and the like by a curiously prescient critique of hyperrealistic sculpture:

> Incidentally it is interesting to note by means of this example how true art, in wise moderation, avoids the absolute and complete imitation of nature and living things, knowing full well that they provoke slight feelings of uneasiness: the existence of polychromatic sculptures in wood and stone does not in any way alter this fact, no more than does the possibility of preventing to some extent such disagreeable side-effects, if this mode of representation is nevertheless chosen. Moreover, the production of the uncanny can, of course, be attempted in true art, but again with artistic means and intentions.[12]

Neither Hanson's artistic means nor his intentions are today any longer in question. Indeed, it has been convincingly argued that far from being the unrepentant realist we have been making him out to be, Hanson is in fact a conceptual artist. What Jentsch could not have anticipated is that taken to its logical conclusion (and beyond), realism in sculpture can only self-deconstruct, give rise to a sort of metasculpture that comments on its own means of deception. As Gerrit Henry has put it: "The viewer's search for the esthetic reasonableness of Duane Hanson's work ends, then, with the recognition of the joke behind it. Unlike the joke behind much conceptual art, Hanson's is not on the viewer, or on art in general, but it is a joke *on the joke* of fallacious and single-minded ways of perceiving, and the results, both artistic and human, of those fallacies."[13] Finally then, the pleasure of the uncanny effect produced by Hanson's figures is the pleasure of the after-effect, the infantile pleasure that comes from taking the doll apart and seeing how it is made, in other words, the pleasure of the critic.

# 10.
## DETAILS AND REALISM:
## The Curé De Tours

... our civilization is infinite in its detail ...
Balzac, Preface, *A Daughter of Eve*

To say that realism, in particular French nineteenth-century realism, is a "detailism" (to recall again Lewes's term), is to rehearse a topos which runs through all of the critical discourses on realism from Brunetière to Barthes, from Lewes to Lukács.[1] Whether the association is positively or negatively valorized, whether the detail is said to be in the service of a conservative or a revolutionary aesthetics, producing its mimetic effect by means of a referential emptiness or plenitude, the detail occupies—despite or perhaps because of its insignificance—a privileged position in the theory of realism.[2] Now recently, at least in France, a pronounced tendency has developed to restrict the field of the realist detail or, rather, of the discourse on that detail. This restriction involves two complementary gestures. On the one hand, the assimilation of the detail to the category of the descriptive detail; on the other, the affirmation that the descriptive detail is somehow a defective sign, either on the level of referentiality,[3] or that of signification.[4] One of the consequences, not to say symptoms, of this double restriction is the privilege the Flaubertian detail enjoys following Barthes, whereas the Balzacian detail, considered as exemplary by Lukács, has been relegated to the function of foil.

If it seems to me timely and even urgent to return to the Balzacian detail at the close of this book, it is once again for reasons of an archaeological order. The very beautiful myth of the origins of modernity which is Barthes's "reality effect" has resulted in the occultation of the revolutionary thrust, that is, the modernity of the Balzacian detail. Studied *in statu nascendi*, as it were, Balzacian realism—which is entirely centered on details, referring to what Hegel calls "the prose of the world"—turns out to be an *anxious detailism*, preoccupied with ensuring its own legitimacy. To return to the crisis in legitimation which Balzacian realism underwent, at least in its early stages, may serve to shed some light on a critical turning point in the history of the detail as aesthetic category.

This being said, let me hasten to add that my concern at this moment is not descriptive details, but rather a category of details which I will call *diegetic details*. By that I do not mean the "good" details of Homeric descriptions, so highly prized by Lessing or Hegel[5] as well as other aestheticians and rhetoricians who have always made special allowances for details borne by a praxis or better yet a *technē*. By diegetic details I mean that class of details which is situated on the evenmential plane of the text, and which involves those prosaic objects whose exchange and communication constitute the classical realist narrative. One example among others: the sugar bowl which figures in the breakfast scene in *Eugénie Grandet*, where it serves both as an agent of psychological revelation and as a narrative catalyst. The struggle that arises over this humble container confirms what the reader already knows of Grandet's avarice, while bringing to light both the daughter's incipient rebellion against the hard law of the father, and Charles's blindness. It is precisely by means of the sugar, but viewed as a signifier, that Grandet announces to his nephew that he has some unpleasant revelation to make to him: "When you have finished, we will take a turn in the garden together. I have things to tell you which sugar won't make any sweeter."[6] Thus the sugar contained in the bowl is doubly inscribed in the text: first as a reference to a precious commodity which becomes a stake in the Oedipal struggle—demonstrating the imbrication of capitalism and patriarchy—then as a signifier endowed with proleptic qualities.

But it is in another text by Balzac, *The Curé de Tours*, that I would like to study the process of legitimation or naturalization of the diegetic detail, for this text can be read as a sort of allegory of that process. In fact, realism is as much a discourse *on* the detail as a discourse *of* the detail, and, at least in Balzac, the promotion of the detail often involves an apologetic metalinguistic commentary. for, contrary to what one might believe, the priority accorded to the diegetic detail by Balzac is not a matter of course. Thus, at the outset, this novel appears to be not so much an apology for the detail as a rather surprising satire of so-called Balzacian realism. This satirical intent takes the form of an insistent lack of solidarity between the narrator and the character he explicitly designates in the opening sentence as the "main character" of his "story,"[7] the Abbé Birotteau, vicar of the Cathedral of Saint-Gatien. From the first page of the novel where one joins the Abbé *in medias res*, returning home in the rain, to the end of the exposition, the narrator seems intent on discrediting the eminently myopic *Weltanschauung* of his protagonist. This satire culminates in the scene where, back home, the Abbé becomes aware of the persecution directed against him by means of four diegetic details:

> . . . since it is in the nature of narrow minds to dwell on trivial details, he suddenly began to ponder very seriously upon these four incidents, which everyone would have overlooked, but which to him were major catastrophes. His entire happiness was obviously at stake, jeopardized by the misplaced slippers, by Marianne's lies in regard to the fire, by the unwar-

ranted transfer of his candlestick to the table in the vestibule, and by the discomfort to which he had been subjected, forced to wait out in the rain (191).

In this remarkable passage Balzac takes great pains to multiply the marks of distanciation, widening (and, of course, by the same gesture, bridging) the gap which (supposedly) separates the poor Abbé from the narratee, a Parisian with far loftier preoccupations. One would have to submit this passage to a microscopic analysis to bring out the diverse means Balzac employs to isolate his character. I will mention only the most telling: devalorizing value judgments; an emphasis on the disproportion between sign and interpretation; hyperbole; slippage into free indirect discourse. By insisting on the attention and the significance the Abbé attributes to details which are situated beneath the normal threshold of vision, Balzac does more than discredit his character. He ridicules any scale of values which grants minute daily occurrences the status of Events or any inflationary linguistic practice which swells minutiae into catastrophes. In light of this passage, as well as all that precedes it, the reader cannot but see in the Abbé Birotteau a new incarnation of a typical character in modern fiction, which he indeed is on one level: the failed "interpretant." (The interpretant is the term I have proposed in Chapter 8 to distinguish the interpreting fictional character from the interpreting reader, for whom I reserve the term interpreter). One could even speak of Birotteau's "bêtise."

But the reader would be well advised to defer his interpretation—if interpretation there be—for the rest of the novel will entirely justify the Abbé, accredit his rather peculiar vision of the stuff of everyday life, and, in so doing, reaffirm the foundations of the realist novel which were somewhat shaken by the initial derision of the protagonist's myopia. For, obviously, however great the ironic distance maintained by the narrator vis-à-vis this character whose profession is "dissecting trivia" (192), the very fact of representing him in such "loving" detail signifies that we are very much in a detailist literary mode, and that the gap advertised between narrator and character masks the most intimate of complicities. This reversal of perspective occurs at that nexus, always critical in Balzacian narrative, the point at which the exposition is joined with the narration:

> If the great things in life are easy to understand, simple to describe, its petty incidents require endless details. This elaborate introduction was necessary to explain the background to a drama which, bourgeois though it may be, inspired passions as violent as any brought about by loftier motives. Even an experienced historian would have found it difficult to condense all its minute developments. (201)

Ever since Genette, we have learned to view with suspicion the strategies enlisted by Balzac to institute and ensure the (pseudo-)verisimilitude of his fiction. But the maxim invoked here is of a special nature; it constitutes a limit-case, since it is designed to dissimulate not the psychological, but rather what we might call the generic arbitrariness of the story.[8] Rather than calling into play some law supposedly drawn from the reservoir of the cultural code in order to make his fiction "passable," it would seem as though, in *The Curé de Tours*, the narrator had fabricated a fiction whose purpose is to demonstrate the worthiness of a law which is precisely the law which regulates realist writing. A law which, let us note in passing, rests on a perfectly classical aesthetic principle: the adequation, indeed the necessary commensurability, of the represented and the representing. If the representation of a bourgeois drama involves a synecdochic proliferation, it is because a certain excess of signifiers must of necessity compensate a certain indigence of the subject-matter. Thus the legitimation of detailism is bound up with the recognition of the split between low and trivial subject-matter and "high writing," which will be one of the mainsprings of Flaubert's style.

Whatever the significance of this maxim, however, the revalorization of the diegetic detail rests essentially on a penetrating critique of the disciplining, or mapping, of the social body during the period when the events recounted unfold. What Birotteau's persecution demonstrates, is that in the France of the Restoration, with its tentacular systems of surveillance, it is impossible to be overly attentive to details. Not only was the Abbé quite justified in drawing far-ranging consequences from the minutiae of his life, but, if failure there is, it is rather a factor of his incapacity to read details *in detail*. The Abbé is insufficiently nearsighted or, to move from the ophthalmologic code to the psychiatric, he is insufficiently paranoid; he suffers from an interpretative deficiency:

> If someone had found it at all worthwhile to probe Birotteau's conscience and show him that in the infinitesimal details and petty duties towards other of his private life he was lacking in the very selflessness which he believed to profess, he would have punished himself . . . (193).

If the Abbé does not attend sufficiently to details, the same does not hold true for the other characters. In fact the revalorization of the detail is inseparable from another reversal which concerns the very notion of protagonist. Indeed, the narrator's metalinguistic commentary which designates Birotteau as the "main character" should have aroused our suspicions, for as the narrative progresses, another character comes to occupy the center of the text, displacing the Abbé both in the space represented (the apartment), and the space of representation (the novel). I am, of course, alluding to the Abbé Troubert, a sinister character who, like all of Balzac's demonic figures, advances masked. Presented at the outset as a creature hovering between the canine and the human, Troubert turns out to be "the most influential person in the province, where he represents the Congregation"; "Archbishop, Superior-general, Prefect, the mighty and the lowly, all lay beneath his sinister sway" (232). The corollary of the revelation of Troubert's supreme and occult power is that the apparently insignificant quarrel between Birotteau and his landlady Mademoiselle Gamard becomes an affair of state and, through a series of mediations, has an effect on higher interests: "In the presence of such powerful conflicts of interest, Birotteau felt like a worm. He was not mistaken" (236).

The word in French for worm is *ciron*. We need only recall that the "Ciron" functions in Pascal's *Pensées* as the hyperbole of smallness to understand that the opposition of Birotteau and Troubert figures the opposition of the two infinities, and that the real stake in their confrontation is *the epistemological status of the detail*. The fundamental question posed by *The Curé de Tours*—and it is for this reason that it is from my perspective exemplary—is: what is a detail? At what point does a detail cease to be, in a pejorative sense, a "detail"? To the extent, as we have seen, that the exclusion of the detail from the field of representation in classical and neo-classical aesthetics is based on the sure discrimination of the great and the small, the rise of realism cannot but involve an interrogation of that hierarchy.

The stake of the novel emerges clearly in the conclusion, which is surely one of the trickiest of Balzac's generally enigmatic conclusions. Troubert, who has been portrayed all along as evil incarnate, suddenly appears here in a new light. Unfortunately, this passage is much too long to be quoted in its entirety. I will simply quote the beginning and the concluding sections so that one may measure the extent of the reversal:

> In another age Troubert would probably have been a Hildebrand, or an Alexander the Sixth. Today the Church is no longer a political power and can no longer absorb the energies of solitary men. Celibacy thus leads to that capital sin which, merging all a man's powers into a single passion, egotism, makes him either destructive or useless . . .
>
> Is not the apparent egotism of the man who bears an entire science, a nation, or a code of laws in his bosom the most noble of passions, a kind of maternal love for the masses? To give birth to new ideas, is it not necessary to combine the compassionate breast of a woman and the power of God? The lives of men like Innocent the Third, or Peter the Great, and all the other leaders of a century or a country, might be called upon as examples, on a very high level, of that great design which Troubert represented, tucked away in the Cloister of Saint-Gatien. (244–45)

What one must note here is the way in which Balzac succeeds in the space of a page and a half in reversing the very thesis he has argued throughout this veritable "roman à thèse," namely, that celibacy and egotism are inextricably linked. *The Curé de Tours* is, let us recall, the second panel in a tryptich embedded in the *Scenes of Provincial Life*, entitled *The Celibates*, and whose two other panels are *Pierrette* and *The Batchelor's House*. In fact, originally, *The Curé de Tours* bore the title of the series. What we have here then is a sort of *Aufhebung* of egotism and thus of celibacy. What appears on one plane as a socially harmful condition appears on the higher plane on which the narrator suddenly places himself—and I must emphasize the suddenness of this elevation—as the "noblest of passions." Troubert's apotheosis—there is no other word to describe his final transformation—suggests that what is finally at stake in this novel is not so much the fine and hazy line between the great and the small, as between the sublime and the ridiculous. For the terrifying grandeur of Troubert—who is doubly inadequate, exceeding both his spatial and his temporal framework—is indeed of the order of Kant's "dynamic sublime." The conclusion of *The Curé de Tours* is a meditation on the disturbing and irresistible beauty of what one might call, anachronistically, totalitarianism.[9]

What is then illuminated in *The Curé de Tours* is the danger that is always hidden in synecdoche: the part may be out of proportion with the whole, and when that happens, one comes under the sway of the sublime. For, if synecdoche presupposes a classical ideal of proportionality, indeed of harmony, the sublime always implies a radical disproportion between part and whole.

It would appear that we have strayed very far from our topic. In fact, only now are we in a position to understand one of the mainsprings of the relationship between details and realism, for what emerges from our reading of *The Curé de Tours* is the fact that realism, at least at the outset, is intimately bound up with the *sublimation of details*, and this sublimation constitutes the very condition of the passage of the detail into the field of artistic representation. If, as we have seen, one reads the writings of certain aestheticians and rhetoricians of the eighteenth century—especially those of the Augustans whose normative discourse weighed heavily on the rise of realism in England and France—one discovers that one of the decisive arguments given to justify the censure of the detail is its fundamental incompatibility with the production of a "sublime-effect." Thus what Reynolds says of painting is equally applicable to literature:

> . . . it is impossible for a picture composed of so many parts to have that effect so indispensably necessary to grandeur, that of one complete whole. However contradictory it may be in geometry, it is true in taste, that many little things will not make a great one. The Sublime impresses the mind at once with one great idea; it is a single blow: the Elegant indeed may be produced by repetition; by an accumulation of many minute circumstances.[10]

Implicitly, realism in its formative stages had as its mission to demonstrate that the neo-classical opposition of particularity and the Sublime is not insuperable; in fiction this demonstration will take the form of a sublimation, indeed, a sacralization of the detail. The dispersion of attention caused by synecdochic proliferation will be offset by the absorption of the details in an overarching whole. At the same time, the prosaic quality of the diegetic details will be overcome by their insertion in a framework which ensures their transcendence.

I would then advance *very tentatively* the following hypothesis: it is perhaps not a coincidence that a novel dedicated to the legitimation of detailism is set in a clerical milieu. One could, of course, point out the absence of any allusion to the spiritual lives of the characters, and take it as consonant with a materialist critique of a post-revolutionary society in the throes of de-christianization. But that would be missing the point. For, if one reads carefully the narrator's description of the rather bizarre situation of Mademoiselle Gamard's house, one realizes that this topographical mapping bodies forth the necessary link between the realist detail and Christianity: "lying to the north of Saint-Gatien, the house is always in the shadow of that great cathedral," "the magnificent structure to which it is united" (184), in French: "avec lequel elle est *mariée.*" *The realist detail is then the shadow projected by the theological detail.*[11]

If one accepts this hypothesis as valid, one is led to revise somewhat the history of representation as it appears first in Hegel, then in Auerbach. Both, let us recall, argue that realist representation could only develop under the aegis of Christianity; according to them, one might say, all modern realist texts originate in the Gospels. Now, if one reads *The Curé de Tours* in an archaeological perspective, it appears that the effects of divine protection extend well into the nineteenth century. And if, as I believe, the detail can not at first have full access to the field of representation without God's guarantee, it follows that far from constituting a threat to the hegemony of the sublime, Balzacian detailism only reinscribes it by sublimating the prose of the world.

Doubtless, it has taken our modernity to shake the hegemony of the sublime—that is, the last vestige of classicism. Thus, since the beginning of the twentieth century, we have witnessed a far-ranging attempt to desublimate what was sublimated, an attempt spearheaded by all those, aestheticians and artists, who make up the avant-garde. In conclusion then, the recent promotion of a detail which is desacralized, detotalized and definalized, however salutary it may be, should not blind us to the revolutionary role of Balzac's sublime details. For whatever the tribute Balzac pays to the aesthetic of the sublime, he does succeed by the same gesture in representing what had previously belonged to the order of the unrepresentable.

# NOTES

## Introduction

1. Jürgen Habermas, "Remettre le mobile en mouvement," *Le monde d'aujourd'hui*, August 6, 1984, xiii. All translations mine except where otherwise noted.

2. The principal references here are to the following: George Wilhelm Friedrich Hegel, *Aesthetics: Lectures on Fine Art*, trans. T. M. Knox, 2 vols. (Oxford: Clarendon Press, 1975); Erich Auerbach, *Mimesis: The Representation of Reality in Western Literature*, trans. Willard R. Trask (Princeton: Princeton University Press, 1953); Ian Watt, *The Rise of the Novel* (Berkeley: University of California Press, 1957); Jean Baudrillard, *Le système des objets* (Paris: Gallimard, "Tel," 1968); Michel Foucault, *Discipline and Punish: The Birth of the Prison*, trans. Alan Sheridan (New York: Pantheon Books, 1977); Henri Lefebvre, *La vie quotidienne dans le monde moderne* (Paris: Gallimard, "Idées," 1968); Walter Benjamin, *Illuminations*, trans. Harry Zohn, ed. Hannah Arendt (New York: Shocken Books, 1969). This listing of some of the major sociopolitical, economic, and technological developments that have shaped the history of the detail is not meant as a dismissive gesture; I mean to signal an immense intellectual debt. Rather than repeat the brilliant analyses of these great thinkers, my concern within the limited scope of this work is to draw attention to the impact on the fate of the detail of a revolution neglected by my predecessors. In short my goal is to add to the list one more historical factor: feminism.

3. Jorge Luis Borges, *Ficciones* (New York: Grove Press, 1962), 114, 115.

4. Ibid., 114.

5. Friedrich Nietzsche, *The Gay Science*, trans. Walter Kaufman (New York: Vintage Books, 1974), 290.

6. See my "Female Paranoia: The Case for Feminist Psychoanalytic Criticism," in *Breaking the Chain: Women, Theory, and French Realist Fiction* (New York: Columbia University Press, 1985), 149–62, and "Female Fetishism: The Case of George Sand," in Susan Suleiman, ed., *The Female Body in Western Culture* (Cambridge: Harvard University Press, 1986), 363–72.

## 1.   Gender: In the Academy

1.   This marvelous neologism was coined by G. H. Lewes who deplores his contemporaries' "reaction against conventionalism which calls itself Idealism," in favour of *"detailism* which calls itself Realism" (*Principles of Success in Literature* [Boston: Allyn and Bacon, 1891], 83). My use of the term differs from Lewes's in two related respects: it is not pejorative, nor is it synonymous with Realism.

2.   Ernst Cassirer, *The Philosophy of the Enlightenment*, trans. Fritz C. A. Koelln and James P. Pettegrove (Princeton: Princeton University Press, 1951), 287.

3.   Women were not entirely absent from the Royal Academy. Among its founding members were two women artists: Angelica Kauffmann (1741–1807) and Mary Moser (1744–1819). At the same time, however, the Royal Academy "systematically excluded women from its schools and privileges for the next hundred years" (Rozcika Parker and Griselda Pollock, *Old Mistresses: Women, Art and Ideology* [New York: Pantheon Books, 1981], 28). In a witty and persuasive illustration of women's ambiguous status in the Academy—admitted as objects of representation, but barred from the all-important life drawing classes—Parker and Pollock gloss Johann Zoffany's painting, "The Academicians of the Royal Academy," pointing out that, "in the painting of the Academicians in the life-class discussing the principles of the nude in classical art, the two women Academicians are excluded," or rather displaced, represented by two nearly unrecognizable portraits hanging on the right-hand wall (87 and 90; see also 88, fig. 49). See also, Ann Sutherland Harris and Linda Nochlin, *Women Artists: 1550–1950* (New York: Alfred A. Knopf, 1977), 174–75.

4.   Sir Joshua Reynolds, *The Literary Works of Sir Joshua Reynolds*, 2 vols. (London: Henry G. Bohn, 1852), 2:352.

5.   M. H. Abrams, *The Mirror and the Lamp: Romantic Theory and the Critical Tradition* (New York: Oxford University Press, 1953), 41.

6.   William Hazlitt, *Essays on Reynolds' Discourses*, as quoted in Sir Joshua Reynolds, *Discourses on Art*, ed. Robert R. Wark (New Haven: Yale University Press, 1975), 326.

7.   Reynolds, *Discourses*, 7. All future references to the *Discourses* will be included in the body of the text and will include the number of the discourse, as well as of the pages cited.

8.   Reynolds, *The Literary Works*, 2:352.

9.   Ibid., 350.

10.   Pliny the Elder, *The Elder Pliny's Chapters on the History of Art*, trans. K. Jox-Blake (London: Macmillan and Co., 1890), 109–11. "To this ancient example," notes Hegel with unwonted humor, "we could add the modern one of Büttner's monkey which ate away a painting of a cockchafer in Rösel's *Insektbelustigungen* [Amusements of Insects] and was pardoned by his master because it had proved the excellence of the pictures in this book, although it had thus destroyed the most beautiful copy of this expensive work" (G. W. F. Hegel, *Aesthetics: Lectures on Fine Art*, trans. T. M. Knox, 2 vols. [Oxford: Clarendon Press, 1975], 1:42–43). Though often cited, what Norman Bryson refers to as the "central anecdote of Western aesthetics" (*Tradition and Desire* [New Haven: Yale University Press, 1985], 8), is generally cited (viz.

Bryson himself) in a significantly skewed form: what is retained or highlighted is the story of Zeuxis's paradigmatic mimetic triumph, while what is conveniently forgotten or downplayed is Parrhasios's upset victory, so humiliating for the (male) artist. The play between the birds and the grapes and the veil is not, however, lost on Lacan who in a recent postscript to the ancient anecdote, enlists it to illustrate the difference between "the natural function of the lure" (Zeuxis's grapes) and "trompe-l'oeil" (Parrhasios's veil). Whereas all that is needed to fool the birds is a lure, which is to say *not* an exact imitation of the real object, "if one wishes to deceive a man, what one presents to him is the painting of a veil, that is to say, something that incites him to ask what is behind it." Plato, according to Lacan, condemns painting not because it "gives an illusory equivalence to the object," but because it passes itself off as something which it is not. And that something is on the order of the object small a, which is to say the fetish (Jacques Lacan, *The Four Fundamental Concepts of Psychoanalysis*, trans. Alan Sheridan, ed. Jacques-Alain Miller [New York: W. W. Norton, 1978], 67–68).

11.  Reynolds, *The Literary Works*, 2:135. Emphasis added.

12.  Aristotle's *Physics*, as quoted by Sylviane Agacinski in her feminist deconstruction of Aristotle's theories of sexual reproduction, "Le tout premier écart," in *Les fins de l'homme*, eds. Philippe Lacoue-Labarthe and Jean-Luc Nancy (Paris: Galilée, 1981), 123. In his "new translation" of Aristotle's *Physics* (Lincoln: University of Nebraska Press, 1961), Richard Hope renders I. 9. 192a thus: "But as *the female or the ugly* inclines to the *male or beautiful* (albeit not essentially but incidentally), so what [naturally] tends to a form is matter" (22; emphasis added). See also Genevieve Lloyd, *The Man of Reason: "Male" and "Female" in Western Philosophy* (Minneapolis: University of Minnesota Press, 1984), especially 2–9.

13.  Sherry Ortner, "Is Female to Male as Nature is to Culture?" in *Woman, Culture & Society*, eds. Michelle Zimbalist Rosaldo and Louise Lamphere (Stanford: Stanford University Press, 1974), 79 and 81.

14.  Jean Larnac, *Histoire de la littérature féminine en France* (Paris: Krà, 1929), 267–68, translation mine. Cf. the strikingly similar language and conclusions reached by Rae Carlson, quoted by Nancy Chodorow: "males represent experiences of self, others, space and time in individualistic, objective, distant ways, while females represent experiences in relatively interpersonal, subjective, immediate ways," Nancy Chodorow, "Family Structure and Feminine Personality," in *Woman, Culture, & Society*, 56–57. The temptation must be resisted here to accumulate other formulations of woman's innate affinity for particularity and her consequent inaptitude to produce universal works of art. One particularly coherent theory grounding woman's cultural inferiority in her weak physiological constitution should suffice. It is that of J. J. Virey, author of two significant works on the relationship between female anatomy and female contributions to culture: *De l'Influence des femmes sur le goût dans la littérature et les beaux-arts, pendant le XVIIe et le XVIIIe siècle* (1810) and *De la Femme, sous ses rapports physiologiques, moral, et littéraire* (1825), as well as of the influential article "Femme" in the *Dictionnaire des science médicales* (Paris: Panckoucke, 1819), 14:547. Basing himself on the theories of Pierre Roussel, the eighteenth-century physician who produced the most systematic articulation of woman's irreducible physiological difference and cultural inferiority, Virey was a prime contributor to the medicalization—or "hysterization" (Foucault)—of the nineteenth-century discourse on woman. Drawing both on eighteenth-century theory of temperaments and on recently exhumed Aristotelian theories of sexual difference, Virey makes

explicit the process whereby woman's incapacity to transcend particularity is nat-uralized. He writes: "with a soft and all-impressible imagination, more apt to un-derstand than to create and to succeed in pursuits requiring skill than in the arts of invention, she receives more sentiments than ideas . . . Hence *she perceives details better than the masses*"; "As man considers the species and general things, woman fastens on the individual and settles on particular objects"; "All that is strong, vast, *sublime* is better perceived by the one, all that is delicate, gracious, and fine is better felt by the other." J. J. Virey, *De l'Influence des femmes sur le goût dans la littérature et les beaux-arts, pendant le XVIIe et le XVIIIe siècle* (Paris: Deterville, 1810), 13, 14, and 15; emphasis added. Translations mine except where otherwise noted. For an ex-cellent feminist reading of Roussel's *Système physique et moral de la femme* (1777), see Michèle Le Doeuff, "Les chiasmes de Pierre Roussel," in *L'imaginaire philosophique* (Paris: Payot, 1980), 181–222.

15. Paul Valéry as quoted by Larnac, 268. Cf. Léon Lagrange, "Du rang des femmes dans l'art," as quoted in Parker and Pollock, *Old Mistresses*, 13.

16. John Baillie, *An Essay on the Sublime*. Introduction by Samuel Holt Monk (Los An-geles: The Augustan Reprint Society, #43, 1953), 9–10. Cf. Lord Kames, *Elements of Criticism*, 3 vols. (New York: Johnson Reprint Corporation, 1967), 1:247–48 passim. The following quotations from Kames ring the changes on the minimalism, so to speak, of the sublime object: "The strongest emotion of grandeur is raised by an object that can be taken in at one view" (1: 281); "A subject that fills the mind with its loftiness and grandeur, appears best in dress altogether plain" (2:9–10).

17. Baillie, *An Essay*, 5.

18. Edmund Burke, *A Philosophical Enquiry into the Origin of our Ideas of the Sublime and Beautiful*, ed. James Boulton (Notre Dame: University of Notre Dame Press, 1968), 72. Smoothness is, conversely, an essential attribute of beauty (114), and beauty is in Burke the province of the female sex and the love its weakness inspires. Indeed, Burke fetishizes women's displays of self-mutilation, for the weakness of the "weaker sex" is in Burke an *artificial imperfection*. Recognizing the aesthetic appeal of the weak, women, "*learn* to lisp, to totter in their walk, to *counterfeit* weakness, and even sickness" (110; emphasis added). Burke's feminization of beauty leaves little doubt as to the gender of the more prestigious term with which it is coupled. As W. J. T. Mitchell has recently put it: "Sublimity, with its foundations in pain, terror, vigorous exertion, and power, is the masculine aesthetic mode" (*Iconology: Image, Text, Ideology* [Chicago: University of Chicago Press, 1986], 129).

19. Burke, *Enquiry*, 75.

20. E. H. Gombrich, *The Sense of Order: A Study in the Psychology of Decorative Art* (Ithaca: Cornell University Press, 1979), 116.

21. A more modern case in point cited by Gombrich is Christopher Wren's account of Versailles:

> The Palace, or if you please, the *Cabinet of Versailles* call'd me twice to view it; the Mixture of Brick, Stone, blue tile and Gold makes it look like a rich Livery: Not an Inch within but is crowded with little Curiosities of Ornaments: the Women, as they make here the Language and Fashions, and meddle with Politicks and Philosophy, so they sway also in Architecture; Works of Filgrand and little Knacks are in great Vogue; but Building certainly ought to have the Attribute of eternal, and therefore the only Thing uncapable of new Fashions. The masculine

Furniture of *Palais Mazarin* pleas'd me much better where is a great and noble Collection of antique Statues and Bustos . . . (Gombrich, 23).

Cf. Virey, *De l'influence*, for more on women's influence on taste.

22.   Kames, 3:300.

23.   Reynolds, *The Literary Works*, 2:130.

24.   Michelangelo as quoted by Alpers in "Art History and Its Exclusions: The Example of Dutch Art," in *Feminism and Art History: Questioning the Litany*, eds. Norma Broude and Mary D. Garrard (New York: Harper & Row, 1978), 194. Similarly, Virey associates women's dominant influence on taste with a preference for genre painting.

25.   Alpers, 195.

26.   William L. Courtney, *The Feminine Note in Fiction* (London: Chapman & Hall, 1904), x–xi and xxxii.

27.   Courtney, xii. Women's penchant for going into detail and losing sight of the essential leads them, by the same logic, to digress, that is to stray from the main storyline, to inflate the incidental episode. Thus Vico writes: "Digressions were born of the grossness of the heroic minds, unable to confine themselves to those essential features of things that were to the purpose at hand, as we see to be naturally the case with the feeble-minded and above all with women." Giambattista Vico, *The New Science of Giambattista Vico*, trans. Thomas Goddard Bergin and Max Harold Fisch (Garden City, N.Y.: Anchor Books, 1961), 111. Carried to an extreme, the detailism of "lady novelists" results in the failure to produce either plots or characters altogether: "we may be prepared to find women succeeding better in *finesse* of detail, in pathos and sentiment, while men generally succeed better in the construction of plots and the delineation of character" (George H. Lewes as cited in Elaine Showalter, *A Literature of their Own* [Princeton: Princeton University Press, 1977], 87).

28.   Charles Baudelaire, *The Painter of Modern Life and Other Essays*, trans. and ed. Jonathan Mayne (Greenwich: Phaidon, 1964), 16. Emphasis added.

29.   Reynolds, *The Literary Works*, 2:353.

## 2.   Sublimation: Hegel's *Aesthetics*

1.   Paul de Man, "Sign and Symbol in Hegel's *Aesthetics*," *Critical Inquiry*, 8 (Summer 1982), 763. Also pertinent is Paul de Man, "Hegel on the Sublime," in *Displacement: Derrida and After*, ed. Mark Krupnik (Bloomington: Indiana University Press, 1983), 139–53.

2.   Hegel, *Aesthetics: Lectures on Fine Art*, trans. T. M. Knox, 2 vols. (Oxford: Clarendon Press, 1975), 1:254–55. All subsequent references will be included in the text. *Aesthetik*, intro. Georg Lukács (Berlin: Aufbau-Verlag, 1955), 267. All German quotations are drawn from this edition and references will be included in the text.

3.   Stephen Bungay, *Beauty and Truth: A Study of Hegel's Aesthetics* (Oxford: Oxford University Press, 1984), 115. Bungay's study—which appeared after the drafting of this chapter—is easily the best introduction to Hegel's *Aesthetics* currently available in English. See also: Jack Kaminsky, *Hegel on Art* (New York: State University of New York Press, 1962) and Charles Karelis, "Hegel's Concept of Art: An Interpretive

Essay" in *Hegel's Introduction to Aesthetics*, trans. T. M. Knox (Oxford: Oxford University Press, 1979).

4.  De Man, "Sign and Symbol in Hegel's *Aesthetics*," 763.

5.  René Wellek, *A History of Modern Criticism*, 4 vols. (New Haven: Yale University Press, 1955), 2:318.

6.  Fredric Jameson, *Marxism and Form: Twentieth-Century Dialectical Theories of Literature* (Princeton: Princeton University Press, 1971), 44.

7.  Sir T. M. Knox, "The Puzzle of Hegel's Aesthetics," in *Art and Logic in Hegel's Philosophy*, eds. Warren E. Steinkraus and Kenneth I. Schmitz (New Jersey: Humanities Press, 1980), 1–10. This volume also contains a fairly comprehensive bibliography of "Studies of Hegel's Aesthetics" (239–49).

8.  De Man, "Sign and Symbol in Hegel's *Aesthetics*," 773.

9.  Wellek, 334.

10. G. W. F. Hegel, *Hegel's Philosophy of Right* as quoted by Patricia Jagentowicz Mills, "Hegel and 'The Woman Question': Recognition and Intersubjectivity," in *The Sexism of Social and Political Theory: Women and Reproduction from Plato to Nietzsche*, eds. L. Clarke, and L. Lange (Toronto: University of Toronto Press, 1979), 94.

11. G. W. F. Hegel, *Esthétique*, trans. S. Jankélévitch, 4 vols. (Paris: Garnier-Flammarion, 1979), 1:222. *Se non e vero e ben trovato*. The vaccination scar can only allude to the smallpox vaccination discovered by Jenner in 1801. The beauty of this made-up detail is that it further specifies Hegel's detailing, inscribing it in time, at the same time as it extends its progression from the pathological to the prophylactic.

12. Sir Joshua Reynolds, *Discourses on Art*, ed. Robert R. Wark (New Haven: Yale University Press, 1975), 187.

13. On German Romanticism as an aesthetics of the fragment, see Philippe Lacoue-Labarthe and Jean-Luc Nancy, *L'absolu littéraire* (Paris: Seuil, 1978), especially 55–80.

14. Bungay, *Beauty*, 137.

15. Roland Barthes, *S/Z*, trans. Richard Miller (New York: Hill and Wang, 1974), 55.

16. See, for example, Mario Praz's very Hegelian introductory chapter, "Genre Painting and the Novel," in *The Hero in Eclipse in Victorian Fiction*, trans. Angus Davidson (London: Oxford University Press, 1956). Cf. in Chapter 1, the association of Dutch and genre painting with the lower order of taste displayed by women.

17. If this reconstruction sounds very familiar to the literary critic, it is because the preeminent twentieth-century writings on realism—I am thinking, of course, of Auerbach's *Mimesis* and Ian Watt's *The Rise of the Novel*—are shot through with Hegelianism.

18. When I speak of sublimation in Hegel I shall not be referring to his writings on the sublime. The tendency to occult the significance of Dutch Art in Hegel's *Aesthetics* persists in the high deconstructionist tendency to focus almost exclusively on Hegel's writings on sublime Egyptian art.

19. Sigmund Freud, *The Standard Edition of the Complete Psychological Works of Sigmund*

*Freud*, ed. James Strachey, trans. James Strachey et al., 24 vols. (London: Hogarth, 1953–74), 14:89.

20.  Marcel Proust, *Remembrance of Things Past*, trans. C. K. Scott Moncrieff and Terence Kilmartin; and by Andreas Mayor, 3 vols. (New York: Random House, 1981), 3:185.

## 3.  Decadence: Wey, Loos, Lukács

1.  Bernard Weinberg, *French Realism: The Critical Reaction 1830–1870* (London: Oxford University Press, 1937) provides an invaluable and exhaustive dossier of contemporary critical responses.

2.  Wey is also known to art historians as Courbet's patron, friend, and correspondent. On Wey's role in Courbet's career see T. J. Clark, *Image of the People: Gustave Courbet and the 1848 Revolution* (Princeton: Princeton University Press, 1982).

3.  Francis Wey, *Remarques sur la langue française au dix-neuvième siècle*, 2 vols. (Paris: Firmin Didot, 1845), 2:374. Translations mine except where otherwise noted.

4.  Paul Bourget, *Essais de psychologie contemporaine*, 2 vols. (Paris: Plon, 1920), 1:20.

5.  On the ornamental style of decadence see "Salammbô unbound," in my *Breaking the Chain: Women, Theory, and French Realist Fiction* (New York: Columbia University Press, 1985), especially 115–16.

6.  Quintilian, *Institutio Oratoria*, III, trans. H. E. Butler, ed. T. E. Page et al. (London: William Heinemann, 1922), Book 8, 3:6.5–7.1.

7.  Cicero, *Orator*, trans. H. M. Hubbell, in *Cicero: Brutus and Orator*, ed. T. E. Page et al. (London: William Heinemann, 1929), 23:78.8–79.8. Cf. in Michel Foucault, *Histoire de la sexualité* 2: *L'Usage des plaisirs* (Paris: Gallimard, 1984), on the significance of make-up in ancient ethics (178–81).

8.  Francis Wey, "Comment le soleil est devenu peintre," *Musée des Familles* (July 1855), 290–91.

9.  In *The Colonial Harem*, trans. Myrna Godzich and Wlad Godzich (Minneapolis: University of Minnesota Press, 1986), Malek Alloula studies a sub-genre of orientalist iconography: postcards of colonized Algeria. The colonial postcard represents the clearest confirmation of the link between photography and the colonialist enterprise.

10. In his *History of Photography* (New York: The Museum of Modern Art, 1982), Beaumont Newhall cites "the French diplomat Baron Jean Baptiste Louis Gros" as one of the first international travelers to record what he saw by daguerreotypes (27). Newhall's chapters on the birth of the new technology contain numerous quotations from contemporaries dazzled by the detail of the earliest prints.

11. Francis Wey, "Photographes et Lithographes," *La Lumière* (October 1851), 146. On the "mimetic rivalry" between landscape painters and photographers, see Aaron Scharf, *Art and Photography* (New York: Viking Penguin, 1986), esp. "Landscape and genre," 77–118. According to Scharf many landscape painters dedicated to absolute pictorial veracity, especially the French orientalists and the English pre-Raphaelites, appropriated photography to their own representational ends. For Scharf on Wey, see 344.

12. Gisèle Freund, *Photography & Society*, trans. Richard M. Dunn et al. (Boston: David

R. Godine, 1980), 64. Disdéri, who dominated the field of early commercial daguerreotype portraiture, made quite explicit his adherence to classical pictorial aesthetic canons and often sacrificed accuracy in order to flatter his predominantly
bourgeois clientele. For an interesting Marxist history of the birth of photography,
see André Rouillé, *L'empire de la photographie: photographie et pouvoir bourgeois 1839–
1870* (Paris: Le Sycomore, 1982). August Sanders, whose *Men of the Twentieth Century*
records the faces of pre-Nazi Germany in chilling detail, represents the modern
refusal of idealization. The story is told that when he made the first print of the
"Barman"—using orthochromatic plates—the model protested vigorously against
the pockmarks the print exposed to view. Using the more popular panchromatic
plate, Sanders made a second print, more flattering to the model. In *Faces of Our
Times*, however, Sanders chose to reprint the first because he judged it more "characteristic" (August Sanders, *Hommes du XXè siècle*, text by Ulrich Keller [Chêne/
Hachette, 1980]).

13. Francis Wey, "Théorie du portrait (II)," *La Lumière* (May 1851), 51.

14. Charles Baudelaire, "Salon of 1846," in *Art in Paris 1845–1862: Salons and Other
Exhibitions*, trans. and ed. Jonathan Mayne (London: Phaidon Press, 1965), 49.

15. Wey, "Théorie du portrait (II)," 51. Cf. Lady Elizabeth Eastlake on "Photography"
in Alan Trachtenberg, ed., *Classic Essays on Photography* (New Haven: Leete's Island
Books, 1980), 60–63.

16. Wey, "Comment le soleil est devenu peintre," 298.

17. G. W. F. Hegel, *Aesthetics: Lectures on Fine Art*, trans. T. M. Knox, 2 vols. (Oxford:
Clarendon Press, 1975), 1:31.

18. Adolf Loos, "Ornament and Crime," in Ludwig Münz and Gustav Künstler, *Adolf
Loos, Pioneer of Modern Architecture* (New York: Praeger, 1966), 226. All subsequent
references to this essay will be incorporated in the text.

19. On Loos's bourgeois puritanism, see Theodor W. Adorno, "Functionalism Today,"
trans. Jane O. Newman and John H. Smith, *Oppositions*, 17 (Summer 1979), 34.
Adorno's essay is a subtle deconstruction of functionalism and its Kantian under-
pinnings, namely the grounding opposition between the purposeful and the pur-
pose-free.

20. Loos, *Spoken in the Void: Collected Essays 1897–1900*, trans. Jane O. Newman and John
H. Smith (Cambridge: The MIT Press, 1982), 102.

21. Loos, *Spoken in the Void*, 99.

22. Ibid., 103.

23. Ibid., 35.

24. In the light of this passage, it is difficult to understand how Benedetto Gravagnuolo,
with whose perceptive analysis of this essay I am otherwise in total agreement, can
state that Loos failed to understand "the logic of capitalist production": "What
stands out, in the end, is his essential failure to understand the mechanisms of
planned and rapid obsolescence of merchandise, dictated by the need to accelerate
the consumption of products" (*Adolf Loos: Theory and Works* [New York: Rizzoli,
1982], 66). It seems to me, on the contrary, that Loos lays bare this mechanism,
which is not to say, of course, that he accepts it with equanimity as an inalterable,
which is to say natural law of consumption.

25.   Loos, *Spoken in the Void*, 99.

26.   The elitism of modernist designers is central to Brent Brolin's recent attempt to account for ornament's virtual disappearance at the beginning of the twentieth century, *Flight of Fancy: The Banishment and Return of Ornament* (New York: St Martin's Press, 1985). According to Brolin, the answer to the mystery of the disappearing ornament is to be found in the class struggle between a newly elevated artistic elite and a newly affluent middle class: because the *nouveau riche* had an "unrestrained love of ornament" (5), which they sought to impose on the artistic marketplace, the only strategy available to designers to assert their "good taste" was to renounce "all ornament as part of a program that rejected virtually all middle-class values" (12).

27.   Hubert Damisch, *Ruptures/Cultures* (Paris: Minuit, 1976), 150. Cf. Baudelaire's observation: "Absolute simplicity which is, in fact, the best way to distinguish oneself."

28.   Jean Baudrillard, *Le système des objets* (Paris: Gallimard, "Tel," 1968), 207.

29.   Roland Barthes, *The Fashion System*, trans. Matthew Ward and Richard Howard (New York: Hill and Wang, 1983), 243.

30.   Georg Lukács, *The Theory of the Novel*, trans. Anna Bostock (Cambridge: MIT Press, 1971), 18 and 15.

31.   Georg Lukács, *Studies in European Realism* (New York: Grosset and Dunlap, 1964), 143–44.

32.   Charles Augustin Sainte-Beuve, "*Madame Bovary* by Gustave Flaubert," trans. Paul de Man in *Madame Bovary* (New York: Norton, A Norton Critical Edition, 1965), 334. As the link established here between details and eroticism suggests, the repression of the detail, as well as of the ornament, is always carried out in the name of a certain moral code; it is a form of *aesthetic Puritanism*. That the detail should figure prominently in pornography—in pornography, writes Baudrillard in *De la séduction*, "the hallucination of the detail reigns supreme"—only serves to confirm Sainte-Beuve's sense that highly detailed descriptions, especially of a woman in the throes of death-agony, can be sexually arousing. A note in passing: there is nothing particularly surprising about the agreement between Sainte-Beuve and Lukács on this point. Lukács's condemnation of Flaubert's *Salammbô* in *The Historical Novel* is nothing but an extrapolation from the debate between Sainte-Beuve and Flaubert provoked by Sainte-Beuve's famous critique of the novel.

33.   Lukács's condemnation of Flaubert's description of Madame Bovary's suicide—especially when set side by side with Sainte-Beuve's—raises, if somewhat obliquely, the question of the relationship which obtains in Lukács between his contempt for the merely contingent detail of naturalist prose and sexual difference. That Lukács's poetics is implicitly phallocentric was convincingly argued some years ago by Michael Danahy in his fundamental article, "Le roman est-il chose femelle?" Commenting on Lukács's theory of the rise of the novel in the wake of the decline of the epic, that virile genre par excellence, Danahy writes: "Having considered the subordination of the novel to poetry and drama, the problem of its subjection to epic narration remains. Lukács provides, in a theoretical vein, the example of an author who attributes just such a fate to the novel. He does so via a detour, when, defining the novel in relationship to authentic and classical genres, he introduces a concept of woman which makes of her a failed man, one who is incomplete and imperfect. What has been lost in the passage from the solid epic narrative to the

novel is a vigorous heroic figure. Tolstoy is to be praised for having been epic. Lukács's declarations about him are positive and imply through their connotations, power and masculinity" (*Poétique*, 25 [1976], 97).

That the privileging of the patriarchal epic over the feminized novel is but the obverse side of the idealist conviction that man is *the* form-giver is admirably confirmed by this passage drawn from an early book review by Lukács: "There have existed in history highly talented women writers and painters, and yet, the remark of a German art historian still remains true that there are few women who do not besmirch themselves when they take a paint brush in hand. It is a curious but irrefutable fact: but the work of art enriches the man, what is more, it even brings to light from the depth of his being values which, without the work, would have forever remained unknown even to himself. But woman is always lovelier and richer than that which she is destined to achieve and the most she can hope for is if her writing or painting vaguely suggests the kind of person behind the work of art. And the lives of even beautiful, sensitive and deep women appear noisily fussy or awkwardly lumpish if they attempt to give form to it in the work of art. I think the great women romanticists clearly understood . . . that this is how it is and how it has to be. And they were satisfied to carry on conversations, to hold salons, to write letters and in these letters and conversations there glows the memory of all those qualities for which they were once loved. Where can we find the inner humanity of the great and famous women writers? We can sense something of George Sand's human beauty and elegance from her correspondence with Flaubert and we would love her dearly for it—if the clarity of our feelings were not muddied by the memory of her novels. It seems that men have invented forms, exclusively for the intensification of male emotions; it is probably men who first invented the need to give form to things." Lukács, "Kaffka Margit-rol," in *Magyar Hirlap*, Jan. 27, 1910, vol. 20, #22, 2–4, reprinted in *Lukács Gyorgy Ifjukori muvek* [Early Works of George Lukács] (Budapest: Magveto, 1977), 275–76. My thanks to my colleague Mary Gluck for having brought this passage to my attention and for having provided me with a translation of it.

34.   Georg Lukács, *Realism in our Time: Literature and the Class Struggle*, trans. John and Necke Mander (New York: Harper Torchbooks, 1971), 43.

35.   In his *Allegory: The Theory of a Symbolic Mode* (Ithaca: Cornell University Press, 1964), Angus Fletcher insists repeatedly on the affinity of allegory for the ornamental detail: "The texture of allegory is 'curiously inwrought,' worked in ornamental detail. This is not realism; it is surrealism" (198). Elsewhere Fletcher emphasizes the ornamentalism of naturalist texts. Paul de Man, writing of allegory in Proust, assigns to the "allegorical" or "iconic detail" (i.e. the kitchen maid's gravid belly in "Combray") a strategic role in the proper functioning of allegory: the fascinating detail is a lure which "sidetracks our attention" and binds us to the "potential resemblance" between the allegorical icon and the abstract idea it represents. If I understand de Man's meaning, allegory is the failure of the resemblance which founds metaphor. To paraphrase Freud, to succeed allegory must fail where metaphor succeeds. (*Allegories of Reading: Figural Language in Rousseau, Nietzsche, Rilke, and Proust* [New Haven: Yale University Press, 1979], 74).

36.   G. W. F. Hegel, *The Logic of Hegel*, trans. William Wallace (Oxford: Clarendon Press, 1874), 252.

37.   Stephen Bungay, *Beauty and Truth* (Oxford: Oxford University Press, 1984), 55. One of the most recent avatars of Hegel's triad occurs in the opening pages of Barthes's

*Writing Degree Zero.* Crossbred with Saussurean linguistics, the universal, the particular, and the individual produce *langue, parole,* and *écriture.* For more on Barthes and Hegel, see Chapter 5.

38.    "Das Besondere als zentrale Kategorie der Ästhetik," *Über die Besonderheit als Kategorie der Aesthetik* (Neuwied: Luchterhand, 1967), 209. I have relied heavily in what follows on the French translation of this text, "Le particulier comme catégorie centrale de l'esthétique," trans. Georges Kassai and Gérard Spitzer, *Les Lettres nouvelles,* Special issue on "Ecrivains hongrois d'aujourd'hui" (September-October 1964), 76–99. The references included in the text are first to the French, then to the German. On Lukács's late aesthetics, see: Bela Királyfalvi, *The Aesthetics of George Lukács* (Princeton: Princeton University Press, 1975); G. H. R. Parkinson, *George Lukács* (London: Routledge & Kegan Paul, 1977), 125–44.

39.    T. W. Adorno, *Aesthetic Theory,* trans. C. Lenhardt, eds., Gretel Adorno and Rolf Tiedemann (London: Routledge & Kegan Paul, 1984), 420. "Independent details" (420), argues Adorno in his characteristically dense reflection on the part-whole relationship, are an essential component of the work of art, which for him (as for Hegel and Lukács) is a "resultant of centripetal and centrifugal forces" (420). The "instant . . . of being touched" particularity provides makes possible the aesthetic experience, for "aesthetic experience can never grasp the whole in its immediacy, and yet immediacy is constitutive of aesthetic experience" (420). Modern art, notably uninspired constructivist modern music, is threatened by a traceless disappearance of the detail into the whole, a particularly unfortunate development because in the detail resides a possible point of resistance to the oppression of the individual by society. Particularization in art "undoes the enduring injustice that society perpetrates against the individual" (422).

40.    Charles Carlut, *La correspondance de Flaubert: Etude et répertoire critique* (Columbus: Ohio State University Press, 1968), 408.

41.    Flaubert, *Madame Bovary,* 52.

## 4.    Displacement: The Case of Sigmund Freud

1.    Nicholas Meyer, *The Seven-Per-Cent Solution* (New York: Ballantine Books, 1974), 181. The Holmes—Freud—Morelli connection is the object of a fascinating article on the emergence of a detail-based epistemology in late nineteenth-century social sciences. In "Clues: Morelli, Freud, and Sherlock Holmes" (in Eco, Umberto and Thomas A. Sebeok, eds., *The Sign of Three: Dupin, Holmes, Peirce* [Bloomington: Indiana University Press, 1983], 81 118), an article that appeared some years after the publication of the original French version of this chapter (1980), Carlo Ginzburg traces the root of what he calls the "symptomatic" or "semiotic" paradigm all the way back to man's origins as a hunter and, less fancifully, to the early conjuncture of diagnostic flair and art expertise represented by a prominent seventeenth-century Sienese physician and art collector, Giulio Mancini, the author of the first treatise on what was to come to be known a century later as "connoisseurship." It is no accident then that Morelli, Freud, and Conan Doyle were all doctors, trained in the practice of "medical semiotics" (87). Ginzburg hints at but does not develop the argument that the "low intuition" rooted in the senses which is at work in the interpretation of clues is a peculiarly female gift: "It was the heritage, he writes in his conclusion, of the Bengalis whom Sir William Herschel expropriated, of hunters, of mariners,

of women. It forms a tight link between the human animal and other animal species" (110–11). In n. 23, Ginzburg promises more on women and their presence in the domain of Metis in the expanded version of this piece.

2. Michel Foucault, *Discipline and Punish: The Birth of the Prison*, trans. Alan Sheridan (New York: Pantheon Books, 1977), 141.

3. See Roman Jakobson and Morris Halle, *Fundamentals of Language* (The Hague: Mouton, 1956); Edgar Wind, *Art and Anarchy*, revised and enlarged (New York: Knopf, 1964); Edward Said, "The Problem of Textuality: Two Exemplary Positions," *Critical Inquiry*, 4 (Summer 1978), 712, and *Orientalism* (New York: Pantheon Books, 1978).

4. Sigmund Freud, *The Standard Edition of the Complete Psychological Works of Sigmund Freud*, ed. James Strachey, trans. James Strachey et al., 24 vols. (London: Hogarth, 1953–74), 2:6. All German quotations refer to the *Gesammelte Werke*, 18 vols. (London: Imago Publishing Co. Ltd, 1940–1968), 1:85. All subsequent references to these editions will be included in the text.

5. Tzvetan Todorov, *Théories du symbole* (Paris: Seuil, 1977), 303. All translations mine except where otherwise noted. See also, Jacques Lacan, "The agency of the letter in the unconscious or reason since Freud," in *Ecrits*, trans. Alan Sheridan (New York: W. W. Norton, 1977), in particular 177, n. 20, and Jakobson, *Fundamentals*, 55–82.

6. Freud's analogy calls to mind Pliny's anecdote about the contest between Zeuxis and Parrhasios, where what the illusionistic veil screens off—if anything—remains forever hidden. The recurrence of the detail of the veil in such vastly different contexts suggests that Freud's seemingly absurd analogy is motivated at least partially by the association of screens and veils, both of which serve as means of concealment.

7. Wladimir Granoff, *La pensée et le féminin* (Paris: Minuit, 1976), 363–64. Cf. the remark of Laplanche and Pontalis: "French translators occasionally use the term *souvenir de couverture*." (Jean Laplanche and J.-B. Pontalis, *Vocabulaire de la psychanalyse* [Paris: Presses Universitaires de France, 1967], 451). This note does not appear in the English translation of the *Vocabulaire*.

8. Granoff, *La pensée*, 364.

9. Jacques Derrida, *Glas* (Paris: Galilée, 1974), 52.

10. Granoff, 358.

11. In French: *"on jette un voile, on dit la chose avec des fleurs."*

12. Alain Robbe-Grillet, "Du réalisme à la réalité," in *Pour un nouveau roman* (Paris: Gallimard, 1963), 177–78.

13. The relationship between details and deception is a complex one, for if the detail is the fulcrum of truth two seemingly contradictory principles follow: one, enunciated above, that the detail must be falsified to ensure deceit, two, as illustrated below, that a true detail must be mixed in with the false to enable deceit. This second principle is the one that informs Odette's lie to Swann in Proust's *Swann in Love*: "Swann could at once detect in this story one of these fragments of literal truth which liars, caught off guard, console themselves by introducing into the composition of the falsehood which they have to invent, thinking that it can safely be incorporated and will lend the whole story an air of verisimilitude" (Marcel Proust,

*Remembrance of Things Past*, trans. C. K. Scott Moncrieff and Terence Kilmartin, 3 vols. [New York: Random House, 1981], 1:303). In fact, the hoped for metonymic contagion, what Freud refers to as the "protection" exerted by truth over error, perversely backfires and the poor fit between the true detail and the false context gives away the deception: "But she was wrong; it *was* what gave her away; she had failed to realise that this fragmentary detail of the truth had sharp edges which could not be made to fit in, except with those contiguous fragments of the truth from which she had arbitrarily detached it, edges which, whatever the fictitious details in which she might embed it, would continue to show, by their overlapping angles and by the gaps she had forgotten to fill in, that its proper place is elsewhere" (ibid.). In the case of the failed deception, Freud's as well as Odette's, contiguity is undone by the lack of similarity which introduces a fissure between the true and the fictitious details.

14.  Ernest Jones, *The Life and Work of Sigmund Freud*. Vol. 1. *The Young Freud 1856–1900*. 2 vols. (London: Hogarth, 1953), 27–28. See also Siegfried Bernfeld, "An Unknown Autobiographical Fragment by Freud," *American Imago* 4 (1946), reprint.

15.  Jones, 28.

16.  Sigmund Freud, letter 70 (October 4 1897), *The Origins of Psychoanalysis: Letters to Wilhelm Fliess*, trans. Eric Mosbacher and James Strachey (New York: Basic Books, Harper Colophon Books, 1954), 220. In her provocative study of Freud's renunciation of his seduction theory, *L'homme aux statues: Freud et la faute cachée du père* (Paris: Grasset, 1979), Marie Balmary proposes another, less "easy" interpretation of this dream-detail, one in keeping with her reconstruction of Freud's father's secret crime: the suicide of his repudiated second wife, the mysterious Rebecca Freud (231).

## 5.   Desublimation: Roland Barthes's Aesthetics

1.  Sir Joshua Reynolds, *Discourses on Art*, ed. Robert R. Wark (New Haven: Yale University Press, 1975), 58.

2.  Roland Barthes, *Roland Barthes by Roland Barthes*, trans. Richard Howard (New York: Hill and Wang, 1977), 94. Cited hereafter as *RB*.

3.  Roland Barthes, *The Eiffel Tower and Other Mythologies*, trans. Richard Howard (New York: Hill and Wang, 1979), 19. Cited hereafter as *ET*.

4.  Roland Barthes, *Mythologies*, trans. Annette Lavers (New York: Hill and Wang, 1972), 57. Cited hereafter as *M*.

5.  M. H. Abrams, *Natural Supernaturalism: Tradition and Revolution in Romantic Literature* (New York: W. W. Norton, 1971), 391.

6.  Roland Barthes, "The Reality Effect," in Tzvetan Todorov, ed., *French Literary Theory Today*, trans. R. Carter (Cambridge: Cambridge University Press, 1982), 11 (translation modified). Cited hereafter as *RE*. The notion that realist fiction is replete with superfluous details does not, of course, originate with Barthes; it is, as we have seen, a recurrent complaint among realism's detractors. Closer to Barthes is George Orwell who, in his essay on Dickens, makes much of what he calls, "the outstanding, unmistakeable mark of Dickens's writing . . . the *unnecessary detail*" (George Orwell, "Charles Dickens," in *Collected Essays* [London: Secker and Warburg, 1961], 75); the example Orwell cites of such a detail could serve equally well to illusstrate the reality

effect. But, having identified this characteristic stylistic effect of Dickens', Orwell is less concerned with taking apart its mechanism than with defending Dickens's piling on of such "florid squiggles on the edge of the page" (76): "Everything is piled up and up, detail on detail, embroidery on embroidery. It is futile to object that this kind of thing is rococo—one might as well make the same objection to a wedding cake" (78; cf. the wedding cake in *Madame Bovary*).

7. Barthes, *Critical Essays*, trans. Richard Howard (Evanston: Northwestern University Press, 1972), 159. Cited hereafter as *CE*.

8. Barthes, *L'empire des signes* (Paris: Champs-Flammarion, 1970), translation mine.

9. Barthes, *Empire of Signs*, trans. Richard Howard (New York: Hill and Wang, 1982), 79. Cited hereafter as *EoS*.

10. In his article "Review of the Arts and Crafts" (*Die Wage*, 1898), Adolf Loos writes: "The Rococo had to go as far as China; for us, only Japan still remains." He goes on to say in terms that distantly presage Barthes's: " 'Japanese' . . . means the de-materialization of the objects being represented. The Japanese represent flowers, but they are pressed flowers . . . It is a kind of stylizing that is expressly meant to decorate the surface. But at the same time naturalism is maintained," *Spoken in the Void*, trans. Jane O. Newman and John H. Smith (Cambridge: MIT Press, 1982), 105.

11. Barthes, *Camera Lucida: Reflections on Photography*, trans. Richard Howard (New York: Hill and Wang, 1981), 4–5. Hereafter cited as *CL*. Cf. G. W. F. Hegel, *Phenomenology of Spirit*, trans. A. V. Miller (Oxford: Oxford University Press, 1977), 58–66. Hegel's *Phenomenology of Spirit* opens with a consideration of the *this* and its two principal modalities, the *here* and the *now*. For Hegel the *this*'s apparent designation of the sensual world in its absolute particularity is nothing but an illusion grounding man's "sense-certainty." In fact, the *this* is a *universality*, a plurality of thises, in the lexicon of structuralist linguistics, a *shifter*. From Hegel's perspective, as I understand it, Barthes's error here would lie not so much in his belief in the "sovereign Contingency" of what is pointed to, as in—surprisingly—Barthes's forgetting of the linguistic properties inherent in the deictic sign itself: "They speak of the existence of *external* objects, which can be more precisely defined as *actual*, absolutely *singular*, *wholly personal*, *individual* things, each of them absolutely unlike anything else; this existence, they say, has absolute certainty and truth. They *mean* 'this' bit of paper on which I am writing—or rather have written—'this'; but what they mean is not what they say. If they actually wanted to *say* 'this' bit of paper which they mean, if they wanted to *say* it, then this is impossible, because the sensuous This that is meant *cannot be reached* by language, which belongs to consciousness, i.e. to that which is inherently universal" (Hegel, *Phenomenology*, 66).

12. Barthes, "The Third Meaning" in *Image—Music—Text*, trans. Stephen Heath (New York: Hill and Wang, 1977), 56. Cited hereafter as I-M-T.

13. Barthes, *The Pleasure of the Text*, trans. Richard Miller (New York: Hill and Wang, 1975), 45. Cited hereafter as *PoT*.

14. Randolph Runyon, *Fowles/Irving/Barthes: Canonical Variations on an Apocrypha Theme* (Oxford, Ohio: Ohio State University Press for Miami University, 1981).

15. Barthes, *A Lover's Discourse: Fragments*, trans. Richard Howard (New York: Hill and Wang, 1979), 20, 72, and 191.

16. Cf. in *Camera*, Barthes's comments on the self-portrait of the photographer Robert

Mapplethorpe: "The photographer has caught the boy's hand (the boy is Mapplethorpe himself, I believe) at just the right degree of openness, the right density of abandonment" (59). See also Barthes's remarks regarding Mapplethorpe's photograph of Robert Wilson and Philip Glass: "Wilson *holds* me, though I cannot say why; i.e. say *where*: is it the eyes, the skin, the position of the hands . . ." (51). On the V see Sigmund Freud, *S. E.*, 17:89–95. See also Serge Leclaire, *Psychanalyser* (Paris: Seuil, 1968), 90–93.

17.    For more on Barthes's erasure of sexual difference and more specifically femininity, see my "Dreaming Dissymmetry: Barthes, Foucault, and Sexual Difference," forthcoming in *Men in Feminism*, eds. Alice Jardine and Paul Smith (New York: Methuen, 1987).

## 6.  Dali's Freud

1.    André Breton, as quoted by Salvador Dali in *The Conquest of the Irrational*, trans. David Gascoyne (Paris: Maison Ramlot, 1935), 7. For a more recent evaluation of Dali's method, see Haim Finkelstein, "Dali's Paranoia-Criticism or The Exercise of Freedom," *Twentieth-Century Literature*, 21 (February 1975), 59–70.

2.    These expressions are drawn from Freud's letter to Stefan Zweig *re* Dali: "I really have reason to thank you for the introduction which brought me yesterday's visitors. For until then I was inclined to look upon surrealists, who have apparently chosen me for their patron saint, as absolute (let us say 95 per cent, like alcohol) cranks. The young Spaniard, however, with his candid fanatical eyes and his undeniable technical mastery, has made me reconsider my opinion." In *Letters of Sigmund Freud*, ed. Ernst Freud, trans. Tania and James Stern (New York: Basic Books, 1960), 448–49. Cf. Dali's account of this same meeting in *The Secret Life of Salvador Dali*, trans. Haakon Chevalier (New York: Dial Press, 1942), 24–25; this account is, in turn, the necessary companion piece to Dali's account of his first meeting with Lacan, quoted below.

3.    Dali, *The Secret Life*, 18.

4.    As quoted by Henri-François Rey in *Dali dans son labyrinthe* (Paris: Grasset, 1974), 187–88. All translations mine except where otherwise noted.

5.    Freud, *The Standard Edition of the Complete Psychological Works of Sigmund Freud*, ed. James Strachey, trans. James Strachey et al., 24 vols. (London: Hogarth Press, 1953–74), 6:255.

6.    Jean-Paul Sartre, *Saint Genêt, Comédien et martyr* (Paris: Gallimard, 1952), 26.

7.    Dali, *Le mythe tragique de l'Angélus de Millet* (Paris: Pauvert, 1963), 17. All subsequent quotations from this work will be included in the text.

8.    Freud, *The Standard Edition*, 13:229.

9.    James Thrall Soby, "Freud and Modern Art," *Saturday Review*, May 5, 1956, 12.

10.    An irresistible—because singularly apt—example comes to mind; I am referring to Richard Klein's review article on Paul de Man's *Blindness and Insight*, "The Blindness of Hyperboles: The Ellipses of Insight," *Diacritics*, 3 (Summer 1973), 33–44. In an attempt to explain the "repression" (43) of Freud in de Man's work, Klein constructs a hypothesis based on the presumption that Henri de Man—"the first serious Marx-

ist thinker to apply explicitly Freudian categories to the analysis of alienation" (42)—is Paul de Man's father: "The sketch on the father allows us to dream the shape of a *psycho-critical narrative*: The work of the son manipulates the proto-Freudian categories of blindness and insight, all the while systematically refusing to read Freud, the father's text" (43; italics mine). The seductions of the Oedipal solution must, however, be abandoned when Paul de Man informs Klein that Henri is his uncle and not his father. In a postscript which attests to the remarkable resiliency of the paranoiac-critical construction, Klein muses, by way of conclusion: "What, after all, is an uncle?" (44).

11. The question of Leonardo's kite/Freud's vulture has become a psycho-critical topos; see, for example, Meyer Shapiro, "Leonardo and Freud: An Art-Historical Study," *Journal of the History of Ideas*, 17 (1957), 147–78, and, more recently, Charlotte F. Johnson, "Leonardo and Dante," *American Imago*, 29 (Spring 1972), 177–85.

12. Freud, *The Standard Edition*, 23:265. The peculiar difficulties of transcoding the fundamental questions raised by Freud in this essay, from the therapeutic to the critical domain, are discussed by Sarah Kofman in *L'enfance de l'art* (Paris: Payot, 1970), 96–104.

13. See Whitney Chadwick, "Masson's *Gradiva*: The Metamorphosis of a Surrealist Myth," *Art Bulletin*, 52 (December 1970), 415–23.

14. André Breton, *Manifestes du surréalisme* (Paris: Gallimard, "Idées," 1969), 76.

## 7. The Delusion of Interpretation: *The Conquest of Plassans*

1. See Michel Foucault, *Madness and Civilization*, trans. Richard Howard (New York: Random House, 1965), and *Discipline and Punish*, trans. Alan Sheridan (New York: Pantheon Books, 1977), especially III (Discipline) and IV (Prison).

   A somewhat different version of this text appears in my *Zola's Crowds* (Baltimore: The Johns Hopkins University Press, 1978), 54–63.

2. Zola, *Le Docteur Pascal* in Henri Mitterand, ed., *Les Rougon-Macquart*, 5 vols. (Paris: Pléiade, 1960–67), 5:977. All subsequent references to this edition will be indicated in the text by *R-M* followed by volume and page numbers.

3. Zola, *The Conquest of Plassans*, ed. E. A. Vizetelly (London: Chatto and Windus, 1900), 212. All subsequent references to this work are included in the text. T. M. stands for Translation Modified.

4. Cf. Robert Ricatte, "Les romans des Goncourt et la médecine," *Revue des Sciences Humaines*, 69 (January-March 1953), 27–43, especially the notes on *Charles Demailly*, 37–39. If the novel begins to resemble psychiatric manuals, these manuals are equally indebted to the novel, as is evidenced in a remark made by one of the characters in *The Conquest*: "The doctor here has just been reciting to us a page out of a book on lucid madness, which I have read, and which is as interesting as a novel" (239). In addition, in his resumé of the works of Kraepelin, Lacan writes: "We mention only one trait, which Kraepelin notes as characteristic, common to the French work on the subject (paranoia). Above all, their efforts are aimed at depicting the clinical details by the liveliest description possible." Jacques Lacan, *De la psychose paranoïaque dans ses rapports avec la personnalité* (Paris: Seuil, 1975), 24.

5. Maxime Du Camp, *Paris, ses organes, ses fonctions et sa vie*, 4 vols. (Paris: Hachette,

1873), 4:325. Let us note that the praise of the asylum leads (inevitably) to the positive valorization of perpetual surveillance of the ill, 347. Translation mine except where otherwise noted (TN).

6.   René Girard, *La violence et le sacré* (Paris: Grasset, 1972), 375.

7.   Zola, *Le roman expérimental*, in Henri Mitterand, ed., *Oeuvres complètes*, 15 vols. (Paris: Cercle du Livre Précieux, 1962–69), 10:1181.

8.   Cf. the internment of Aunt Dide, which is situated outside the text, between *The Fortune of the Rougons* and *The Conquest of Plassans*. It is otherwise impossible to fix the date of this internment, because on the family tree of 1893, it takes place in 1831, while on that of 1878, Zola indicates the year 1851.

9.   Sigmund Freud, *The Standard Edition of the Complete Psychological Works of Sigmund Freud*, ed. James Strachey, trans. James Strachey et al., 24 vols. (London: Hogarth Press, 1953–74), 6:255.

   The technical equivalent of "le délire d'interprétation" is "the delusion of reference," a type of paranoia wherein a fact or detail is seized upon as having great personal ramifications, leading to all manner of erroneous conclusions. Because the psychiatrically correct equivalent does not render the intended pun, I have preferred to translate literally. (TN)

10.   See Oswald Ducrot and Tzvetan Todorov, *Encyclopedic Dictionary of the Sciences of Language*, trans. Catherine Porter (Baltimore: The Johns Hopkins University Press, 1979), 105.

11.   I borrow this expression from Philippe Hamon, "What Is Description?" in *French Literary Theory Today*, ed. Tzvetan Todorov, trans. R. Carter (Cambridge: Cambridge University Press, 1982).

12.   See Freud, *The Standard Edition*, 4:242–48.

13.   The French for "the worker of the hat"—*le travailleur du chapeau*—is an idiomatic expression used to describe someone who is considered mad. (TN) The persistence of the association *hat-madness* throughout Zola's *oeuvre* is simply astonishing. Already Maurin in "Story of a Madman" is considered mad because he goes for a walk "on the place du Panthéon *without a hat* on a rainy day" (*R-M*, 1:1643; emphasis added). Approximately twenty-five years later, during Dr. Pascal's visit to the asylum of the Tulettes, the problem is with one of his guinea-pigs: "a hatter, Sarteur, who had been in the Asylum for a year, where he had himself come begging to be locked up so that he would not commit a crime," *R-M*, 5:977. Let us recapitulate in tabular form:

| HAT | MADNESS |
| --- | --- |
| hat (-) | sign of madness |
| hatter | judge of madness |
| hatter | agent of madness |
| hatter | madman |

14.   Zola, *Correspondance (1872–1902)* in Maurice Leblond, ed., *Oeuvres complètes*, 50 vols. (Paris: Bernouard, 1927–29), 636–37; emphasis added.

15.   Zola, "La mort d'Olivier Bécaille," *Naïs Micoulin* in *Oeuvres complètes* (Paris: Cercle du Livre Précieux, 1968), 9:750.

16.   Zola, *Germinal*, trans. Leonard Tancock (Harmondsworth: Penguin Books, 1954), 352; emphasis added.

8.  Fiction as Interpretation/Interpretation as Fiction

1.  In Sontag, *Against Interpretation* (New York: Dell, 1966), 15. Cf. Tzvetan Todorov, *Poétique de la prose* (Paris: Seuil, 1971), 245. All subsequent references will be included in the text.

2.  Franz Kafka, *The Trial*, trans. Willa and Edwin Muir (New York: Schocken, 1968), 217.

3.  Theodor Adorno, "Notes on Kafka," in *Prisms*, trans. S. and S. Weber (London: Spearman, 1967), 246; as quoted by Stanley Corngold in "The Hermeneutic of 'The Judgement,'" in Angel Flores, ed., *The Problem of "The Judgement": Eleven Approaches to Kafka's Story* (Staten Island, N.Y., 1977), 139. This chapter owes more to Professor Corngold than a mere footnote can convey; it has benefited overall from his generous and learned commentary.

4.  Erich Heller, *Franz Kafka* (New York: Viking, 1974), 72 and 71.

5.  Roland Barthes, *S/Z*, trans. Richard Miller (New York: Hill and Wang, 1974), 5.

6.  Genette, *Figures of Literary Discourse*, trans. Alan Sheridan, intro. Marie-Rose Logan (New York: Columbia University Press, 1982); Todorov, *Poétique de la prose* (Paris: Seuil, 1971).

7.  In addition to the critics cited throughout this chapter, others might be mentioned. Several recent examples of this trend: Paul de Man, "Proust et l'allégorie de la lecture," in *Mouvements premiers: Etudes critiques offertes à Georges Poulet* (Paris, 1972); Max Byrd, "Reading in *Great Expectations*," PMLA, 91 (1976), 259–65; and Philippe Hamon, "Texte littéraire et métalangage," *Poétique*, 31 (1977), 261–84. In an altogether different paradigm: Algirdas Julien Greimas, *Maupassant: La sémiotique du texte* (Paris: Seuil, 1976), in particular 175–89 ("La Réinterprétation"). In this work Greimas introduces a new descriptive term, "le faire interprétatif," which, while not synonymous with our notion of "interpretation as performance" (the differences being those of scale—sentence versus novel—and methodological preoccupations—narratology versus hermeneutics), is to be retained for dealing with interpretation as manifested in microunits of the text.

8.  Kafka, *The Trial*, 126.

9.  Green, *Un oeil en trop* (Paris: Minuit, 1969), 282. Translation mine.

10. See Charles Sanders Peirce, *Collected Papers*, ed. Charles Hartshorne and Paul Weiss, vols. 1–2 (Cambridge: Harvard University Press, 1960): "A sign stands *for* something *to* the idea which it produces, or modifies. Or, it is a vehicle conveying into the mind something from without. That for which it stands is called its *object*; that which it conveys, its *meaning*; and the idea to which it gives rise, its *interpretant*" (1:171). It might be, indeed it already has been suggested, that I would do better to develop a new terminology and leave the interpretant to the linguists. If I have chosen to maintain the term it is partly because of the interpretant/analysand homophony, and partly because, as I hope to show in my conclusion, my meaning and Peirce's are not so far apart as they at first appear.

11. See Gerald Prince, "Introduction à l'étude du narrataire," *Poétique*, 14 (1973), 178–96.

12. See Walter J. Ong, S. J., "The Writer's Audience is Always a Fiction," PMLA, 90 (1975), 9–21.

13. See Wolfgang Iser, *The Implied Reader* (Baltimore: The Johns Hopkins University Press, 1974).

14. This formulation is not restrictive: secondary characters can and do perform important interpretative functions; indeed there are novels where the main protagonist, because he is either an "innocent" or an enigma or both, while not ceasing all interpretative activities, plays a largely passive role in the hermeneutic script. Two examples that come to mind, Balzac's *Le Cousin Pons* and Zola's *Le Ventre de Paris*, share a common feature: interpretation as practiced by the secondary characters is a form of persecution; the hermeneutic object is a scapegoat.

15. Doubrovsky, *La place de la madeleine* (Paris: Mercure de France, 1974), 153.

16. Lyall H. Powers, ed., *Henry James's Major Novels: Essays in Criticism* (East Lansing: Michigan State University Press, 1973), xxxii.

17. Tony Tanner, "Henry James's Subjective Adventurers: *The Sacred Fount*," in *Henry James's Major Novels*, 225.

18. Henry James, *In the Cage and Other Tales* (New York: Norton, 1969), 182. All subsequent page references in the text are to this edition.

19. James, *The Art of the Novel* (New York: Scribner, 1962), 157; emphasis added.

20. Ibid., 64.

21. James, *In the Cage*, 187.

22. Gilles Deleuze, *Proust and Signs*, trans. Richard Howard (New York: George Braziller, 1972), 1.

23. Ibid., 160–61 and 16.

24. Marcel Proust, *Remembrance of Things Past*, trans. C. K. Scott Moncrieff and Terence Kilmartin, 3 vols. (New York: Random House, 1981), 1:293. All subsequent references are to this edition.

25. The interpretant's class, gender and occupation are determining factors second in importance only to his place in literary history. Swann's "advantages" have jaded his interpretative appetite, while the postal clerk's deprivations have whet hers. If in James (and in Proust, too, viz. Charlus) male interpretants do often belong to Swann's class and age group, they operate out of some imperative affective constraint (though nothing so vulgar as jealousy—see, for example, Lambert Strether in *The Ambassadors*), or function as the author's persona which Swann, the narrator's foil, is most emphatically not. The case of female interpretants of this class is altogether different: they are always compelled by some sort of erotic constraint. As for the lower- and lower-middle-class characters, the male interpretants tend to be bureaucrats (as in Dostoyevsky), and the female, professional busybodies such as old maids and concierges (as in Balzac). The female bureaucrat, the young lady "in the cage," represents a super-interpretant, syncretizing as she does the "natural" interpretative attributes of her sex with the interpretative opportunities inherent in her position.

26. Charles Bernheimer, "Symbolic Bond and Textual Play: The Structure of Kafka's

*Castle,"* in *The Kafka Debate,* ed. Angel Flores (Staten Island, N.Y.: Gordian Press, 1977), 367.

27.  Kafka, *The Trial,* 44. All subsequent page references in the text are to the Schocken edition.

28.  See Stanley Corngold, *The Commentators' Despair* (Port Washington, N.Y.: Kennikat Press, 1973), 31–38.

29.  See Michael Riffaterre, *Essais de stylistique structurale* (Paris: Flammarion, 1971), 68–78.

30.  J. Hillis Miller, "The Interpretation of *Lord Jim,"* in *The Interpretation of Narrative: Theory and Practice,* ed. Morton W. Bloomfield (Cambridge: Harvard University Press, 1970), 211.

31.  James, *The Art of the Novel,* 63.

32.  Peirce, *Collected Papers,* 1:171.

33.  Said, *Beginnings: Intention and Method* (New York: Basic Books, 1975), 315.

## 9.  Duane Hanson: Truth in Sculpture

1.  Michael Greenwood, "Current Representational Art: Five Other Visions," *artscanada,* 210–11 (December 76–January 77), 24.

2.  Honoré de Balzac, *The Quest of the Absolute,* trans. Ellen Marriage (New York: A. L. Burt, 1899), 2.

3.  Roland Barthes, "The Reality Effect" in Todorov, Tzvetan, ed., *French Literary Theory Today,* trans. R. Carter (Cambridge: Cambridge University Press, 1982).

4.  Brian O'Doherty, *Art Forum,* and Jürgen Beckelmann, *Erlanger Tagblatt,* as quoted by Martin H. Buoh, *Duane Hanson* (Wichita, Kans · Wichita State University Press, 1976).

5.  Sigmund Freud, "The 'Uncanny'," in *The Standard Edition of the Complete Psychological Works of Sigmund Freud,* ed. James Strachey, trans. James Strachey et al., 24 vols. (London: Hogarth Press, 1953–74), 17:219–20. All subsequent references to this edition are included in the text.

6.  Hélène Cixous, "Fiction and Its Phantoms: A Reading of Freud's *Das Unheimliche* (The 'uncanny')," trans. Robert Dennomé, *New Literary History,* 7 (Spring 1976), 534. All subsequent references to this article are included in the text.

7.  An inexplicable move on the part of the author of *The Moses of Michelangelo.* Indeed, Freud's failure to deal specifically with the uncanny in sculpture is all the more regrettable as in his single essay devoted entirely to a work of sculpture, the status of the detail is very much in question. His (re)interpretation of the enigmatic stone figure rests on nothing more substantial than the revalorization of two details: "Now in two places in the figure of Moses there are certain details which have hitherto not only escaped notice—but, in fact, have not even been properly described" (*S. E.,* 13:222). And these details are very emphatically sculptural details, which is to say convexities which stand out and catch the onlooker's eye: the "loop of the beard" (224) and "a protuberance like a horn" (226) on the bottom of the Tablets of the Law. It is no coincidence that it is in his unique essay on sculpture that Freud deals

most explicitly with the hermeneutics of the detail, because the sculptural detail enjoys paradigmatic status—unlike the literary detail whose prominence relies on stylistic effects (the form of the expression) and/or derives from an extratextual connection (the form of the referent) and is thus in some way mediated, the sculptural detail stands out directly, can be apprehended by both the eye and the hand.

8.  Ernst Jentsch, "Zur Psychologie des Unheimlichen," *Psychiatrisch-Neurologische Wochenscrift* (1906), 22:198.

> Bekannt ist der unangenehme Eindruck, der bei manchen Menschen durch den Besuch von Wachsfigurencabinetten, Panopticis und Panoramen leicht ensteht. Es ist namentlich im Halbdunkel oft schwer, eine lebensgrosse Wachs- oder ähnliche Figur von einer Person zu unterscheiden. Für manche sensitive Gemüther vermag eine solche Figur auch nach der vom Individuum getroffenen Entscheidung, ob sie belebt sei oder nicht, ihre Ungemüthlichkeit zu behalten. Wahrscheinlich handelt es sich hier um halbbewusste secundäre Zweifel, die durch die erneute Betrachtung und die Wahrnehmung der feineren Einzelheiten immer wieder von neuem automatisch ausgelöst werden, vielleicht auch nur um ein blosses lebhaftes Nachschwingen der Erinnerung an den ersten peinlichen Eindruck. Dass solche Wachsfiguren oft anatomische Einzelheiten zur Darstellung bringen, mag zur Steigerung der gedachten Gefühlswirkung beitragen, ist aber durchaus nicht die Hauptsache: ein wirkliches anatomisches Leichenpräparat braucht nicht entfernt so widerwärtig auszusehen, als die entsprechende Modelirung in Wachs.

The translations of Jentsch are my own; I do want, however, to thank my colleague William Crossgrove for his help in elucidating some tricky details. Although the greater part of Jentsch's two-part article is concerned with what one might call the uncanny in everyday life, it forms an essential complement to Freud's text and should be translated in its entirety.

9.  Joseph Mashek, "Verist Sculpture: Hanson and de Andrea," in Gregory Battcock, ed., *Super Realism: A Critical Anthology* (New York: Dutton, 1975), 196.

10.  Harold Rosenberg, "Reality Again," *Super Realism*, 139.

11.  Jacques Derrida, "The Parergon," trans. Craig Owens, *October*, 9 (Summer 1979), 18.

12.  Jentsch, 198:

> Es ist nebenbei bemerkt von Interesse, an diesem Beispiel zu sehen, wie die echte Kunst in weiser Mässigung die absolute und vollständige Nachahmung von Natur und Lebewesen, wohl wissend, dass bei einer solchen leicht Missbehagen entstehen kann, vermeidet: die Existenz einer polychromen Plastik in Holz und Stein ändert nichts an dieser Thatsache, ebenso die Möglichkeit, solchen unangenehmen Nebenwirkungen, falls diese Art der Darstellung dennoch gewählt wird, einigermaassen vorzubeugen. Uebrigens kann die Erzeugung des Unheimlichen in der echten Kunst zwar auch versucht werden, aber immer nur wieder mit künstlerischen Mitteln und in künstlerischer Intention.

13.  Gerritt Henry, "The Soho Body Snatcher," *ARTnews*, 71 (March 1972), 61.

## 10.  Details and Realism: The *Curé De Tours*

1.  See Ferdinand Brunetière, *Le roman naturaliste* (Paris: Calmann-Lévy, 1886); Roland Barthes, "The Reality Effect" in Todorov, Tzvetan, ed., *French Literary Theory Today:*

*A Reader*, trans. R. Carter (Cambridge: Cambridge University Press, 1982), 11–17; Georg Lukács, *Studies in European Realism* (New York: Grosset and Dunlap, 1964). Two further references might be adduced to indicate the prevalence and the persistence of the association of details and realism. The first is drawn from George Sand's review of Flaubert's *Salammbô*: "We would readily qualify realism as quite simply the science of details," *Questions d'art et de littérature* (Paris: Calmann-Lévy, 1878). The second occurs in the context of Bertolt Brecht's debate with Lukács over theories of realism: "There are a few generally recognized distinctive criteria of realism, such as the true detail . . . ," *Über Realismus* (Frankfurt: Suhrkamp, 1971), 124. All translations mine except where otherwise noted.

2.  See Marshall Brown, "The Logic of Realism: A Hegelian Approach," *PMLA*, 96 (March 1981), 228 in particular.

3.  See Michael Riffaterre, "Système du genre descriptif,' *Poétique*, 9 (1972), 15–30; Philippe Hamon, *Introduction à l'analyse du descriptif* (Paris: Hachette, 1981).

4.  Barthes, art. cit. supra; Jonathan Culler, *Flaubert: The Uses of Uncertainty* (Ithaca, NY: Cornell University Press, 1974).

5.  See Gotthold Lessing, *Laocoön* (Indianapolis: Bobbs-Merrill, 1962), in particular chap. 18; G. W. F. Hegel, *Aesthetics: Lectures on Fine Art*, trans. T. M. Knox, 2 vols. (Oxford: Clarendon Press, 1975), 2:1054–55.

6.  Honoré de Balzac, *Eugénie Grandet*, trans. Marion Ayton Crawford (Harmondsworth: Penguin, 1977), 114.

7.  Balzac, *The Curé de Tours*, trans. Merloyd Lawrence (New York: Houghton Mifflin, Riverside Editions, 1964). All subsequent page references in the text are to this edition.

8.  Perhaps not coincidentally, *The Curé de Tours* functions as the paradigm of Balzac's "artificial verisimilitude" in Gérard Genette's classical essay, "Vraisemblance et motivation" in *Figures II* (Paris: Seuil, 1969), 78–85.

9.  Consider in this regard Kant's remarks on the sublimity of the warrior, indeed of war itself: "And so, comparing the statesman and the general, men may argue as they please as to the pre-eminent respect which is due to either above the other; but the verdict of the aesthetic judgement is for the latter. War itself, provided it is conducted with order and a sacred respect for the rights of civilians, has something sublime about it . . . ," *The Critique of Judgment*, trans. James Creed Meredith (Oxford: Clarendon Press, 1973), 112–13.

10.  Sir Joshua Reynolds, *Discourses on Art*, ed. Robert R. Wark (New Haven: Yale University Press, 1975), IV, 65.

11.  See Michel Foucault, *Discipline and Punish: The Birth of the Prison*, trans. Alan Sheridan (New York: Pantheon Books, 1977).

# BIBLIOGRAPHY

Abrams, M. H. *The Mirror and the Lamp: Romantic Theory and the Critical Tradition.* New York: Oxford University Press, 1953.
*Natural Supernaturalism: Tradition and Revolution in Romantic Literature.* New York: W. W. Norton, 1971.

Adorno, T. W. *Aesthetic Theory.* Trans. C. Lenhardt. Ed. by Gretel Adorno and Rolf Tiedemann. London: Routledge & Kegan Paul, 1984.
"Functionalism Today." Trans. Jane O. Newman and John H. Smith. *Oppositions,* 17 (Summer 1979), 31–41.
*Prisms.* Trans. S. and S. Weber. London: Spearman, 1967.

Agacinski, Sylviane. "Le tout premier écart." In Lacoue-Labarthe, Philippe and Jean-Luc Nancy, eds. *Les fins de l'homme.* Paris: Galilée, 1981.

Alloula, Malek. *The Colonial Harem.* Trans. Myrna Godzich and Wlad Godzich. Minneapolis: University of Minnesota Press, 1986.

Alpers, Svetlana. "Art History and Its Exclusions: The Example of Dutch Painting." In Broude, Norma and Mary D. Garrard, eds. *Feminism and Art History: Questioning the Litany.* New York: Harper & Row, 1978, Pp. 183–200.

Aristotle. *Physics.* Trans. Richard Hope. Lincoln: University of Nebraska Press, 1961.

Auerbach, Erich. *Mimesis: The Representation of Reality in Western Literature.* Trans. Willard R. Trask. Princeton: Princeton University Press, 1953.

Baillie, John. *An Essay on the Sublime.* Introduction by Samuel Holt Monk. Los Angeles: The Augustan Reprint Society, 43, 1953.

Balmary, Marie. *L'homme aux statues: Freud et la faute cachée du père.* Paris: Grasset, 1979.

Balzac, Honoré de. *The Curé de Tours.* Trans. Merloyd Lawrence. New York: Houghton Mifflin, Riverside Editions, 1964.
*Eugénie Grandet.* Trans. Marion Ayton Crawford. Harmondsworth: Penguin, 1977.
*The Quest of the Absolute.* Trans. Ellen Marriage. New York: A. L. Burt, 1899.

Barthes, Roland. *Camera Lucida: Reflections on Photography.* Trans. Richard Howard. New York: Hill and Wang, 1981.
*Critical Essays.* Trans. Richard Howard. Evanston: Northwestern University Press, 1972.

*The Eiffel Tower and Other Mythologies*. Trans. Richard Howard. New York: Hill and Wang, 1979.

*Empire of Signs*. Trans. Richard Howard. New York: Hill and Wang, 1982.

*L'empire des signes*. Paris: Champs-Flammarion, 1979.

*The Fashion System*. Trans. Matthew Ward and Richard Howard. New York: Hill and Wang, 1983.

*Image—Music—Text*. Essays selected and translated by Stephen Heath. New York: Hill and Wang, 1977.

*A Lover's Discourse: Fragments*. Trans. Richard Howard. New York: Hill and Wang, 1978.

*Mythologies*. Trans. Annette Lavers. New York: Hill and Wang, 1972.

*The Pleasure of the Text*. Trans. Richard Miller. New York: Hill and Wang, 1977.

"The Reality Effect." In Todorov, Tzvetan, ed. *French Literary Theory Today: A Reader*. Trans. R. Carter. Cambridge: Cambridge University Press, 1982, Pp. 11–17.

*Roland Barthes by Roland Barthes*. Trans. Richard Howard. New York: Hill and Wang, 1977.

*Sade, Fourier, Loyola*. Paris: Seuil, 1971.

*S/Z*. Trans. Richard Miller. New York: Hill and Wang, 1974.

*Writing Degree Zero, and Elements of Semiology*. Preface by Susan Sontag. Trans. Annette Lavers and Colin Smith. Boston: Beacon Press, 1970.

Battcock, Gregory, ed. *Super Realism: A Critical Anthology*. New York: Dutton, 1975.

Baudelaire, Charles. *Art in Paris: 1845–1862. Salons and Other Exhibitions*. Trans. and ed. Jonathan Mayne. London: Phaidon Press, 1965.

*The Painter of Modern Life and Other Essays*. Trans. and ed. Jonathan Mayne. Greenwich: Phaidon, 1964.

Baudrillard, Jean. *De la séduction*. Paris: Denoël/Gonthier, 1981.

*La société de consommation: ses mythes, ses structures*. Paris: Gallimard, "Idées," 1970.

*Le système des objets*. Paris: Gallimard, "Tel," 1968.

Benjamin, Walter. *Illuminations*. Edited and with an Introduction by Hannah Arendt. Trans. Harry Zohn. New York: Schocken Books, 1969.

Bensmaïa, Réda. "Du fragment au détail." *Poétique*, 47 (September 1981), 355–70.

Bernfeld, Siegfried. "An Unknown Autobiographical Fragment by Freud." *American Imago*, 4 (August 1946). Reprint.

Bernheimer, Charles. "Symbolic Bond and Textual Play: The Structure of Kafka's *Castle*." In Flores, Angel, ed. *The Kafka Debate: New Perspectives for Our Time*. Staten Island, N. Y.: Gordian Press, 1977.

Borges, Jorge Luis. *Ficciones*. Edited and with an Introduction by Anthony Kerrigan. New York: Grove Press, 1962.

Bourget, Paul. *Essais de psychologie contemporaine*. 2 vols. Paris: Plon, 1920.

Brecht, Bertolt. *Über Realismus*. Frankfurt: Suhrkamp, 1971.

Breton, André. *Manifestes du surréalisme*. Paris: Gallimard, "Idées," 1969.

Brolin, Brent. *Flight of Fancy: The Banishment and Return of Ornament*. New York: St. Martin's Press, 1985.

Brown, Marshall. "The Logic of Realism: A Hegelian Approach." *PMLA*, 96 (March 1981), 224–41.

Brunetière, Ferdinand. *Le roman naturaliste.* Paris: Calmann-Lévy, 1886.

Bryson, Norman. *Tradition and Desire.* New Haven: Yale University Press, 1986.

Buck-Morss, Susan. *The Origins of Negative Dialectics: Theodor W. Adorno, Walter Benjamin, and the Frankfurt Institute.* New York: Free Press, 1977.

Bungay, Stephen. *Beauty and Truth: A Study of Hegel's Aesthetics.* Oxford: Oxford University Press, 1984.

Burke, Edmund. *A Philosophical Enquiry into the Origin of our Ideas of the Sublime and Beautiful.* Edited with an Introduction and Notes by James T. Boulton. Notre Dame: University of Notre Dame Press, 1968.                                                          \

Bush, Martin H. *Duane Hanson.* Wichita: Wichita State University Press, 1976.

Carlut, Charles. *La correspondance de Flaubert: Etude et répertoire critique.* Columbus: Ohio State University Press, 1968.

Cassirer, Ernst. *The Philosophy of the Enlightenment.* Trans. Fritz C. A. Koelln and James P. Pettegrove. Princeton: Princeton University Press, 1951.

Chodorow, Nancy. "Family Structure and Feminine Personality." In Rosaldo, Michelle Zimbalist and Louise Lamphere, eds. *Women, Culture & Society.* Stanford: Stanford University Press, 1974. Pp. 43–66.

Christ, Carol T. *The Finer Optic: The Aesthetic of Particularity in Victorian Poetry.* New Haven: Yale University Press, 1975.

Christensen, Jerome C. "The Sublime and the Romance of the Other." *Diacritics,* 8 (Summer 1978), 10–23.

Cicero. *Orator.* Trans. H. M. Hubbell. In *Cicero: Brutus and Orator.* Ed. T. E. Page et al., trans. H. M. Hubbell. London: William Heinemann, 1929.

Cixous, Hélène. "Fiction and Its Phantoms: A Reading of Freud's *Das Unheimliche* (The 'uncanny')." Trans. Robert Dennomé. *New Literary History,* 7 (Spring 1976), 525–48.

Clark, L. and L. Lange, eds. *The Sexism of Social and Political Theory: Women and Reproduction from Plato to Nietzsche.* Toronto: University of Toronto Press, 1979.

Clark, T. J. *Image of the People: Gustave Courbet and the 1848 Revolution.* Princeton: Princeton University Press, 1982.

Corngold, Stanley. *The Commentators' Despair: The Interpretation of Kafka's "Metamorphosis."* Port Washington N. Y.: Kennikat Press, 1973.
"The Hermeneutic of 'The Judgement'." In Flores, Angel, ed. *The Problem of "The Judgement":* *Eleven Approaches to Kafka's Story.* Staten Island, N. Y.: Gordian Press, 1977.

Courtney, William L. *The Feminine Note in Fiction.* London: Chapman & Hall, 1904.

Culler, Jonathan. *Flaubert: The Uses of Uncertainty.* Ithaca: Cornell University Press, 1974.

Daemmrich, Horst S. "The Aesthetic Function of Detail and Silhouette in Literary Genres." *Yearbook of Comparative Criticism* 3. Theories of Literary Genre, ed. Joseph P. Strelka. University Park: Penn State University Press, 1978.

Dali, Salvador. *The Conquest of the Irrational.* Trans. David Gascoyne. Paris: Maison Ramlot, 1935.
*Le mythe tragique de l'Angélus de Millet.* Paris: Pauvert, 1963.
*The Secret Life of Salvador Dali.* Trans. Haakon Chevalier. New York: Dial Press, 1942.

Damisch, Hubert. "L'autre 'ich' ou le désir du vide: pour un tombeau d'Adolf Loos." In *Ruptures/Cultures*. Paris: Minuit, 1976. Pp. 143–59.
"Le gardien de l'interprétation." *Tel Quel*, 44 (1971), 70–84.
"La partie et le tout." *Revue d'esthétique*, 23 (1970), 168–88.

Danahy, Michael, "Le roman est-il chose femelle?" *Poétique*, 25 (1976), 85–106.

Davis, Robert Gorham. "The Sense of the Real in English Fiction." *Comparative Literature*, 3 (1951), 200–17.

Deleuze, Gilles. *Proust and Signs*. Trans. Richard Howard. New York: George Braziller, 1972.

de Man, Paul. *Allegories of Reading: Figural Language in Rousseau, Nietzsche, Rilke, and Proust*. New Haven: Yale University Press, 1979.
*Blindness and Insight: Essays in the Rhetoric of Contemporary Criticism*. Second Edition, Revised. Introduction by Wlad Godzich. Minneapolis: University of Minnesota Press, 1983.
"Hegel on the Sublime." In *Displacement: Derrida and After*. Mark Krupnick, ed. Bloomington: Indiana University Press, 1983. Pp. 139–53.
"Sign and Symbol in Hegel's *Aesthetics*." *Critical Inquiry*, 8 (Summer 1982), 761–75.

Derrida, Jacques. *Glas*. Paris: Galilée, 1974.
"Les morts de Roland Barthes." *Poétique*, 47 (1981), 269–92.
"La mythologie blanche." *Marges de la philosophie*. Paris: Minuit, 1972. Pp. 247–324.
"The Parergon." Trans. Craig Owens. *October*, 9 (Summer 1979), 3–41.
*La vérité en peinture*. Paris: Champs-Flammarion, 1976.

Diderot, Denis. "Eloge de Richardson." *Oeuvres esthétiques*. Paris: Garnier, 1959.

Doubrovsky, Serge. *La place de la madeleine*. Paris: Mercure de France, 1974.

Du Camp, Maxime. *Paris, ses organes, ses fonctions et sa vie*. 4 vols. Paris: Hachette, 1873.

Ducrot, Oswald and Izvetan Todorov *Encyclopedic Dictionary of the Sciences of Language*. Trans. Catherine Porter. Baltimore: The Johns Hopkins University Press, 1979.

Eisler, K. R. "The Function of Details in the Interpretation of Works of Literature." *The Psychoanalytic Quarterly* (January 1959), 1–20.

Elledge, Scott. "The Background and Development of English Criticism of the Theories of Generality and Particularity." *PMLA*, 62 (1947), 147–82.

Finkelstein, Haim. "Dali's Paranoia-Criticism or The Exercise of Freedom." *Twentieth-Century Literature*, 21 (February 1975), 59–70.

Flaubert, Gustave. *Madame Bovary*. Trans. Paul de Man. New York: A Norton Critical Edition, 1965.

Fletcher, Angus. *Allegory: The Theory of a Symbolic Mode*. Ithaca: Cornell University Press, 1964.

Foucault, Michel. *The Birth of the Clinic: An Archeology of Medical Perception*. Trans. A. M. Sheridan Smith. New York: Pantheon Books, 1973.
*Discipline and Punish: The Birth of the Prison*. Trans. Alan Sheridan. New York: Pantheon Books, 1977.
*Madness and Civilization: A History of Insanity in the Age of Reason*. Trans. Richard Howard. New York: Random House, 1965.

Freud, Sigmund. *Collected Papers.* 5 vols. Trans. and ed. Joan Rivière. New York: Basic Books, 1959–60.
*Gesammelte Werke.* 18 vols. London: Imago Publishing Co., Ltd., 1940–68.
*Letters of Sigmund Freud.* Ed. Ernst Freud, trans. Tania and James Stern. New York: Basic Books, 1960.
*The Origins of Psychoanalysis: Letters to Wilhelm Fliess.* Trans. Eric Mosbacher and James Strachey. New York: Basic Books, Harper Colophon Books, 1954.
*The Standard Edition of The Complete Psychological Works of Sigmund Freud.* 24 vols. Ed. James Strachey and trans. James Strachey et al. London: Hogarth, 1953–74.

Freund, Gisèle. *Photography & Society.* Trans. Richard Dunn, Yong-Hee Last et al. Boston: David R. Godine, 1980.

Galassi, Peter. *Before Photography: Painting and the Invention of Photography.* New York: MOMA, 1981.

Genette, Gérard. *Figures II.* Paris: Seuil, 1969.
*Figures of Literary Discourse.* Trans. Alan Sheridan. Introduction by Marie-Rose Logan. New York: Columbia University Press, 1982.

Ginzburg, Carlo. "Clues: Morelli, Freud, and Sherlock Holmes." In Eco, Umberto and Thomas A. Sebeok, eds. *The Sign of Three: Dupin, Holmes, Peirce.* Bloomington: Indiana University Press, 1983. Pp. 81–118.

Girard, René. *La violence et le sacré.* Paris: Grasset, 1972.

Gombrich, E. H. *Art and Illusion: A Study in the Psychology of Pictorial Representation.* Oxford: Phaidon Press, 1960.
*The Sense of Order. A Study in the Psychology of Decorative Art.* Ithaca: Cornell University Press, 1979.

Granoff, Wladimir. *La pensée et le féminin.* Paris: Minuit, 1976.

Gravagnuolo, Benedetto. *Adolf Loos: Theory and Work.* New York: Rizzoli, 1982.

Green, André. *Un oeil en trop.* Paris: Minuit, 1969.

Greenwood, Michael. "Current Representational Art: Five Other Visions." *artscanada,* 210–11 (December 76–January 77), 23–29.

Greimas, Algirdas Julien. *Maupassant: La sémiotique du texte.* Paris: Seuil, 1976.

Hamon, Philippe. *Introduction à l'analyse du descriptif.* Paris: Hachette, 1981.
"What is description?" In Todorov, Tvetan, ed. *French Literary Theory Today: A Reader.* Trans. R. Carter. Cambridge: Cambridge University Press, 1982. Pp. 147–78.

Harris, Ann Sutherland and Linda Nochlin. *Women Artists: 1550–1950.* New York: Alfred A. Knopf, 1977.

Hegel, Georg Wilhelm Friedrich. *Aesthetics: Lectures on Fine Art.* Trans. T. M. Knox. 2 vols. Oxford: Clarendon Press, 1975.
*Aesthetik.* Introduction by Georg Lukács. Berlin: Aufbau-Verlag, 1955.
*Esthétique.* Trans. S. Jankélévitch. 4 vols. Paris: Garnier-Flammarion, 1979.
*The Logic of Hegel.* Trans. William Wallace. Oxford: Clarendon Press, 1874.
*Phenomenology of Spirit.* Trans. A. V. Miller. Oxford: Oxford University Press, 1977.

Heller, Erich. *Franz Kafka.* New York: Viking, 1974.

Henry, Gerritt. "The Soho Body Snatcher." *ARTnews* 71 (March 1972).

Hertz, Neil. *The End of The Line: Essays on Psychoanalysis and the Sublime.* New York: Columbia University Press, 1985.

Hipple, Walter J., Jr. *The Beautiful, The Sublime, and the Picturesque in Eighteenth-Century British Aesthetic Theory.* Carbondale: The Southern Illinois University Press, 1957.
"General and Particular in the *Discourses* of Sir Joshua Reynolds: A Study in Method." *The Journal of Aesthetics and Art Criticism,* 11 (March 1953), 231–47.

Honour, Hugh. *Neo-Classicism.* Harmondsworth: Penguin, 1968.

Iser, Wolfgang. *The Act of Reading: A Theory of Aesthetic Response.* Baltimore: The Johns Hopkins University Press, 1978.
*The Implied Reader.* Baltimore: The Johns Hopkins University Press, 1974.

Jakobson, Roman. *Fundamentals of Language.* The Hague: Mouton, 1956.
"Du réalisme en art." *Questions de poétique.* Paris: Seuil, 1973.

James, Henry. *The Art of The Novel.* New York: Scribner, 1962.
*In the Cage and other Tales.* New York: Norton, 1969.

Jameson, Fredric. *Marxism and Form: Twentieth-Century Dialectical Theories of Literature.* Princeton: Princeton University Press, 1971.

Jentsch, Ernst. "Zur Psychologie des Unheimlichen." *Psychiatrisch-Neurologische Wochenschrift,* 22 (August 1906), 195–98 and 23 (September 1906), 203–5.

Jones, Ernest. *The Life and Work of Sigmund Freud.* Vol. 1. *The Young Freud 1856–1900.* 2 vols. London: Hogarth Press, 1953.

Kafka, Franz. *The Trial.* Trans. Willa and Edwin Muir. New York: Schocken, 1968.

Kamerbeck, J. "Style de Décadence." *Revue de Littérature Comparée,* 39 (1965), 268–86.

Kames, Lord. *Elements of Criticism.* 3 vols. New York: Johnson Reprint Corporation, 1967.

Kaminsky, Jack. *Hegel on Art.* New York: State University of New York Press, 1962.

Kant, Immanuel. *The Critique of Judgment.* Trans. James Creed Meredith. Oxford: Clarendon Press, 1973.

Karelis, Charles. "Hegel's Concept of Art: An Interpretive Essay." In *Hegel's Introduction to Aesthetics.* Trans. T. M. Knox. Oxford: Oxford University Press, 1979.

Klein, Richard. "The Blindness of Hyperboles: The Ellipses of Insight." *Diacritics,* 3 (Summer 1973), 33–44.

Knox, Sir T. M. "The Puzzle of Hegel's Aesthetics." In Steinhaus, Warren E. and Kenneth I. Schmitz, eds. *Art and Logic in Hegel's Philosophy.* New Jersey: Humanities Press, 1980.

Kofman, Sarah. "Un philosophe 'unheimlich'." In *Ecarts: Quatre essais à propos de Jacques Derrida.* Paris: Fayard, 1973.

Lacan, Jacques. *De la psychose paranoïaque dans ses rapports avec la personnalité.* Paris: Seuil, 1975.
*Ecrits.* Trans. Alan Sheridan. New York: W. W. Norton, 1977.
*The Four Fundamental Concepts of Psychoanalysis.* Trans. Alan Sheridan. Ed. Jacques-Alain Miller. New York: W. W. Norton, 1978.

Lacoue-Labarthe, Philippe and Jean-Luc Nancy. *L'absolu littéraire: Théorie de la littérature du romantisme allemand.* Paris: Seuil, 1978.

Laplanche, Jean. *Life and Death in Psychoanalysis.* Trans. Jeffrey Mehlman. Baltimore: The Johns Hopkins University Press, 1976.

Larnac, Jean. *Histoire de la littérature féminine en France.* Paris: Kra, 1929.

Leclaire, Serge. *Psychanalyser.* Paris: Seuil, 1968.

Le Doeuff, Michèle. *L'imaginaire philosophique.* Paris: Payot, 1980.

Lefebvre, Henri. *La vie quotidienne dans le monde moderne.* Paris: Gallimard, "Idées," 1968.

Le Goff, Jacques and Pierre Nora, eds. *Faire de l'histoire.* 3 vols. Paris: Gallimard, 1974.

Lessing, Gotthold. *Laocoön: An Essay on the Limits of Painting and Poetry.* Trans. Edward Allen McCormick. Indianapolis: Bobbs-Merrill, 1962.

Lewes, George H. *Principles of Success in Literature.* Boston: Allyn and Bacon, 1891.

Lloyd, Genevieve. *The Man of Reason: 'Male' and 'Female' in Western Philosophy.* Minneapolis: University of Minnesota Press, 1984.

Loos, Adolf. "Ornament and Crime." In Münz, Ludwig and Gustav Künstler. *Adolf Loos, Pioneer of Modern Architecture.* Introduction by Nikolaus Pevsner, New York: Praeger, 1966.
*Spoken in the Void: Collected Essays 1897–1900.* Trans. Jane O. Newman and John H. Smith. Cambridge: The MIT Press, 1982.

Lukács, Georg. *Ästhetik, Teil 1. Die Eigenart des Ästhetischen.* 2 vols. In Georg Lukács, *Werke,* vol. 12. Neuwied: Luchterhand, 1963.
"Le particulier comme catégorie centrale de l'esthétique." Trans. Georges Kassai and Gérard Spitzer. *Les Lettres nouvelles.* Special Issue, "Ecrivains hongrois d'aujourd'hui" (September–October 1964), 76–99.
*Lukács Gyorgy Ifjukori Muvek.* Budapest: Magveto, 1977.
*Realism in Our Time: Literature and the Class Struggle.* Trans. John and Necke Mander. New York: Harper Torchbooks, 1971.
*Studies in European Realism.* Introduction by Alfred Kazin. New York: Grosset and Dunlap, 1964.
*The Theory of the Novel.* Trans. Anna Bostock. Cambridge: The MIT Press, 1971.
*Über die Besonderheit als Kategorie der Ästhetik.* Neuwied: Luchterhand, 1967.

Miller, J. Hillis. "The Interpretation of *Lord Jim.*" In Bloomfield, Morton W., ed. *The Interpretation of Narrative: Theory and Practice.* Cambridge: Harvard University Press, 1970. Pp. 211–28.

Mitchell, W. J. T. *Iconology: Image, Text, Ideology.* Chicago: University of Chicago Press, 1986.

Monk, Samuel. *The Sublime: A Study of Critical Theories in XVIII-Century England.* New York: MLA, 1935.

Mukařovský, Jan. "Detail as the Basic Semantic Unit in Folk Art." In *The Word and Verbal Art: Selected Essays.* Trans. and ed. John Burbank and Peter Steiner. Foreword by René Wellek. New Haven: Yale University Press, 1977. Pp. 180–204.

Newhall, Beaumont. *The History of Photography from 1839 to the Present.* New York: The Museum of Modern Art, 1982.

Nietzsche, Friedrich. *The Gay Science.* Trans. Walter Kaufman. New York: Vintage Books, 1974.

*Noésis* 1 (1985). Special Issue. "El detalle-le détail."

Ogilvie, John. *Philosophical and Critical Observations on the Nature, Characters and Various Species of Composition (1774)*. Vol 2. Hildesheim: Georg Olms Verlag, 1968.

Ong, Walter, J., S. J. "The Writer's Audience is Always a Fiction." *PMLA*, 90 (1975), 9–21.

Ortner, Sherry. "Is Female to Male as Nature is to Culture?" In Rosaldo, Michelle Zimbalist and Louise Lamphere, eds. *Woman, Culture & Society*. Stanford: Stanford University Press, 1974. Pp. 67–87.

Orwell, George. *Collected Essays*. London: Secker and Warburg, 1961.

Parker, Rozcika and Griselda Pollock. *Old Mistresses: Women, Art and Ideology*. New York: Pantheon Books, 1981.

Peirce, Charles Sanders. *Collected Papers*. Ed. by Charles Hartshorne and Paul Weiss. 8 vols. Cambridge: Harvard University Press, 1960.

Pliny the Elder. *The Elder Pliny's Chapters on the History of Art*. Trans. K. Jox-Blake. London: Macmillan and Co., 1890.

Powers, Lyall H., ed. *Henry James's Major Novels: Essays in Criticism*. East Lansing: Michigan State University Press, 1973.

Praz, Mario. *The Hero in Eclipse in Victorian Fiction*. Trans. Angus Davidson. London: Oxford University Press, 1956.

Price, Martin. "The Irrelevant Detail and the Emergence of Form." In J. Hillis Miller, ed. *Aspects of Narrative: Selected Papers from the English Institute*. New York: Columbia University Press, 1971. Pp. 69–91.

Prince, Gerald. "Introduction à l'étude du narrataire." *Poétique*, 14 (1973), 178–96.

Proust, Marcel. *Remembrance of Things Past*. Trans. C. K. Scott Moncrieff, Terence Kilmartin et al. 3 vols. New York: Random House, 1981.

Quintilian. *Institutio Oratoria* 3 4 vols. Ed. T. E. Page et al., trans. H. E. Butler. London: William Heinemann, 1922.

Rey, Henri-François. *Dali dans son labyrinthe*. Paris: Grasset, 1974.

Reynolds, Sir Joshua. *Discourses on Art*. Ed. Robert R. Wark. New Haven: Yale University Press, 1975.
*The Literary Works of Sir Joshua Reynolds*. 2 vols. London: Henry G. Bohn, 1852.

Riffaterre, Michael. *Essais de stylistique structurale*. Paris: Flammarion, 1971.
"Système du genre descriptif." *Poétique*, 9 (1972), 15–30.

Robbe-Grillet, Alain. *Pour un nouveau roman*. Paris: Gallimard, 1963.

Rouillé, André. *L'empire de la photographie: Photographie et pouvoir bourgeois 1839–1870*. Paris: Le Sycomore, 1982.

Runyon, Randolph. *Fowles/Irving/Barthes: Canonical Variations on an Apocrypha Theme*. Oxford, Ohio: Ohio State University Press for Miami University, 1981.

Said, Edward, *Beginnings: Intention and Method*. New York: Basic Books, 1975.
*Orientalism*. New York: Pantheon Books, 1978.
"The Problem of Textuality: Two Exemplary Positions." *Critical Inquiry*, 4 (Summer 1978), 673–714.

Sand, George. *Questions d'art et de littérature.* Paris: Calmann-Lévy, 1878.

Sanders, August. *Hommes du XXè siècle.* Intro. Ulrich Keller. Paris: Chêne/Hachette, 1980.

Sartre, Jean-Paul. *Saint Genêt, Comédien et martyr.* Paris: Gallimard, 1952.

Scharf, Aaron. *Art and Photography.* New York: Viking Penguin, 1986.

Schor, Naomi. *Breaking the Chain: Women, Theory, and French Realist Fiction.* New York: Columbia University Press, 1985.
"Details and Decadence: End-troping in *Madame Bovary.*" *Sub-Stance,* 26 (1980), 27–35.
"Female Fetishism: The Case of George Sand." In Suleiman, Susan, ed. *The Female Body in Western Culture: Contemporary Approaches.* Cambridge: Harvard University Press, 1986. Pp. 363–72.

Showalter, Elaine. *A Literature of their Own.* Princeton: Princeton University Press, 1977.

Soby, James Thrall. "Freud and Modern Art." *Saturday Review* (May 5, 1956), 11–12.

Sontag, Susan. *Against Interpretation.* New York: Dell, 1986.
*On Photography.* New York: A Delta Book, 1973.

Sterling, Elwyn F. "Toward a Theory of Detail in the French Novel: 1630–1830." *Agora,* 3 (1976), 91–109.

Taylor, Houghton, W. "'Particular Character': An Early Phase of a Literary Evolution." *PMLA,* 60 (1945), 161–74.

Todorov, Tzvetan. "Synecdoques." *Communications,* 16 (1970), 26–35.
*Poétique de la prose.* Paris: Seuil, 1971.
*Theories of the Symbol.* Trans. Catherine Porter. Ithaca: Cornell University Press, 1982.

Trachtenberg, Alan, ed. *Classic Essays in Photography.* New Haven: Leete's Island Books, 1980.

Ulmer, Gregory L. "Fetishism in Roland Barthes's Nietzschean Phase." *Papers on Language and Literature,* 14 (Summer 1978), 334–55.

Vico, Giambattista. *The New Science of Giambattista Vico.* Trans. Thomas Goddard Bergin and Max Harold Fisch. Garden City, New York: Anchor Books, 1961.

Virey, J. J. *De l'influence des femmes sur le goût dans la littérature et les beaux-arts pendant le XVIIè et XVIIIè siècle.* Paris: Déterville, 1810.

Watt, Ian. *The Rise of the Novel.* Berkeley: University of California Press, 1957.

Weinberg, Bernard. *French Realism: The Critical Reaction 1830–1870.* London: Oxford University Press, 1937.

Wellek, René. *A History of Modern Criticism.* 4 vols. New Haven: Yale University Press, 1955.

Wey, Francis. "Comment le soleil est devenu peintre." *Musée des Familles* (July 1855).
"Photographes et Lithographes." *La Lumière* (October 1851).
*Remarques sur la langue française au dix-neuvième siècle.* 2 vols. Paris: Firmin Didot, 1845.
"Théorie du Portrait (II)." *La Lumière* (May 1851).

Williams, Rosalind H. *Dream Worlds: Mass Consumption in Late Nineteenth-Century France.* Berkeley: University of California Press, 1982.

Wind, Edgar. *Art and Anarchy.* Revised and Enlarged. New York: Knopf, 1964.

Zola, Emile. *The Conquest of Plassans*. Trans. E. A. Vizetelly. London: Chatto and Windus, 1900.

*Correspondance (1872–1902)*. In *Oeuvres Complètes*. Ed. Maurice Leblond. 50 vols. Paris: Bernouard, 1927–29.

*The Fortune of the Rougons*. Trans. E. A. Vizetelly. London: Chatto and Windus, 1898.

*Germinal*. Trans. Leonard Tancock. Harmondsworth: Penguin Books, 1954.

*Oeuvres complètes*. Ed. Henri Mitterand. 15 vols. Paris: Cercle du Livre Précieux, 1962–69.

*Les Rougon-Macquart*. Ed. Henri Mitterand. 5 vols. Paris: Pléiade, 1960–67.

# INDEX